The Dessert Book

by Duncan Hines

Edited by Louis Hatchett

Mercer University Press
Macon, Georgia | 2002

ISBN 0-86554-810-2
MUP/H630

© 2002 Mercer University Press
6316 Peake Road
Macon, Georgia 31210-3960
All rights reserved

First Edition.

∞The paper used in this publication meets the minimum requirements
of American National Standard for Information Sciences—
Permanence of Paper for Printed Library Materials, ANSI Z39.48-1992.

Library of Congress Cataloging-in-Publication Data

The Dessert Book
edited by Louis B. Hatchett, Jr.
1st ed.
p. cm.
ISBN 0-86554-810-2 (hardcover: alk paper)
1. Desserts
I. Hatchett, Louis
TX773 .D818 2002
641.8'6–dc21
2002151070

Dedication

For Linda Priscilla

Acknowledgments

I WANT TO THANK CORA JANE SPILLER, DUNCAN HINES'S GREAT NIECE, FOR PROVIDING ME WITH MUCH OF THE information found in these pages concerning the individuals who contributed these recipes. She has always made herself available whenever I've needed some help in tracking down some arcane matter pertaining to Duncan Hines, and I want to record my sincere thanks here.

I ALSO WANT TO THANK MARC JOLLEY FOR HIS EDITORSHIP IN GUIDING THIS BOOK FROM START TO FINISH, AS WELL AS the entire production staff at Mercer University Press for doing a fine job.

Introduction to the 2002 Edition

FOR THOSE WHO ARE UNAWARE, IN THE 1940s AND 1950s SURVEYS SHOWED THAT THE MOST respected name in the food industry was Duncan Hines. Beginning in 1936, he published *Adventures in Good Eating*, an annual restaurant guide that eventually forced the restaurant industry—particularly those eating establishments in out-of-the-way places—into the modern era; with that single book he helped pave the way for the quality restaurant meals that we expect today. In 1938 he began publishing an annual guide for travelers seeking quality overnight lodgings, one which he called *Lodging for a Night*. In 1948 he published *Duncan Hines Vacation Guide*, which was a guidebook for people seeking that era's quality vacation spots throughout America. And in 1939 he began publishing an annually updated cookbook, *Adventures in Good Cooking*, which consisted of recipes taken from many of the nation's finest restaurants as well as from individuals who were as discriminating about quality food as he was. ▶

When Procter and Gamble bought the rights to Duncan Hines name in August 1956 and began putting his name on its cake mix packages, a lot of this history was forgotten by the American public. When Hines died in 1959, he was soon forgotten as a celebrity, but his name lives on today via America's supermarket shelves.

In my book *Duncan Hines: The Man Behind the Cake Mix* (Macon, Georgia: Mercer University Press, 2001), I described two books that Duncan Hines published in 1955. In July 1953 Duncan Hines, then 73, wanted to semi-retire; so he sold his publishing operation, Adventures in Good Eating, Inc., to Roy Park, his business partner in Hines-Park Foods. At the time of the sale and transfer, Hines was publishing his three annual guidebooks and cookbook, which were all still popular.

Later that year Park moved the operations of Adventures in Good Eating, Inc. from Bowling Green, Kentucky to Ithaca, New York and changed its name to The Duncan Hines Institute. From this location, he was responsible not only for sales of the books, but he was also the CEO for Hines-Park Foods, which produced about 250 products for the Duncan Hines label.

While Park continued to update and expand the annual editions of Hines' popular guidebooks and kept the cookbook fresh with new contributions, he also put together a couple of other publishing ventures featuring Duncan Hines. With his business partner's co-operation, Park arranged to have published Hines's autobiography, *Duncan Hines' Food Odyssey* (New York: Thomas Y. Crowell, 1955), but even more popular was their other effort *Duncan Hines' Dessert Book* (New York, Pocket Books, 1955), which sold hundreds of thousands of copies over the next decade.

Duncan Hines Dessert Book was originally a standard paperback book which sold for 35 cents. Depending on the edition, the cover carried a picture of chocolate cake (or some other tantalizing edible) along with the familiar "Duncan Hines" logo emblazoned across the top. The *Dessert Book*'s organization was a simple one. The recipes were arranged in the same manner and style as they had been in his other popular cookbook *Adventures in Good Cooking*, with the ingredients on the left side of the page and the directions on the right. The book was distributed in early 1955 and had an initial print-run of 250,000 copies.[1]

Duncan Hines' Dessert Book, like its older sister publication, was compiled from recipes submitted from restaurants and assorted individuals. Contributions submitted by both individuals and restaurants were given credit. As was the case with *Adventures in Good Cooking*, any blank areas that made a page look awkward were filled with household hints, suggestions, admonitions, and an assortment of Duncan Hines's famous *bon mots*. In subsequent editions, picture sketches were provided when it was thought to be of value to the reader.

By early July 1954 the editorial outline had taken shape. The book began with 100 recipes for cake. This consisted of various recipes for conventional cakes, mix cakes, sponge, chiffon and angel food cakes, fruit cakes, coffee and up-side-down cakes, tortes and cheese cakes. Next came dessert cakes not frequently produced in American

[1] In later additions of *The Duncan Hines Dessert Book*, every attempt was made to ensure that there was no confusion when a sugary concoction was being described; each recipe had dotted lines that connected its ingredients to the cooking directions. Some of these directions, incidentally, were more elaborate and detailed than they had been in *Adventures in Good Cooking*. Because it was estimated that it could reach a larger cross section of the population than *Adventures in Good Cooking* ever had, Park believed that easy-to-read instructions were essential to the book's success. No doubt many readers of *Adventures in Good Cooking* occasionally wished they had been blessed with dotted lines to keep track of the book's sometimes elaborate instructions. Indeed, when one compares the two volumes side-by-side, it quickly becomes clear that *Adventures in Good Cooking* was not for the kitchen novice; occasionally some of the recipes are quite difficult. Thanks to Park's efforts, however, the *Dessert Book's* uncomplicated instructions resolved this difficulty.

homes: recipes for petit fours, cupcakes, meringues, cream puffs and éclairs, among many others. Finally, there came 40 selections of the many things that one could pour onto a cake: frostings, icings, fillings, and sauces.

Having exhausted the subject of cakes, the book next turned to other dessert forms: cobblers, dumplings, shortcakes and turnovers. The number of these four dessert groups came to 25. This was followed first by 25 variations of corn-starch pudding and then 40 recipes for custard-styled desserts. The latter came in two forms: 1) baked puddings, as in bread pudding, and 2) soft pudding, as in soft custard.

As the user turned the pages, he next found recipes for ten forms of fruit dessert, including frozen fruit dishes, ambrosia, baked fruit, and a recipe for Apple Brown Betty. Next came 20 recipes of various cheese desserts, such as cheese cracker specialties and cheese cakes; this was accompanied with serving suggestions. The book's next section was a compilation of 40 gelatin desserts that covered charlottes, bavarians, whips, and sponges, among other delectable treats. This

was followed by five recipes for whips and sponges not using gelatin.

Recipes for 100 types of pie encompassed the next category. After a discussion on pie crusts, came concoctions for nearly every pie known to mankind, including apple pie, crumb meringue pie, and coconut pie. There were also recipes for the many things that could be poured into a pie crust: fruit filling, cream filling, custard filling, chiffon, parfait, and sponge filling. Concluding this section were recipes for tarts, turnovers, and "refrigerator pies."

The next to the last section of the book consisted of ten recipes for souffles and fondues, ten more for assorted steamed puddings, and another fifteen which covered tapioca, cereal, and rice desserts. Finally came 50 recipes for cookies of all kinds, 20 recipes for cooked and uncooked sauces and rounding off the book's contents came ten miscellaneous recipes, including Swedish pancakes, crepe suzette, waffles, waffle brownies, shortcake, fruit fritters, and doughnuts. The book contained a total of 555 recipes.

Many of these recipes had been tested in the

kitchen of the wife of his brother's son, Geraldine Hines. Clara Hines, who took her place, tested many more. Those that came after the business transfer in 1953 were tested in the Duncan Hines Test Kitchen in Ithaca, New York.

I'd like to include in this spot a little information as to the origin of some of these recipes. In the companion book to this volume, *The Duncan Hines Cookbook*, I've included some information about the restaurants from where many of the recipes in that volume and this one came. Below I'd like to identify some of the individuals who contributed the recipes found in both volumes.

Mrs. Thomas A. Williams, Nashville, Tennessee, was the wife of a vice-president of the Williams Printing Company which published Duncan Hines's guidebooks and his cookbook. The Williams firm continued to publish his books from 1939 until Roy Park took over Hines's operation in July 1953.

Francis E. Fowler, Jr., Los Angeles, California, was an entrepreneur and lifelong art collector whose greatest commercial success was in developing and marketing a sweet whiskey he named Southern Comfort. Every Christmas the Fowlers sent Duncan Hines a case of Southern Comfort, which he generously distributed among members of his family. When Hines and his wife went to Los Angeles, they always saw the Fowlers and dined with them as frequently as they could. The Fowlers owned a set of gold dishes that had belonged to a Czar of Russia, and on special occasions they served meals on them. Fowler is best remembered today as the namesake of the Fowler Museum of Cultural History on the UCLA campus, which holds a major portion of his silver collection.

Mrs. Louis (Idella) Weathers, Elkton, Kentucky, was a woman whose daughter, Elizabeth Ann, was married to Duncan Hines's nephew, Duncan Ludlow Hines. Mrs. Weathers was known to be a wonderful cook who presided over the kitchen with the help of a faithful black cook named Donie (pronounced DOUGH-NEE).

Charlie Grider, Bowling Green, Kentucky, was a distant Hines relative. Grider was considered by many to be an excellent cook.

Mrs. Edmund H. Singmaster, Philadelphia,

Pennsylvania, was the wife of perhaps Hines' most cherished "dinner detective." Edmund Singmaster was an elderly gentlemen whose exacting demands for good eating may have even exceeded Duncan Hines's own. He actually lived in Germantown, a suburb of Philadelphia. The two got to know each other so well that by 1941 Singmaster and his wife would accompany the Hineses on several gustatory prowls when the Kentucky couple came to town. Sometimes the Singmasters would go with them to far-flung eateries, even as far away as Maine or Wisconsin. Singmaster became in Hines' estimation something close to the word of God when it came to restaurant recommendations. If Singmaster recommended a restaurant, the place went into Hines' book and no questions were asked. Hines knew Singmaster would recommend only those restaurants that were both heavenly to dine in as well as immaculately clean.

Mrs. W[ill]. B. (Louise) Taylor, Bowling Green, Kentucky, was the granddaughter of John J. Valentine, the President of the Wells Fargo Company, who was the man who obtained for Duncan Hines a job with his firm in December 1898. Hines's father and Mr. Valentine were close friends, and as evidence of these recipes attest, that friendship between the two families continued long after the two elder men had passed away.

Mrs. Taylor had a wonderful cook named Antha who made delicious corncakes. The problem with duplicating recipes from the likes of Antha is that women of her kind prepared their meals with no measures; a pinch of salt here, another pinch of sugar there, a handful of corn-meal, and perhaps a half-dozen other ingredients were the only measurements they knew; it was all done by feel, and Duncan Hines marveled at their skill and wondered how they made it taste so good. Hines's own maid, Myrtle Potter, was just such a person, and at one time or another over the many years she was employed by the Hines she prepared practically all of the recipes found in this and its companion book, *The Duncan Hines Cookbook*. It could very well be that some of the recipes listed here under Duncan Hines's name may have originated with Mrs. Potter herself.

The Duncan Hines Dessert Book

Elsie Smythe, Bowling Green, Kentucky, was also a grand-daughter of John J. Valentine and is the sister of Mrs. W. B. Taylor and Mrs. R. T. Cooksey. She had lived in California and moved back to her hometown of Bowling Green in her later years. On her return, she brought back several recipes from out west, and Duncan Hines thought enough of many of them for inclusion here.

Mrs. R[ichard]. T. Cooksey, Madison, Wisconsin, was the third grand-daughter of John J. Valentine. She married a doctor who moved to Wisconsin. She was also an excellent cook, and a few of her contributions are included here along with her sisters.

Mrs. C[larence]. H. Welch, Tucson, Arizona, (whose maiden name was Annie Fore Hines) is the daughter of Duncan Hines's only sister. She married Clarence H. Welch, a young man in the United States Army Air Corps, who retired to become the personnel manager of a Howard Hughes firm in Tucson and then later became a stockbroker before he retired. Mrs. Welch had a reputation as a wonderful cook, and because she was with her husband in so many places over the years, her recipes came from as many locations as the recipes in this book.

Mrs. Roy (Jane) Morningstar, Bowling Green, Kentucky, was Duncan Hines's niece. She was his brother Porter's daughter. When Mrs. Morningstar first saw her name listed as the originator of the recipe for "Scalloped Oysters" in the *Duncan Hines Cookbook* (# 196), she told him, "This isn't my recipe for scalloped oysters." Duncan Hines replied that "No, it's not. The recipe came from a can of oysters. But I couldn't say that, so I put your name on it." What brand he got it from, no one knows, but it's mighty good just the same.

Charlot[te] C[ombs]. Moore, Henderson, Kentucky, was the sister-in law of Duncan Hines's brother, Porter, as well as a distant cousin.

Marion Flexner, Louisville, Kentucky, wrote a popular regional cookbook called *Out of Kentucky Kitchens* (University Press of Kentucky, 1949), for which Duncan Hines wrote the Preface. She and Duncan Hines had some correspondence and greatly admired each other.

Fred Waring, New York, New York, was a famous musical entertainer from the early 1920s until his death on July 29, 1984. Not only was he the inventor of the popular Waring Food Blender, but he was also one of Duncan Hines's dinner detectives. Always on the lookout for a good recipe, several dishes created by his own hand are included here.

Mrs. H[enry]. H. (Nell) Baird, Bowling Green, Kentucky, whose husband headed that town's Scott Tobacco Company, was a popular hostess in the middle half of the 20th century. She and Nellie, her faithful servant of many years who originally hailed from Tennessee, created scores of heavenly dishes for her many luncheons and dinners.

Mrs. Rhea G. Price, Bowling Green, Kentucky, was a friend of Duncan and Clara Hines. With help from her cook Annie Covington, throughout the 1930s and 1940s Mrs. Price created and served many delicious recipes to her guests at her home south of Bowling Green.

Mrs. McKenzie (Louise) Moss, Bowling Green, Kentucky, was the daughter of Duncan Hines's brother, Porter.

Mrs. Bland (Bena) Farnsworth, Bowling Green, Kentucky, was another cousin of Duncan Hines. Noted for her culinary skills, she was also in the same Bowling Green literary and women's clubs as was Clara Hines.

Gertrude Chaffin Wellman, Cleveland, Ohio, was a relative of Duncan Hines's first wife, Florence Chaffin Hines.

Due to neglect, this book has mainly been forgotten. But when its contents are tried, they are guaranteed to pack a wallop on the tongue. As always, Duncan Hines never recommended anything unless it was extraordinarily good. If he recommended it, he really meant it. So when he approved his name to be associated with the delectable desserts found in these pages, the reader can be sure that a rich treat, one never to be quickly forgotten, will delightfully entertain his taste buds and make him pine for more.

—Louis Hatchett
March 2002

The *Duncan Hines*

DESSERT BOOK

Treasures You Can Now Share

Duncan Hines is America's foremost authority on good eating. For many years he has traveled the length and breadth of America sampling and evaluating the finest in food.

His famous guide books, *Adventures in Good Eating* and *Lodging for a Night*, are standard authorities.

Now, from the wealth of his experience he has selected the best of the desserts—more than 500 recipes culled from the treasured secrets of hundreds of the finest chefs.

Easy to Make

Ambrosia
See page 126

Ice Cream Royale
See page 255

White Mountain Frosting
See page 90

Delicious to Eat!

Contents

Introduction

ONE OF THE MOST IMPORTANT COURSES IN ANY MEAL IS THE DESSERT. IT IS THE FINALE IN ANY FULL course Adventure in Good Eating—and, like the final act in a good play, is long remembered with pleasure.

I am in the fortunate position of being a professional taster. I work and eat at the same time. In my work I have sampled thousands of desserts, ranging from the old stand-by, apple pie, to such exotic creations as Zabaglione. When I enjoy a particularly good dessert at one of the places listed in my books, *Adventures in Good Eating, Lodging for a Night,* and *Vacation Guide,* I often ask for the recipe. It is a matter of extreme gratification to me that so many places I recommend have consented to release their prized recipes for publication in my book, *Adventures in Good Cooking and The Art of Carving in the Home.*

This *Duncan Hines Dessert Book* contains a selection of the dessert recipes that I have taken from my private collection which has been built up over the years through the generosity of friends who have been willing to share with me their prized recipes.

You will note that my recipes are easy to follow. I list the ingredients in the order they are used. Opposite the list of ingredients I tell in specific language the steps to be taken. Although some of the creations are exotic and sound mysterious, actually any person who follows the directions carefully can come forth with a delectable dessert.

For the most satisfying results from any recipe you should take precautions from beginning to end. Before you begin, make certain you have on hand the exact ingredients the recipe calls for. Follow directions carefully, use exact level measurements, and know your temperatures. You should have your oven tested occasionally to see that the temperature is the same throughout all corners, front and back. Never proceed by guess.

I should like to acknowledge the assistance that has been given to me in the preparation of this book by:

My wife, Clara, who is an artist with foods as well as a delightful traveling companion, and who often goes into the kitchen to observe a famous chef while he puts together some of his creations.

E. L. Ackley, Director of Quality Control, and Marie W. Layer, Home Economist, Hines-Park Foods, Inc., Ithaca, New York, who have assisted with the testing of the recipes.

Nebraska Consolidated Mills Company, Omaha, Nebraska, manufacturers of the Cake Mixes that bear my name, who put the findings of their Test Kitchen at our disposal in the preparation of this book.

My associate, Roy H. Park, of the Duncan Hines Institute, Ithaca, New York, who has worked with the publishers on the manifold details of bringing out this publication.

…And so, ladies—and gentleman—let's go into the kitchen now and set forth on a new adventure in the preparation of good desserts. May you have fun in the doing as well as in the eating. Good luck!

—DUNCAN HINES

EQUIVALENT MEASURES AND WEIGHTS

Pinch, dash = less than ⅛ teaspoon

3 teaspoons = 1 tablespoon

2 tablespoons = 1 oz. liquid or fat

4 tablespoons = ¼ cup

16 tablespoons = 1 cup or 8 oz.

½ cup = 1 gill

4 gills = 1 pint

1 cup = 8 oz. or ½ lb. liquid or fat

16 oz. = 1 lb.

2 cups = 1 pt.

1 pint = 1 lb. liquid or fat

4 cups = 1 quart or 32 oz.

2 pints = 1 quart

4 quarts = 1 gallon

8 quarts = peck

4 pecks = 1 bushel

1 pony = ⅓ oz.

1 jigger = 1 ½ oz.

1 shell = 1 ½ oz.

1 wine glass = 4 oz. = 8 tablespoons = ½ cup
(This is a claret glass and is most
commonly used in the average home)

1 sherry glass = 3 oz. = 6 tablespoons = ⅓ cup

1 port glass = 2 oz. = 4 tablespoons = ¼ cup

Table silverware spoons do not correspond
accurately with the capacity of measuring spoons.

FOOD WEIGHTS AND MEASURES

This table is for approximate weights and measures of various foods and is intended as a handy guide in estimating quantities. Courtesy of Restaurant Management Magazine, 222 East 42nd Street, New York City, N. Y.

Ingredient	Weights	Approximate Measures
Almonds (shelled, chopped)	1 oz.	¼ cup
Allspice (ground)	1 oz.	5 tablespoons
Allspice (whole)	1 oz.	6 tablespoons
Apple (juice)	8 oz.	1 cup
Apples (dried)	1 lb.	5 cups
Apricots (dry)	1 lb.	3 cups
Apricots (soaked and cooked)	1 lb.	4 cups and juice
Baking powder	1 oz.	3 tablespoons
Bananas (mashed)	1 lb.	2 cups
Bread	1 lb.	12 slices ½ inch thick
Bread crumbs (dried, sifted)	4 oz.	1 cup
Butter	1 lb.	2 cups
Butter	1 oz.	2 tablespoons
Butter	Size of an egg	¼ cup
Cashew nuts	1 lb.	4 cups
Cheese (cream)	1 lb.	2 cups

FOOD WEIGHTS AND MEASURES

Cheese (cream, Philadelphia)	6 oz.	1 pkg.
Cheese (cubed)	1 lb.	2 2/3 cups
Cherries (candied)	1 lb.	3 cups
Chestnuts (in shell)	1 lb.	2 cups - meats
Chocolate (grated)	1 oz.	4 tablespoons
Chocolate (melted)	1 lb.	2 cups
Cider	8 oz.	1 cup
Cinnamon (ground)	1 oz.	4 tablespoons
Cinnamon (stick)	¾ oz.	4 (5-inch size)
Cloves (ground)	1 oz.	4 tablespoons
Cloves (whole)	1 oz.	6 tablespoons
Cocoa (ground)	1 oz.	4 tablespoons
Coconut (shredded)	1 lb.	6 cups
Coffee (ground fine)	1 lb.	5 cups
Cornmeal	1 lb.	3 cups
Cornstarch	1 oz.	3 tablespoons
Cracker crumbs	2 ½ oz.	1 cup
Crackers (graham, crushed)	1 cup	12 crackers
Cranberries	1 lb.	4 cups
Cranberry sauce (strained)	1 lb.	2 cups
Cream of Tartar	1 oz.	3 tablespoons

FOOD WEIGHTS AND MEASURES

Currants (dried)	1 lb.	3 cups
Currants (dried)	10 oz.	1 pkg.
Dates (pitted)	1 lb.	3 cups
Eggs (1 unbeaten)	1 ½ oz.	3 tablespoons
Eggs (whole)	1 cup	4 to 6 medium
Eggs (whites) - 1 cup	8 oz.	8 to 10
Eggs (yolks) - 1 cup	8 oz.	12 to 16
Figs (dried, cut-up)	1 lb.	2 ¾ cups
Filberts (shelled)	1 lb.	3 ½ cups
Flour (bread, sifted)	1 lb.	4 cups
Flour (graham, sifted)	1 lb.	3 ½ to 3 ¾ cups
Flour (rye, sifted)	1 lb.	5 ½ cups
Flour (whole wheat)	1 lb.	3 ¾ cups
Flour (bread)	1 oz.	3 to 4 tablespoons
Flour (pastry, sifted)	4 oz.	1 cup
Flour (rice)	1 lb.	2 cups
Flour (cake, sifted)	1 lb.	4 ½ cups
Gelatin (granulated)	1 lb.	4 cups
Gelatin (prepared)	1 oz.	2 ½ cups
Ginger (ground)	1 lb.	6 tablespoons
Grapes (cut and seeded)	8 oz.	2 to 3 cups

The Duncan Hines Dessert Book

FOOD WEIGHTS AND MEASURES

Grapefruit juice	11 oz.	1 cup
Honey	1 lb.	1 cup
Lard	8 oz.	1 cup
Lemons	1 lb.	3 to 5 lemons
Lemon juice	1 cup	4 to 5 lemons
Lemon rind	1 lemon	2 teaspoons
Milk (condensed, sweetened)	11 oz.	1 cup
Milk (evaporated)	1 lb.	2 cups
Molasses	12 oz.	1 cup
Mixed spices	1 lb.	4 ⅔ cups
Nutmeg (ground)	1 oz.	4 ⅔ tablespoons
Oats (rolled, quick-cook)	2 ¾ oz.	1 cup
Oatmeal (quick-cook)	1 lb.	3 cups
Oils	1 lb.	2 cups
Orange (rind, grated)	½ oz.	2 tablespoons
Peaches (dried)	1 lb.	3 cups
Peaches (fresh, sliced)	1 lb.	2 to 2 ½ cups
Peanuts (shelled, jumbo)	1 lb.	3 cups
Peanut butter	1 lb.	1 ⅔ cups
Pecans (shelled)	1 lb.	4 cups
Pineapple (canned, tidbits)	1 lb.	2 cups

FOOD WEIGHTS AND MEASURES

Pineapple (canned, sliced and diced)	3 slices	1 cup
Pineapple (candied)	1 lb.	7 rings
Pineapple (juice)	8 oz.	1 cup
Prunes (cooked, pitted)	1 lb.	3 cups
Raisins (seedless)	1 lb.	3 cups
Raisins (seeded)	1 lb.	2 cups
Raisins (seedless)	5 ⅓ oz.	1 cup
Rhubarb (edible part cooked)	1 lb.	2 ¼ cups
Rye Meal	2 ⅓ oz.	1 cup
Salt	1 oz.	1 ¾ tablespoons
Soda	1 oz.	2 ½ tablespoons
Strawberries (whole)	1 qt.	3 ½ cups
Sugar (brown, loosely packed)	1 lb.	3 cups
Sugar (brown, firmly packed)	1 lb.	2 ¼ cups
Sugar (confectioners' sifted)	1 lb.	3 ½ cups
Sugar, confectioners'	4 ½ oz.	1 cup
Sugar, granulated	1 lb.	2 cups
Sugar, powdered	6 ½ oz.	1 cup
Tapioca (minute)	1 lb.	2 ½ cups
Tapioca (pearl)	5 oz.	1 cup
Tea (dry)	2 oz.	1 cup

FOOD WEIGHTS AND MEASURES

Vanilla	1 oz.	2 tablespoons
Vinegar	8 oz.	1 cup
Walnuts (English, shelled)	4 oz.	1 cup
Water	8 oz.	1 cup
Yeast	½ oz.	1 cake

SWEETENING VALUE OF SUGAR SUBSTITUTES

Equivalents of 1 cup Sugar:

¾ to 1 cup honey

1 cup brown sugar

1 cup maple sugar

1 cup maple syrup

1 ½ cups sorghum or molasses

1 ½ cups cane syrup

2 cups corn syrup

RECOMMENDED TEMPERATURES

Simmering water	180° F.	Slow oven	300° F. - 325° F.
Boiling water	212° F.	Moderate oven	350° F. - 375° F.
Boiled icings	238° F. - 240° F.	Hot oven	400° F. - 425° F.
Jellying stage	218° F. - 222° F.	Very hot oven	450° F. - 475° F.
Very slow oven	250° F. - 275° F.	Extremely hot oven	500° F. - 525° F.

DEEP FAT FRYING

Doughnuts	370° F. - 380° F.
Fritters	370° F. - 380° F.

BREADS

Baking powder biscuits	450° F. - 475° F.	12 - 15 minutes

CAKES

Angel food cake	325° F.	60-75 minutes
Cupcakes	350° F.-375° F.	20-30 minutes
Layer cake	375° F.	25-35 minutes
Loaf Cake	350° F.	45-60 minutes
Sponge cake	325° F.	40-60 minutes
Pie shells	450° F.	12-15 minutes
Prebaked shell with filling	350° F.	25-30 minutes
One-crust pie (custard type)	400° F. or 450° F. And reset to 325° F. and 25-30 minutes at 325° F.	25-30 minutes 10 minutes at 450° F.
Two-crust pie (fruit pies)	425° F. or 450° F. and reset to 350° F. and 35-45 minutes at 350° F.	45-50 minutes 15 minutes at 450° F.

It is always best to use the ingredients stated in the recipe; however, if they are not on hand, here is a list of satisfactory substitutes.

FOR	USE
1 cup sifted all-purpose flour	1 cup plus 2 tablespoons sifted cake flour
1 cup sifted cake flour	1 cup minus 2 tablespoons sifted all-purpose flour
1 cup sifted pastry flour	1 cup minus 2 tablespoons sifted all-purpose flour
1 tablespoon cornstarch (for thickening)	2 tablespoons flour (approximately)
1 teaspoon baking powder	¼ teaspoon soda plus ½ teaspoon cream of tartar
1 cup fresh sweet milk	½ cup evaporated milk plus ½ cup water
1 cup fresh sweet milk	1 cup sour milk or buttermilk plus ½ teaspoon soda (decrease baking powder by 2 teaspoons)
1 cup sour milk or buttermilk	1 cup fresh sweet milk with 1 tablespoon lemon juice or vinegar added
1 square (1 oz.) unsweetened chocolate	3 to 4 tablespoons cocoa plus 1/2 teaspoon shortening

Bake: To cook by dry heat, usually in the oven.

Batter: A mixture of flour and liquid usually in combination with other ingredients thin enough to pour.

Beat: To mix vigorously with an over-over motion.

Blanch: To remove the skins from fruits or nuts by dipping in boiling water.

Blend: To mix thoroughly together two or more ingredients.

Boil: To cook in water, or in a liquid consisting of mostly water, in which bubbles rise continually and break on the surface.

Broil: To cook directly under a hot heated unit or flame, or over live coals.

Brush: To spread thinly, usually with a brush, but sometimes done with a piece of cloth or paper.

Caramelize: To melt sugar to a golden brown color over low heat.

Chill: To allow a mixture to become thoroughly cold but not frozen.

Chop: To cut into coarse or fine pieces with a chopper or knife.

Combine: See blend.

Core: To remove the core from certain fruits.

Cream: To soften fat, butter, cheese, etc., until it is light and creamy.

Cream together: To work one or more foods together until soft. Usually this applies to sugar and shortening.

Crumble: To break into smaller particles usually using the fingers.

Cube: To cut into small squares.

Cut in: To mix fat with dry ingredients using two knives, a fork, or pastry blender.

Defrost: To bring a food to room temperature.

Dice: To cut into cubes.

Dip: To coat a food with a dry or moist substance like flour or beaten egg.

Dissolve: To make a solution from a dry and liquid ingredient.

BAKING AND COOKING TERMS

Dot: To scatter bits of fat or cheese over the surface of food.

Drain: To remove the liquid from foods usually using a sieve or strainer.

Dust: To sprinkle lightly with flour or sugar.

Envelope: Usually refers to gelatin. 1 envelope equals 1 tablespoon.

Flake: To break lightly apart into small pieces with a fork.

Flour: To sprinkle or cover with a thin film of flour.

Fold in: To mix by cutting down through the batter, lifting up, and then folding over before cutting down again. It is usually done with a large spoon, flat wire whip, rubber scraper, etc.

Fry: To cook in hot fat.

Grate: To rub against a grater to tear food into small pieces or shreds.

Grind: To change a food into small particles by the cutting and crushing motion of a food grinder.

Halve: To cut into two equal parts.

Heat: To cause a mixture or liquid to become hot by the use of a flame.

Knead: To work into a smooth, satiny mass with the hands, using a rolling, pressing, and folding-over motion.

Macerate: To soften or separate parts of a substance by steeping in liquid.

Marinate: To let food stand in a marinade, usually an oil and acid mixture like French dressing.

Mash: To reduce a food to a soft, smooth state by crushing or beating.

Melt: To change a solid to a liquid by heating.

Mix: To combine two or more ingredients until evenly blended.

Pare: To cut off the outside covering with a knife.

Peel: To strip off the outside covering.

Pinch: Amount of substance that can be contained between thumb and forefinger.

Preheat: To heat the oven to the desired temperature before putting in the food.

Press: To pack down a mixture, with the fingers or the bottom of a cup, into a pan.

Purée: To press through a fine sieve.

Quarter: To cut into four equal parts.

Roll: To place on a board and spread thin with a rolling pin.

Rub: To smear two substances together.

Sauté: To brown or cook in a small amount of fat.

Scald: To heat a liquid to just below the boiling point.

Scrape: To remove the outside skin by rubbing the surface with a sharp knife.

Sift: To put dry ingredients through a sieve.

Simmer: To cook in liquid just below the boiling point. It is done on the top of the stove.

Skin: To remove the outer covering.

Slightly beaten: To mix together lightly (a few strokes).

Sliver: To cut or shred into long pieces.

Soak: To suck up and absorb liquid.

Sprinkle: To scatter a dry ingredient over the surface of a food.

Steam: To cook in the steam which arises from a pan of boiling water or other liquid.

Stir: To mix, usually with a spoon, using a circular motion.

Stuff: To fill a cavity or hole with a mixture.

Sugaring: To sprinkle with sugar.

Toast: To brown by means of dry heat.

Top: To crown or cap.

Warm: To heat to moderate degree.

Whip: To beat rapidly, using a flat wire whisk, rotary egg beater, or electric mixer at high speed, to incorporate air and to increase the volume.

USEFUL KITCHEN UTENSILS
FOR DESSERT PREPARATION

Measuring

1. Set of standard measuring spoons

2. Nest of measuring cups with lips for liquids and plain rims for dry ingredients

3. Pint and quart measuring cups

4. Utility tray

5. Metal spatula

Mixing

6. Kitchen fork and knife

7. Flat wire whip

8. Pastry blender

9. Wooden spoon

10. Rotary egg beater

11. Electric mixer

12. Flour sifter

13. Mixing bowls

14. Rubber spatula

USEFUL KITCHEN UTENSILS
FOR DESSERT PREPARATION

Food Preparation

15. Paring knife

16. Bread knife

17. Straight-edged knives

18. Flexible spatula

19. Grapefruit knife

20. Apple corer

21. Strawberry huller

22. Kitchen scissors

23. Food chopper

24. Wire strainers: very fine, medium, and coarse

25. Pastry brush

26. Set of graters

27. Lemon squeezer

28. Can opener, jar opener, bottle opener, and corkscrew

29. Timer

30. Cookie cutters

31. Cookie press

32. Rolling pin

33. Pastry canvas

34. Bread board

USEFUL KITCHEN UTENSILS
FOR DESSERT PREPARATION

Top of the Stove Cooking

35. Saucepans and covers, several sizes
36. Double boiler: large and small
37. Large kettle with steamer
38. Deep fat frying basket
39. Heavy skillets – large and small
40. Pancake griddle
41. Pancake turner
42. Coffee maker
43. Teakettle
44. Waffle iron

Baking

45. Square pans: 8-inch and 9-inch
46. Round layer pans: 8-inch and 9-inch
47. Oblong pan: 13x9x2-inch
48. Loaf pan: 10x5x3-inch
49. Tube pan: 9-inch and 10-inch
50. Pie pans: 7-inch, 8-inch and 9-inch
51. Baking sheets
52. Jelly roll pan: 15 ½ x 10 ½ x ½ inch
53. Ring molds, several sizes
54. Wire cooling racks
55. Oven thermometer
56. Muffin pans
57. Casserole with covers, several sizes
58. Individual custard cups
59. Pudding molds

How to Freeze Desserts

THERE ARE MANY ADVANTAGES TO THE HOME FREEZER. FOOD CAN BE PREPARED AHEAD WHEN time is available and when it is convenient. For example, fruit pies and other fruit desserts can be made up in season when fresh fruit is easy to find and cheaper to buy. Then too, with a freezer there is no need to worry about what to serve unexpected guests.

Cakes, cookies, fruits, ice cream, ice cream desserts, and most pies can be frozen satisfactorily. Proper choice of material and correct wrapping is very important to successful freezing. The wrapping material should be moisture-vapor-proof, strong and tough, free of odor, and pliable and easy to work with. Aluminum foil, polyethylene, and pliofilm are excellent and readily available. The foods should be very tightly wrapped and sealed. ▶

To protect them against rough handling, it is a good idea to place baked goods in paper plates or on cardboard and then wrap. They may also be wrapped and placed in a sturdy box.

Label and date all packages. Be careful not to overload your freezer as it causes the temperature to rise. Specific directions for cakes, cookies, fruits, ice cream, ice cream desserts, pies, and pastries follow below:

Cakes—All kinds of baked cakes may be frozen. They may be frosted or unfrosted; however they keep better and longer if unfrosted. If frosted, use a butter or penuche-type frosting. Cool cakes first before wrapping, and if frosted freeze before wrapping so as not to upset the frosting. Unwrap frosted cakes before thawing while unfrosted cakes should be left wrapped during the thawing period. Two hours at room temperature are sufficient for thawing. Frozen cakes may be stored 3 to 4 months.

Cookies—Baked cookies or cookie dough may be frozen. Baked cookies should be packed very carefully before freezing to prevent breakage. Freeze baked cookies in covered containers, and thaw the frozen cookies in the original container at room temperature. It takes from 15 to 30 minutes. Cookie doughs, other than refrigerator cookie dough, should be packed into freezer containers. Refrigerator dough should first be molded, then wrapped in sheet wrapping, and sealed with tape, and when used the dough should be thawed in the refrigerator until it is soft enough to slice easily. Other doughs should be thawed until they can be handled easily.

Fruits (general directions)—Freeze only sound, fully ripe fruit. Make a sugar-water syrup and chill before packaging. To prevent darkening, add 1/2 teaspoon ascorbic acid for each quart of syrup. Add syrup to fruit in liquid-tight containers and fill to within 3/4 inch from the top. Freeze according to directions furnished with your freezer or obtained from some other reliable source.

Ice Cream and Ice Cream Desserts—Freeze ice creams in tight containers to prevent loss of flavor and accumulation of ice crystals. The richer the ice cream mixture, the lower the freezing and storing temperature required. Ice cream may be stored for a month. Ice cream desserts should be carefully wrapped to protect the flavor. They should not be kept *too long*.

Pies—Fruit pies, vegetable pies (pumpkin and squash), mince, and chiffon pies all freeze well. Custard pies do not freeze satisfactorily, and meringue toppings shrink and become tough. Some juicy fruits and berries may require more thickening when put in a pie to be frozen. Fruit and mince pie may be frozen baked or unbaked. (Pies frozen unbaked have a slightly fresher flavor). All fruit pies should be thawed in the oven. Chiffon pies should be set before freezing. Baked pumpkin pie may be frozen for a short period of time; however, for longer storage, it is better to freeze the unbaked filling. Be sure to thaw pies before baking. Pie shells may be frozen baked or unbaked. Pies may be made and frozen in regular pie plates or special paper baking plates but if baked, be sure to cool first. Do not slit the top crust of unbaked pies. On a whole it is easier to freeze pie before wrapping. To protect the top of pies, cover with paper pie plate before placing it in the freezer bags or other wrapping material. Be sure pies are setting level while freezing. To thaw chiffon pies, unwrap them and set them in the refrigerator 1 to 1 1/2 hours. Frozen fruit and mince pies should also be unwrapped when thawed. When you use a frozen unbaked pie slit the top crust and bake in hot oven (425° F.) 40 to 60 minutes or until done. Frozen baked pies should be heated in a moderate oven (375° F.) 30 to 50 minutes or until the center is bubbling. Unbaked pie shells should be unwrapped and thawed at room temperature or in a moderate oven. Baked pastry and pastry circles should be thawed completely before using. Pies may be stored up to 2 months.

REDUCING AND INCREASING RECIPES

To make half a recipe use exactly one-half the amount of each ingredient. To double a recipe use exactly twice the amount of each ingredient. Refer to the table of Food Weights and Measures and the table of Equivalent Measures and Weights for help in dividing or multiplying the ingredient.

If the modified recipe calls for uneven amounts of flour, liquid, eggs, etc., remember the following proportions:

⅜ cup = ¼ cup + 2 tablespoons

⅝ cup = ½ cup + 2 tablespoons

⅞ cup = ¾ cup + 2 tablespoons

If the modified recipe figures out to be part of an egg, beat up one whole egg, measure with a tablespoon, and divide.

Baking pans for half recipes of cakes, pies, etc., should measure half the area but have the same depth of those for the whole recipe.

Approximate the baking time and oven temperature. When doubling the recipe use 2 pans of the same size indicated for the original recipe or a pan double in area. Thus the same baking time and temperature may be maintained so that the batter will be the same depth in the pan.

Recipes

Cakes

"My mother keeps in two big books
The secrets of the things she cooks.
If I could ever learn to bake,
I'd send my brother Bill a cake.
But mother says it's hard to learn
To bake cakes that never burn."

THIS OLD NURSERY RHYME APPLIES NO MORE. TODAY ANY WOMAN CAN BE QUEEN OF THE "CASTLE" by making a perfect cake. A perfect cake does not depend upon luck or knack. Our recipes, unlike our grandmother's, are carefully balanced in ingredients and precisely written to give the clearest directions. If you use top quality ingredients, measure accurately, follow the recipe exactly, have proper sized pans, use a good ▶

oven, and follow the baking time and temperature–perfect results will be your reward every time. Those are the secrets of cake baking.

In the 18th century "Animated Specialties" were the pride and joy of French chefs. Huge cakes and pies were made which, when cut, released birds, frogs, or butterflies. The larger, more fantastic cakes concealed dwarfs who jumped out. Strange as it may seem, cakes were part of the entertainment program in the castle.

In early times, particularly in England, every religious occasion was celebrated with a cake.

Many of the original English recipes and traditions continue unchanged. To this day, cakes are thrown from the tower of Biddenden Church in Kent on the Eve of Epiphany. Back in the 12th century two sisters gave money to build this church and the thrown cakes are symbolic of the donors.

There is an interesting tale about Mother's Day and cakes. The origin of our Mother's Day is Mothering Sunday, which is known in the Church of England as Refreshment Sunday or the Fourth Sunday in Lent. Like the evergreen tree at Christmas time, cake was traditional for this event.

Usually sons and daughters (especially those living away) went "a-mothering" with a gift of a cake. The cake was eaten while the family reunited in worship. Eventually, the day became an occasion to honor all mothers.

Two of our familiar cakes, the Plum or Fruit Cake and the Bride's Cake, also have their origins in a religious event. The Fruit Cake made of fruits and spices represented the gifts of the Wise Men to the Christ Child. The present day Bride's Cake is a descendant of the Honey Cake, which was an important part of the marriage ceremony and from which we get the word honeymoon.

We can trace many more of our present-day practices, expressions, and recipes to cakes of one kind or another from the four corners of the earth. I am sure that many a bride in many a land was chosen, by men of good appetite, for her cake-making abilities as much as for her handsome features and ample dowry. And you know, even though it is out of style to say so, I believe that many of today's young prospective husbands keep their eye peeled for a good cake baker. The joke on them is the fact that it is so easy to make excellent cakes.

In fact, the old saying, "you can't eat your cake and have it too," no longer applies. Today you can eat your cake and tomorrow make another identical one. And when you know that friends are coming, whether it is the teen-age crowd, the afternoon bridge club, your husband's poker club, or dinner guests—bake a cake!

1 - 2 - 3 - 4 Cake

Ingredients	Directions (Makes two 9-inch layers)
3 cups sifted flour 4 teaspoons baking powder 1/4 teaspoon salt	Sift together opposite ingredients three times. Set aside.
1 cup butter 2 cups sugar	Cream butter; add sugar gradually, and cream together until light and fluffy.
4 egg yolks 1 cup milk	Add yolks, one at a time, beating well after each addition.
1 teaspoon vanilla 4 egg whites	Fold in vanilla. Beat egg whites until stiff but not dry. Fold in carefully. Pour batter into two round 9-inch layer pans which have been lined on bottoms with paper. Bake in moderate oven 375° about 25 minutes. This cake may also be baked in three 8-inch layer pans. Cool and frost with Orange Butter Cream Frosting and sprinkle with coconut.

Cake pans cost so little that you should have a set of each size
in your kitchen if you wish to be a successful cake maker.

One Egg Cake

Ingredients

Directions (Makes two 8-inch layers)

2 cups sifted cake flour ·················· Sift together opposite ingredients three times. Set aside.

2 teaspoons baking powder

3/4 teaspoon salt

1/3 cup butter ······························· Cream butter; add sugar gradually, and cream together until light and fluffy.

1 cup sugar

1 egg ··· Add egg to the creamed mixture and beat well.

7/8 cup milk ·································· Add flour, alternately with milk, beating well after each addition.

1 teaspoon vanilla ························· Stir in vanilla. Pour batter into two round 8-inch layer pans which have been lined on bottoms with paper. Bake in moderate oven 375° about 25 minutes. This cake may also be baked in the 9x9x2-inch pan.

Economical Gold Cake

Ingredients

Directions (Makes two 8-inch layers)

2 cups sifted cake flour ·················· Sift together opposite ingredients three times. Set aside.

2 teaspoons baking powder

1/2 teaspoon salt

1/2 cup butter ······························ Cream butter; add sugar gradually, and cream together until light and fluffy.

1 cup plus 2 tablespoons sugar

3 egg yolks ·································· Beat yolks until very thick and lemon-colored; add to the above butter mixture and beat well.

3/4 cup milk ································· Add flour, alternately with milk, beating after each addition until smooth.

1 teaspoon vanilla ························· Add vanilla and blend. Pour batter into two round 8-inch layer pans which have been lined on bottoms with paper. Bake in moderate oven 375° for 20 to 30 minutes. This cake may also be baked in the 9x9x2-inch pan at 375° for 35 to 40 minutes.

Rich Butter Cake

Ingredients   **Directions** (Makes two 9-inch layers)

2 1/4 cups sifted cake flour ·········· Sift together opposite ingredients three times. Set aside.
2 1/4 teaspoons baking powder
1/2 teaspoon salt
3/4 cup butter ························· Cream butter; add sugar gradually, and cream together until light and fluffy.
1 1/2 cups sugar
3 eggs ······························· Add eggs one at a time, beating well after each addition.
2/3 cup milk ························· Add flour, alternately with milk, beating after each addition until smooth.
1 teaspoon vanilla ···················· Add vanilla and blend. Pour batter into two round 9-inch layer pans which have
                                     been lined on bottoms with paper. Bake in moderate oven 375° about 25
                                     minutes. This cake may also be baked in two 8x8x2-inch square pans about 30
                                     minutes.

White Cake

Ingredients   **Directions** (Makes two 9-inch layers)

1/2 cup butter ······················· Cream butter and sugar together.
1 3/4 cups sugar–sifted
4 egg yolks ·························· Add yolks to above.
3 cups flour ························· Sift flour three times. Add just a little to mixture
1 cup milk ·························· Add milk alternately with remaining flour. Hold out 1 cup of flour.
1/2 teaspoon salt ···················· Add salt and baking powder to final cup of flour and stir into mixture.
3 teaspoons baking powder
2 egg whites–beaten ················· Fold in beaten egg whites.
2 teaspoons lemon extract ··········· Add extract to mixture. Pour batter into two 9-inch cake pans which have been
                                     greased and floured. Bake in 350° oven for 35 minutes. Fill and frost when cold.

White Cake

Ingredients

2 2/3 cups sifted cake flour ··········

3 teaspoons baking powder

1 teaspoon salt

5 egg whites ·······················

1/2 cup sugar

2/3 cup vegetable shortening ········

1 1/4 cups sugar

1 cup milk ···························

1 teaspoon vanilla ···················

Directions (Makes two 9-inch layers)

Sift together opposite ingredients three times. Set aside.

Beat egg whites until frothy throughout. Add sugar, 2 tablespoons at a time, beating after each addition until blended. Beat only to soft peaks. Set meringue aside.

Cream shortening; add sugar gradually, and cream together until light and fluffy.

Add flour, alternately with milk, beating after each addition until smooth.

Add vanilla and blend. Stir in meringue until well blended. Pour batter into two round 9-inch layer pans which have been lined on bottoms with paper. Bake in moderate oven 375° for 25 to 30 minutes or until done.

White Cake Supreme

Ingredients

1 cup butter ························

2 cups sugar

3 1/2 cups cake flour ···············

4 teaspoons baking powder

1/2 teaspoon salt

1 cup milk

1 teaspoon vanilla

8 egg whites ·······················

Directions (Makes two 9-inch layers)

Beat butter until creamy. Add sugar gradually and blend until very light and creamy.

Sift flour and measure. Add baking powder and salt and sift all together two or three times. Stir into butter mixture alternately with milk. Beat batter until smooth. Add vanilla. Remove from beater.

Beat egg whites until stiff and fairly dry. Fold into batter. Place in two greased, paper lined 9-inch cake pans. Bake in 350° oven for 40 minutes. Can also be baked in three 8-inch pans at 375° for about 25 minutes.

Orange Cake

Francis Fowler, Jr., Los Angeles, California

Ingredients

Directions (Makes two 9-inch layers)

1 tablespoon grated orange rind ······ Put rind in juice and let stand while making the cake. Save the pulp for filling.
1/4 cup orange juice–strained

3/4 cup butter ························· Cream butter; add sugar gradually and cream thoroughly.
1 1/2 cups sugar

3 egg yolks–beaten ··················· Add yolks to mixture.

2 1/4 cups cake flour ················· Sift together dry ingredients. Add water to the orange juice and add alternately
3 1/2 teaspoons baking powder   with the sifted dry ingredients to the above mixture.
1/2 teaspoon salt
3/4 cup water

3 egg whites–beaten ················· Fold egg whites into mixture. Pour into two 9-inch layer pans which have been
                                     well greased. Bake in 350° oven for 30 to 35 minutes. Cool and spread with Clear
                                     Orange Filling.

Hot Milk Cake

Ingredients

Directions (Makes two 9-inch layers)

2 cups sifted flour ··················· Sift together opposite ingredients three times. Set aside.
2 teaspoons baking powder
1/4 teaspoon salt
1 cup milk–scalded

2 tablespoons butter ················· Add butter to scalded milk. Set aside.

4 eggs ······························· Beat eggs until thick and lemon-colored. Add sugar gradually and continue
2 cups sugar   beating until very thick. Quickly add flour mixture and stir until just mixed. Stir
                                     in hot milk.

2 teaspoons vanilla ·················· Add vanilla. Pour batter into two 9-inch layer pans which have been lined on
                                     bottoms with paper. Bake in moderate oven 350° about 35 minutes. Frost with
                                     your favorite frosting.

Orange Juice Cake

Ingredients

2 1/3 cups sifted cake flour ··········
2 3/4 teaspoons baking powder
1/4 teaspoon soda
1 teaspoon salt
1 1/2 cups sugar
2/3 cup butter ·······························
1 3/4 tsp grated orange rind
1/2 cup milk ·································
1/4 cup orange juice
1/4 teaspoon almond extract
3 eggs ····································

Directions (Makes two 9-inch layers)

Sift together opposite ingredients. Set aside.

Stir butter just to soften. Add grated orange rind. Sift in dry ingredients.

Combine milk, orange juice, and almond extract. Add to the above mixture and mix until all flour is dampened. Beat 2 minutes at a low speed of mixer or 300 vigorous strokes by hand.

Add eggs to above mixture and beat 1 minute longer in mixer or 150 strokes by hand. Pour batter into two round 9-inch layer pans which have been lined on bottoms with paper. Bake in moderate oven 375° for 25 to 30 minutes. Cool and frost with Seven Minute Frosting and sprinkle with coconut.

Orange Layer Cake

Use your favorite yellow cake recipe, but when mixing dough, substitute ¼ of the amount of liquid stipulated with orange juice. Cool and frost with Orange Butter Cream Icing.

Damon's, Cleveland, Ohio

Aunt Susan's Clabber Cake

Ingredients

1/2 lb. butter ·······························
2 cups sugar
2 eggs–beaten ·······························
2 cups clabber
3 1/2 cups cake flour ····················
2 teaspoons soda
3 1/3 tablespoons cocoa

Directions (Serves 16)

Cream together.

Add to mixture.

Add to mixture. Stir well. Pour batter into greased and floured pan. Bake in a 350° oven for 45 minutes.

The Anna Maude, Oklahoma City, Oklahoma

Buttermilk Cake

Ingredients

Directions (Makes two 9-inch layers)

2 1/2 cups sifted cake flour ············· Sift together opposite ingredients. Set aside.

1 ½ teaspoons baking powder

1/2 teaspoon soda

1 teaspoon salt

1 2/3 cups sugar

3/4 cup butter ······························· Stir butter just to soften. Sift in dry ingredients.

3/4 cup buttermilk or sour milk ······ Add buttermilk and vanilla to the above and mix until all flour is dampened. Beat

1 teaspoon vanilla   2 minutes at a low speed of electric mixer or 300 vigorous strokes by hand.

3 eggs   Add eggs and beat 1 minute longer in mixer or 150 strokes by hand. Pour batter into two round 9-inch layer pans which have been lined on bottoms with paper. Bake in moderate oven 350° about 35 minutes. This cake may also be baked in two 9x9x2-inch baking pans at 350° for 25 to 30 minutes or in the 13x9x2-inch baking pan 35 to 40 minutes.

Minnehaha Cake

Ingredients

Directions (Makes two 8-inch layers)

3 egg whites ······························· Beat until stiff and add sugar, beating until blended. Set aside.

1/2 cup sugar

1/2 cup butter ······························· Cream butter and sugar.

1/2 cup sugar

1 1/2 cups flour ····························· Sift dry ingredients; add to creamed mixture alternately with milk. Beat smooth.

2 teaspoons baking powder

1/2 teaspoon salt

1/2 cup milk

1 teaspoon vanilla ······················· Add vanilla. Fold in beaten egg whites. Pour batter into two buttered, 8-inch layer cake pans. Bake at 350° for 30 to 35 minutes. Cool and spread with Festive Frosting.

Burnt Sugar Cake

The Anna Maude, Oklahoma City, Oklahoma

Ingredients

1 cup butter

2 cups sugar

4 tablespoons caramelized sugar syrup

3/4 cup milk

3 cups cake flour–sifted

4 eggs

1 tablespoon baking powder

1 teaspoon vanilla

Directions (Makes two 9-inch layers)

Cream butter and sugar together.

Make a syrup by melting granulated sugar in an iron skillet. (May be made up in quantity and kept on hand.) Combine syrup and milk.

Add flour to creamed mixture alternately with milk and syrup.

Add eggs, one at a time, beating well after each addition.

Add baking powder and vanilla last. Pour batter into two 9-inch layer pans which have been greased and floured. Bake in a 350° oven for 40 minutes.

Banana Cake

Ingredients

1/2 cup butter

1 1/2 cups sugar

2 egg yolks

1 scant cup crushed bananas

5 tablespoons buttermilk

1 teaspoon soda

2 cups cake flour

1 teaspoon baking powder

1/2 cup chopped nuts

1 teaspoon vanilla

2 egg whites

Directions (Makes one 10-inch square layer)

Cream together in electric mixer until light and fluffy.

Add yolks to above and beat well.

Add crushed bananas. Dissolve soda in buttermilk and stir into mixture.

Sift flour twice, adding baking powder to second sifting. Add nuts to flour and beat into mixture. Add vanilla and fold in stiffly beaten egg whites. Pour into greased and lined 10-inch square cake pan and bake in 350° oven for 40 to 50 minutes or until cake tester comes out clean. Let cool and ice with Maple Frosting.

Grandma Shield's Montgomery Cake-Pie

Water Gate Inn, Washington, D.C.

Ingredients

1 cup sugar ···

1/4 cup shortening

1 egg–beaten

Directions (Makes two 8-inch layers)

Cream together sugar and shortening until well blended. Add egg and mix well.

1 1/2 cups sifted cake flour ··············

2 teaspoons double-acting

baking powder

1/2 cup milk

1 teaspoon lemon extract

Sift baking powder with flour. Add to above mixture, alternately with milk, in small amounts. Beat well. Add lemon extract and mix well. Pour batter into two greased 8-inch round cake pans and bake in 350° oven for 25 to 30 minutes or until done. Cool and spread filling between layers and on top of cake.

Filling

1 cup sugar ··

4 1/2 tablespoons cornstarch

1/4 teaspoon salt

Mix together.

2 lemons ···

1 cup dark corn syrup

2 cups water

1 teaspoon lemon extract

3 eggs

Grate rinds; then squeeze lemons to extract juice. Add grated rind and juice to water, corn syrup and lemon extract. Add to the above mixture. Beat and add to above. Cook in top of double boiler over hot water, stirring constantly, until thickened. Cool.

Here's a simple way to find out if your cake is done.
Stick in a toothpick and if it comes out clean, it is done.
Or you can lightly touch the top of the cake
with your little finger, and if it leaves no imprint it is done.

Poppy Seed Cake

Ingredients

Directions (Makes three 9-inch layers)

1 cup poppy seeds ·························· Soak together overnight.
3/4 cup scalded milk
1 1/2 cups sugar
3/4 cup butter ···························· Cream butter and sugar together. Stir in milk.
3/4 cup cold milk
3 teaspoons baking powder ·········· Sift together three times and blend all ingredients together.
3 cups flour
4 egg whites–beaten ···················· Fold into mixture. Bake in three layers in 9-inch cake pans in 350° oven for 25 to 30 minutes. Cool and fill with Lemon Filling. Frost with White Icing.

Allenwood Fudge Cake

Ingredients

Directions (Makes two 8-inch layers)

2 squares unsweetened ················· Melt chocolate in milk stirring constantly, until like custard.
  chocolate
1/2 cup milk
1 tablespoon butter ····················· Add to the above mixture. Let cool.
1 egg yolk
1 cup sugar ······························· Add opposite ingredients to the mixture.
1/2 cup milk
1 teaspoon vanilla
1 3/4 cups flour ·························· Blend together and add to mixture. Pour into greased and floured 8-inch cake pans and bake in 375° oven for about 10 minutes, then lower the temperature to about 350° and bake for another 25 to 30 minutes.
1 teaspoon soda

Cooked fruits usually have a better flavor and retain more of their natural sweetness if served hot.

Fudge Cake

Ingredients

4 squares unsweetened ·············· chocolate
1/2 cup hot water

1/2 cup sugar ·······················

2 cups sifted cake flour ···············
1 teaspoon soda
1 teaspoon salt

1/2 cup butter ····················
1 1/4 cups sugar

3 eggs ··························

2/3 cup milk ·····················

1 teaspoon vanilla ··················

Directions (Makes two 9-inch layers)

Heat chocolate with hot water in top of double boiler. Cook and stir over boiling water until chocolate is melted and mixture thickens.

Add to the above mixture and cook and stir 2 minutes longer. Cool to lukewarm while mixing cake.

Sift together opposite ingredients three times. Set aside.

Cream butter; add sugar gradually, and cream together until light and fluffy.

Add eggs one at a time, beating well after each addition.

Add flour, alternately with milk, in small amounts, beating after each addition until smooth.

Add vanilla with chocolate mixture to the batter. Stir until blended. Pour batter into two round 9-inch layer pans which have been lined on bottoms with paper. Bake in moderate oven 350° for 25 to 30 minutes. This cake may also be baked in the 13x9x2-inch pan about 40 minutes. Cool and frost with Sea Foam Frosting or Mocha Butter Cream Frosting.

You cannot expect perfect results in making cake unless you are certain that the ingredients are of top quality and always fresh.

8-Yolk Fudge Cake

Violet Bray Berry, Berkeley, California

Ingredients

Directions (Makes three 9-inch layers)

2 cups sugar–sifted ·························· Cream sugar and butter until light and fine grained.
3/4 cup butter

8 egg yolks ··································· Beat until thick and lemon-colored and add to above.
2 squares unsweetened   Melt chocolate and add to mixture.
  chocolate

2 1/2 cups flour ······························ Sift dry ingredients four times. Alternately add to above mixture with buttermilk.
3/4 teaspoon soda
2 teaspoons baking powder
1/4 teaspoon salt
1 1/4 cups buttermilk

1 teaspoon vanilla ·························· Add to mixture. Pour into three 9-inch layer pans which have been greased and
floured. Bake in 350° oven for 30 minutes.

Fudge Cake à la Anchorage-by-the-Sea

Anchorage-by-the-Sea, Mattapoisett, Massachusetts

Ingredients

Directions

3 eggs–separated ·························· Beat egg yolks with sugar. Add milk and flour which has been sifted with the
1 1/2 cups sugar   baking powder.
3/4 cup milk
1 1/2 cups cake flour
1 1/2 teaspoons baking
  powder
1/2 cup butter

2 squares unsweetened ··············· Melt chocolate with butter and add. Then add stiffly beaten egg whites and
  chocolate   vanilla. Pour batter into two 8-inch layer pans which have been greased and
1 teaspoon vanilla   floured. Bake in moderate oven 350° about 35 minutes. Cool and frost with
Fudge Frosting.

Fudge Pecan Cake Ball

Take a day old chocolate cake without frosting and crumble until very fine. Take a scoop or slice of brick ice cream and roll in crumbs, pressing rather hard so the ice cream will collect as much of the crumbs as possible. Place in a serving dish and cover with chocolate syrup. Top with chopped pecans.

Cocoa Devil's Food Cake

Ingredients

Directions (Makes two 8-inch layers)

1 1/2 cups sifted cake flour ·········· Sift together opposite ingredients. Set aside.

1 teaspoon soda

1 teaspoon salt

1/3 cup sugar

1/2 cup cocoa

1/2 cup butter ···························· Stir just to soften. Sift in dry ingredients.

7/8 cup milk ······························· Add ¾ cup of the milk and vanilla to the above mixture. Mix until all flour is

1 teaspoon vanilla dampened. Beat 2 minutes at a low speed of electric mixer or 300 vigorous strokes by hand.

2 eggs ····································· Add eggs and remaining milk. Beat 1 minute longer in the mixer or 150 strokes by hand. Pour batter into two round 8-inch layer pans which have been lined on bottoms with paper. Bake in moderate oven 350° for about 35 minutes. This cake may also be baked in the 9x9x2-inch pan 35 to 40 minutes.

Part of the success in your cake making lies in using the proper size pan. Never try to crowd a 9-inch cake into an 8-inch pan or you will have cake batter all over the bottom of your oven. If you try to put an 8-inch cake into a 9-inch pan, the result will be a product which is thin and tough. Cake tins cost so little that you should have a set of each in your kitchen if you wish to be a successful cake maker.

Devil's Food Cake

Ingredients

Directions (Makes two 9-inch layers)

2 cups sifted cake flour ·············· Sift together opposite ingredients three times. Set aside.
1 teaspoon baking powder

1/2 cup butter ······················· Cream butter; add brown sugar gradually and cream together until light and
1 1/4 cups firmly packed   fluffy.
  brown sugar

3 egg yolks ··························· Add, one at a time, beating well after each addition.
3 squares unsweetened   Add to the above and blend thoroughly.
  chocolate–melted

1 cup milk ···························· Add flour, alternately with milk, in small amounts, beating after each addition
1 teaspoon vanilla   until smooth.
                                Stir in vanilla. Pour batter into two round 9-inch layer pans, which have been
                                lined on bottoms with paper. Bake in moderate oven 350° about 30 minutes.

Devil's Food Cake

Mrs. K's Toll House Tavern, Silver Springs, Maryland

Ingredients

Directions (Makes two 9-inch layers)

2 cups sugar ························· Cream together sugar and butter.
2 tablespoons butter

4 egg yolks ·························· Beat yolks, add cream, add to above, mix well.
1 cup sour cream

3 squares unsweetened ··········· Melt in water in top of double boiler, add to above.
  chocolate

3/4 cup water

2 1/2 cups cake flour ·············· Sift flour, measure. Dissolve soda in a little water. Add flour to above then stir in
2 teaspoons soda   soda.

4 egg whites ························ Beat until stiff, fold into batter. Bake in two 9-inch layers at 350° until straw
                                comes out dry. Ice with a boiled white icing.

Devil's Food Cake

Ingredients

Directions (Makes two 9-inch layers)

2 cups sugar ·································· Cream together butter and sugar until fluffy. Beat eggs and stir into creamed
2 tablespoons butter   mixture with salt and vanilla.

3 eggs

1/4 teaspoon salt

2 teaspoons vanilla

1 cup buttermilk ······················· Add buttermilk to the above.

3 cups cake flour ······················· Sift together, add to mixture.

2 teaspoons soda

4 squares unsweetened ················· Heat milk and chocolate in double boiler until chocolate is dissolved. Stir into
  chocolate   cake batter; place in two 9-inch pans which have been greased and lined with
1 cup sweet milk   paper and bake in 325° oven for 1 hour.

Sour Cream Devil's Food Cake

Ingredients

Directions (Makes two 9-inch layers)

2 cups sifted cake flour ··············· Sift together opposite ingredients three times. Set aside.

1 1/4 teaspoons soda

1/2 teaspoon salt

1/3 cup butter ···························· Cream butter; add sugar gradually, cream together until light and fluffy.

1 1/4 cups sugar

1 egg ······································· Add to creamed mixture and beat well.
3 squares unsweetened   Stir into the above and blend thoroughly. Add ¼ of the flour mixture and blend.
  chocolate–melted

1 teaspoon vanilla

1/2 cup sour cream ····················· Add to above, beat well.

1 cup sweet milk ······················· Add remaining flour, alternately with milk, beating after each addition until
                                 smooth. Pour batter into two round 9-inch layer pans which have been lined on
                                 bottoms with paper. Bake in moderate oven 350° for 30 to 35 minutes.

Party Devil's Food Cake

Ingredients

2 1/4 cups sifted cake flour ··········
2 teaspoons soda
1/2 teaspoon salt

1/2 cup butter ·······················
2 1/2 cups firmly packed
　brown sugar

3 eggs ·······························

3 squares unsweetened ··············
　chocolate–melted

1/2 cup buttermilk or sour milk ······

1 teaspoon vanilla ·················

1 cup boiling water

Directions (Makes three 8-inch layers)

Sift together opposite ingredients three times. Set aside.

Cream butter; add sugar gradually, cream together until light and fluffy.

Add eggs, one at a time, beating well after each addition.

Add chocolate to the above mixture and blend thoroughly.

Add flour, alternately with milk, beating after each addition until smooth.

Stir in vanilla and water and blend. (Batter will be thin.) Pour batter into three 8-inch layer pans, which have been lined on bottoms with paper. Bake in moderate oven 375° for 25 to 30 minutes. Cool and frost tops and sides with double the Cocoa Whipped Cream recipe.

Chocolate Cake Supreme

Ingredients

1/2 cup butter ·····················
2 cups sugar

4 squares unsweetened ············
　chocolate

2 egg yolks ·······················
1 teaspoon vanilla

2 1/2 cups cake flour ··············
2 teaspoons baking powder
1/2 teaspoon salt

Directions (Makes two 9-inch layers)

Cream butter and sugar together until fluffy.

Melt in double boiler, add to above.

Beat yolks, add vanilla to beaten yolks and add to above.

Sift together opposite ingredients three times.

| 1 1/2 cups sweet milk ·················· | Add milk alternately with flour mixture to the above. |
| 2 egg whites ······························· | Beat stiff and fold into mixture. Place in two 9-inch cake pans which have been greased, paper lined, and lightly greased again. Bake in 350° oven for about 30 minutes or until done. Cool and spread with Chocolate Frosting. |

In order to insure perfect cakes, be sure that your oven temperature is correct. Every good cook should have an oven thermometer and test the stove front and back, top and bottom to see that the oven heats evenly. Always have the oven preheated to the temperature called for in the recipe before putting in the cake or pie. After a cake has cooled, keep it fresh and moist by storing it in a container which has a tight cover.

Buttermilk Chocolate Cake

Ingredients	Directions (Makes two 8-inch layers)
2 cups sifted cake flour ···············	Sift together three times.
1/4 teaspoon salt	
1/2 cup butter ····························	Cream butter; add sugar gradually, cream together until light and fluffy.
1 1/4 cups sugar	
2 eggs ·······································	Add, one at a time, beating well after each addition.
1 cup buttermilk ·························	Add flour, alternately with milk, adding four parts flour and three parts milk, beating well after each addition until smooth.
2 squares unsweetened ··············· chocolate – melted	Add remaining ingredients and blend thoroughly. Pour batter into two 8-inch layer pans which have been lined on the bottoms with paper. Bake in moderate oven 350° about 35 minutes or until done. Cool and frost with Seven Minute Frosting.
1 tablespoon vinegar	
1/2 teaspoon vanilla	
1 teaspoon soda	

Buttermilk Chocolate Cake

Ingredients

3 cups sifted cake flour ················
1/2 teaspoon salt
3/4 cup butter
2 1/4 cups sugar
3 eggs
1 1/2 cups buttermilk
3 squares unsweetened
  chocolate–melted
1 1/2 tablespoons vinegar
1 teaspoon vanilla
1 1/2 teaspoons soda

Directions (Makes three 8-inch layers)

Use directions for Buttermilk Chocolate Cake (two 8-inch layers) substituting the listed ingredients.

Mild Chocolate Cake

Ingredients

1 3/4 cups sifted cake flour ···········
2 teaspoons baking powder
1/4 teaspoon soda
1 teaspoon salt
1 1/2 cups sugar
1/2 cup butter ·····················
1 cup plus 2 tablespoons ···········
  undiluted evaporated milk
1 1/4 teaspoons vanilla
2 eggs ·····························
2 squares unsweetened ···········
  chocolate–melted

Directions (Makes two 9-inch layers)

Sift together opposite ingredients. Set aside.

Stir just to soften. Sift in dry ingredients.

Add and mix until all flour is dampened. Beat 2 minutes at a low speed of electric mixer or 300 vigorous strokes by hand.

Add to above mixture and beat 1 minute longer in mixer or 150 strokes by hand.

Pour batter into two round 9-inch layer pans which have been lined on bottoms with paper. Bake in moderate oven 350° for 30 to 35 minutes. Cool and frost with Butter Cream Frosting.

"My Eureka Cake"

Ingredients

1/2 cup water ···················
2 squares unsweetened
  chocolate
1/4 cup butter

1 cup sugar ·····················
1 cup sifted cake flour
3/4 teaspoon soda ·············
1/4 cup sour milk

1 egg ···························

Directions (Makes one 8-inch square cake)

Pour water in a saucepan with chocolate and butter. Bring to a boil to melt. Let cool

Measure into a bowl.

Combine and add to above mixture. Add cooled chocolate.

Stir quickly into the mixture. (Batter must be thin.) Pour into an 8-inch square pan which has been greased and floured. Bake in 350° oven for 30 minutes or until cake tester comes out clean. Cool and spread with Mocha Frosting or Cocoa Whipped Cream.

Chocolate Chip Cake

The Derings, Green Lake, Wisconsin

Ingredients

1/2 cup shortening ············
1 1/2 cups sugar
1 1/2 teaspoons vanilla
1 teaspoon salt
2 1/4 cups sifted flour ·········
2 1/2 teaspoons baking
  powder
1 cup water ····················
3 egg whites–stiffly beaten ·····
1 square unsweetened
  chocolate–grated

Directions (Makes two 8-inch layers)

Blend together the opposite ingredients.

Sift together the flour and baking powder.

Add sifted dry ingredients alternately with water, to the creamed mixture.
Fold whites into the batter. Then add grated chocolate. Bake in 8-inch layer pans in a 350° oven for 30 to 35 minutes. Cool and frost with Creamy Soft Chocolate Frosting.

Sugar Plum Cake

Ingredients

Directions (Makes two 8-inch layers)

1 tablespoon butter ⋯⋯⋯⋯⋯ Cream butter, sugar, and sour cream together.
1 cup sugar
1 cup sour cream

1/2 cup cocoa ⋯⋯⋯⋯⋯⋯⋯ Add to above.
1/2 cup hot water
2 eggs–beaten

2 cups flour ⋯⋯⋯⋯⋯⋯⋯ Sift flour, baking powder, and salt. Add to mixture.
1 teaspoon baking powder
1/4 teaspoon salt

1 teaspoon soda ⋯⋯⋯⋯⋯ Dissolve soda in cold water. Add to the mixture. Stir well. Bake in two 8-inch
8 teaspoons cold water   pans or one 12x9-inch loaf pan which have been lightly greased and floured. Bake
                            in 350° oven for 30 minutes. While cake is warm spread with Date Nut Frosting.

Spice Cake

Ingredients

Directions (Makes two 9-inch layers)

2 1/2 cups sifted cake flour ⋯⋯ Sift together opposite ingredients. Set aside.
1 teaspoon baking powder
1 teaspoon soda
3/4 teaspoon salt
3/4 teaspoon cinnamon
3/4 teaspoon cloves
1 cup sugar

1/2 cup butter ⋯⋯⋯⋯⋯⋯ Stir just to soften. Sift in dry ingredients.

2/3 cup soft, firmly packed ⋯⋯ Add to the above and mix until all flour is dampened. Beat 2 minutes at a low
  brown sugar   speed of electric mixer or 300 vigorous strokes by hand.

| 1 cup milk | Add remaining ingredients and beat 1 minute longer in mixer or 150 strokes by hand. Pour batter into two round 9-inch layer pans or two 9x9x2-inch square pans which have been lined on bottoms with paper. Bake in moderate oven 375° for 25 to 30 minutes. |

1 cup milk

2 tablespoons milk

2 eggs

Fruits for cake may be cut easily by using a pair of scissors and dipping frequently in water. Fruit that has been soaked in warm water a few minutes blends well with other ingredients.

Spiced Layer Cake with Seafoam Frosting
Williamsburg Inn, Williamsburg, Virginia

Ingredients

Directions (Makes two 8-inch layers)

1/3 cup butter .... Cream butter thoroughly. Add sugar gradually and cream until light and fluffy.

1 cup sugar

1 egg .... Add egg and egg yolk to butter mixture and beat well.

1 egg yolk

2 tablespoons molasses .... Add molasses and mix thoroughly.

2 cups sifted flour .... Sift dry ingredients together three times. Add to creamed mixture alternately with milk, beating after each addition until smooth. Pour batter into two greased 8-inch layer pans and bake in 375° oven for about 25 minutes or until done. Cool and frost with Seafoam Frosting.

2 teaspoons baking powder

1/4 teaspoon salt

1/4 teaspoon ginger

1/4 teaspoon mace

1/4 teaspoon allspice

1/4 teaspoon nutmeg

3/4 teaspoon cloves

3/4 teaspoon cinnamon

3/4 cup milk

Hart's Old Fashioned Spice Cake

Hart's Old Tyme Coffee House, Moose Lake, Minnesota.

Ingredients

2 cups brown sugar
1/2 cup shortening
  (butter preferred)
3 whole eggs or 5 egg yolks
1 teaspoon allspice
1 teaspoon cinnamon
1 teaspoon ground cloves
2 cup pastry flour
1 teaspoon soda
1/2 teaspoon salt
1 cup heavy sour cream

Directions (Makes one 12x7½x2-inch cake)

Cream shortening and sugar together until thoroughly blended.

Beat egg yolks well. Add yolks and spices to above and beat well.

Sift together flour, soda and salt. Add to mixture alternately with sour cream. If whole eggs are used fold in beaten egg whites. Pour batter into a 12x7½x2-inch cake pan. Bake in 350° oven for 50 minutes or until cake starts to shrink from sides of pan. Cool and frost with Sour Cream Frosting.

Spiced Molasses Cake

Ingredients

1 3/4 cups sifted cake flour
2 teaspoons baking powder
3/4 teaspoon salt
1/4 teaspoon cloves
1/2 teaspoon nutmeg
1/2 teaspoon allspice
1 teaspoon cinnamon
1/2 cup butter
2 teaspoons grated orange rind
1 cup sugar

Directions (Makes two 8-inch layers)

Sift together opposite ingredients three times. Set aside.

Cream butter and orange rind. Add sugar gradually, and cream together until light and fluffy.

2 eggs	Add one at a time, beating well after each addition.
2/3 cup milk	Combine remaining ingredients. Add flour, alternately with milk, beating after
1 teaspoon vanilla	each addition. Pour batter into two round 8-inch layer pans which have been
2 tablespoons molasses	lined on bottoms with paper. Bake in moderate oven 375° about 35 minutes.

One of the most important kitchen tools is a set of accurate measuring spoons.
If you would get the best out of every recipe, you must follow it to the letter.

Hickory Nut Cake

Ingredients

Directions (Makes two 9-inch layers)

2 1/2 cups sifted cake flour	Sift together opposite ingredients. Set aside.
3 teaspoons baking powder	
1 teaspoon salt	
1 1/2 cups sugar	
1/2 cup butter	Stir just to soften. Sift in dry ingredients.
7/8 cup milk	Add ¾ cup of the milk and vanilla to the above mixture. Mix until all the flour is
1 teaspoon vanilla	dampened. Then beat 2 minutes at a low speed of electric mixer or 300 vigorous strokes by hand.
2 eggs	Add eggs with remaining milk. Beat 1 minute longer in mixer or 150 strokes by
1 cup chopped hickory nuts	hand. Stir in nuts. Pour batter into two round 9-inch layer pans which have been lined on bottoms with paper. Bake in moderate oven 375° for 20 to 25 minutes. This cake may also be baked in three round 8-inch layers at 375° for about 20 minutes.

Hazel Nut (Filberts) Cake

Mrs. Carl F. G. Neuhaus, Chicago, Illinois

Ingredients

Directions (Makes two 9-inch layers)

1 cup butter ·················· Cream butter and gradually add sugar.

2 cups sugar

3 cups flour ·················· Sift flour three times, last time with salt and baking powder. Add to the above
Pinch of salt   mixture alternately with milk.

2 teaspoons baking powder

1 cup milk

6 egg whites–stiffly beaten ·········· Fold in stiffly beaten egg whites. Then add remaining ingredients. Pour batter

1 1/2 cups chopped hazel nuts   into two 9-inch cake pans which have been greased and floured well. Bake in 375°
(put through No. 2 size meat   oven until top springs back when lightly pressed with fingers. Cool and frost with
chopper)   Butter Cream Frosting.

1 teaspoon cinnamon

1/2 teaspoon cloves

Pecan Cake

Ingredients

Directions (Makes one 10-inch tube cake)

3 cups sifted cake flour ·············· Sift together opposite ingredients three times. Set aside.

2 teaspoons baking powder

3/4 teaspoon salt

1 cup butter ·················· Cream butter; add sugar gradually, and cream together until light and fluffy.

1 3/4 cups sugar

3 eggs ·················· Add eggs and yolk to the above mixture and beat well.

1 egg yolk

3/4 cup milk ·················· Add flour, alternately with milk, beating after each addition until smooth.

1 teaspoon orange extract ·········· Add to the above and mix well. Pour batter into a 9 to 10-inch tube pan which

1 teaspoon almond extract   has been greased and lightly floured. Bake in moderate oven 375° for 60 minutes,

1 cup finely chopped pecans   or until wire cake tester comes out clean and dry. (Cool slightly before removing
from pan.) Serve unfrosted to accompany fruit desserts or ice cream. May be
frosted if desired.

The Duncan Hines Dessert Book

Prune and Nut Spice Cake

The Maine Maid, Jericho, Long Island, New York

Ingredients

1/2 cup butter
1 cup sugar
2 eggs—beaten
1 cup sour milk
2 teaspoons soda
2 cups flour
1 1/2 teaspoons cinnamon
1/2 teaspoon cloves
1/2 teaspoon salt
1/2 teaspoon allspice
3/4 cup chopped stewed prunes
3/4 cup chopped nuts

Directions (Makes two 9-inch layers)

Cream butter and sugar. Add beaten eggs, then sour milk in which soda has been dissolved.

Sift together flour, salt and spices and add to above mixture.

Add nuts to prunes; dust lightly with flour, add to above and mix. Pour batter into two 9-inch layer cake pans which have been greased and floured. Bake in 375° oven for 20 to 30 minutes or until done. Put together with any desired filling.

Fairy Loaf Cake

Dorothy Dean, The Spokesman-Review, Spokane, Washington

Ingredients

8 egg yolks
1 1/4 cups sugar
1/2 cup salad oil
2 3/4 cups sifted cake flour
3 teaspoons double-acting baking powder
1/2 teaspoon salt
1 cup water
1 1/2 teaspoons vanilla or 1 teaspoon vanilla and 1/2 teaspoon lemon or whatever flavoring you prefer.

Directions (Makes one 10-inch tube cake)

Beat egg yolks until fluffy. Add sugar gradually and beat in thoroughly. Add oil and beat until fluffy.

Sift flour with baking powder and salt. Add to first mixture alternately with water and flavoring, beating carefully. The batter will be thin. Bake in a 10-inch tube pan or in a 13x9x2-inch pan, or a 10x16-inch pan at 350° to 375° for 35 to 50 minutes. This is a good cake to cut into small pieces and frost for petits fours. If desired, slice the tube cake crosswise, in three equal layers, and frost with Butter Rum Frosting.

Prune Layer Cake

Mrs. Alonzo Newton Benn, Chicago, Illinois

Ingredients

Directions (Serves 10 to 12)

1/3 cup butter ················· Cream butter and sugar together.

1 1/8 cups sugar

2 egg yolks–beaten ················· Add opposite ingredients to above mixture and stir well.

1 egg–beaten

5 tablespoons milk

1 1/8 cups stewed ················· Add chopped prunes and lemon juice to mixture and stir.
   prunes–chopped

1 teaspoon lemon juice

1 1/2 cups flour ················· Sift together and add to mixture, stir lightly. Pour batter into two 9-inch round

1/2 teaspoon baking soda   cake pans which have been greased and floured. Bake in 375° oven for 25 to 30

1 1/2 teaspoons baking   minutes. Cool and cover with a boiled white icing. This delicious cake remains
   powder   fresh for some time.

1/4 teaspoon salt

1 teaspoon cinnamon

1 teaspoon cloves

1 teaspoon nutmeg

Luncheon Cake

Mrs. H. V. Cameron, Chatham, Ontario, Canada

Ingredients

Directions (Makes two loaf cakes)

1 lb. butter ················· Cream butter until fluffy, add sugar and beat five minutes.

1 lb. sugar

10 eggs ················· Add eggs, two at a time to the above mixture, until six have been added, beat five

1 1/4 lbs. all purpose flour   minutes after each addition. Add the remaining four eggs one at a time, beating

1 1/2 lbs. raisins   five minutes after each one.

1/2 lb. mixed candied fruit peel ···· Combine fruit and flour lightly. Add fruit and remaining flour to the above,
   mixing well. Pour into two 9x5-inch loaf pans. Bake in a 300° F. oven for 1 hour.

Orange Gold Loaf

Ingredients

2 1/4 cups sifted cake flour
2 teaspoons baking powder
3/4 teaspoon salt
1 cup sugar
1/2 cup butter
2 teaspoons grated orange
  rind
5 egg yolks
1/3 cup milk
1/3 cup milk

Directions (Makes one 10 x 3-inch loaf cake)

Sift together opposite ingredients. Set aside.

Stir butter just to soften. Sift dry ingredients.

Add rind, yolks, and milk and mix until all flour is dampened. Beat 2 minutes at a low speed of electric mixer or 300 vigorous strokes by hand.

Add milk to the above mixture and beat 1 minute in electric mixer or 150 strokes by hand. Pour batter into a 10x3-inch loaf pan which has been lined on bottom with paper. Bake in moderate oven 350° for 60 to 70 minutes. (Cake will have a crack on top.)

Angel Peppermint Loaf Cake

Ingredients

1/2 cup sifted cake flour
1/4 cup sifted sugar
2/3 cup egg whites
1/8 teaspoon salt
1/2 teaspoon cream of tartar
1/2 teaspoon vanilla
1/4 teaspoon almond extract
1/2 cup sugar
2 tablespoons finely crushed
  peppermint stick candy

Directions (Serves 8)

Sift together opposite ingredients three times. Set aside.

Combine opposite ingredients in a large bowl. Beat with flat wire whip, egg beater, or at a high speed of electric mixer until soft peaks are formed.

Add sugar to the egg whites, 2 tablespoons at a time, beating after each addition.
Fold in flour mixture, one-half at a time.
Fold crushed candy into batter. Pour batter into ungreased 10x5x3-inch loaf pan. Bake in moderate oven 375° about 25 minutes. Cool upside down 1 hour. Serve plain or with ice cream and Chocolate Sauce.

Hoagy Cake

Ingredients

1 1/4 cups sugar
1/2 cup butter
2 eggs–well beaten
1 1/4 cups buttermilk
1 teaspoon soda
1/2 teaspoon salt
1 teaspoon baking powder
2 cups sifted cake flour
Grated rind of 2 oranges
1/2 cup chopped nuts

Sauce

1 cup sugar
Juice of 2 oranges
Juice of 1 lemon

Directions (Makes one 13x9x2-inch cake)

Cream butter and sugar; add well beaten eggs.

Combine soda, baking powder and salt with flour and add alternately with buttermilk to above.

Add orange rind and chopped nuts to above; pour batter into a 13x9x2-inch pan which has been greased and floured. Bake in 350° oven for 30 minutes or until done.

Combine sugar with juice of oranges and lemon and cook for 5 minutes. While cake is still in pan, pour sauce over cake. Cut and serve immediately.

Sultana Cake

Ingredients

1 lb. butter
1 lb. sugar
8 eggs
1 1/2 cups milk
8 cups cake flour
3 teaspoons baking powder
1 lb. sultana raisins
1/2 lb. orange peel
Orange and lemon to flavor

Directions (Makes 3 loaves)

Cream together butter and sugar.

Mix eggs into the above.
Slowly add milk to the mixture.
Sift cake flour and baking powder and add to mixture.

Add remaining ingredients to mixture. Pour batter into 3 loaf pans which have been greased and lightly floured. Bake in 350° oven for 1 hour or more.

Pound Cake

Ingredients

1/2 lb. butter

1 3/4 cups sugar

5 whole eggs

2 cups flour–measured after
   two siftings

Vanilla

Mace

Directions (Makes one loaf cake)

Cream butter until fluffy. Beat like the Devil.

Add sugar to creamed butter. Cream until fluffy and light.

Drop in one whole egg at a time, while beating, until you have dropped in five.

Stop the beater and fold in flour. Do not beat as that makes it tough. Flavor with a little vanilla and mace. Bake in loaf pan about 45 minutes at 300°. Turn oven up to 325° for fifteen minutes or until brown.

The old-fashioned recipe called for brandy, nutmeg, and mace instead of vanilla. Do you have the brandy?

Applesauce Cake

Ingredients

1 1/2 cups brown sugar

3/4 cup butter

3 teaspoons soda

1 1/2 cups applesauce

3 cups flour

1/2 teaspoon cinnamon

1/2 teaspoon cloves

1/2 teaspoon allspice

1 cup raisins

1 cup nuts

Directions (Makes one 10-inch square layer)

Cream together brown sugar and butter until smooth.

Dissolve soda in applesauce and add to butter and sugar mixture.

Sift flour; measure and sift again with spices. Add raisins and nuts to flour and stir all into batter. Bake in a 10-inch square cake pan or in a 13x9x2-inch pan which has been greased and lined with waxed paper. Bake in 350° oven for 25 to 30 minutes or until done. Ice with boiled white icing.

Here is a simple way to find out if your cake is done. Stick in a toothpick and if it comes out clean it is done. Or lightly touch the tope of the cake with your little finger, and if it leaves no imprint, it is done.

Applesauce Cake

Ingredients

3 cups sifted flour ·····················

2 teaspoons soda

1/4 teaspoon salt

2 teaspoons cinnamon

1 1/2 teaspoons cloves

1/2 cup butter ·····················

3/4 cup brown sugar

2 eggs ·····························

2 cups thick applesauce ···············

2 cups chopped walnuts ············

2 cups chopped raisins

1 cup chopped dates

Directions (Makes two loaf cakes)

Sift together opposite ingredients three times. Set aside.

Cream butter; add brown sugar gradually, and cream together until light and fluffy.

Add eggs, one at a time, beating well after each addition.

Add flour, alternately with applesauce, beating well after each addition until smooth.

Beat in remaining ingredients. Pour batter into two 6x3-inch loaf pans which have been lined on bottoms with paper. Bake in slow oven 325° about 60 minutes. (This cake will keep moist for several days if stored in a tightly covered cake box.)

Gingerbread

Ingredients

1 cup boiling water ·····················

1 cup shortening

1 cup brown sugar ·····················

1 cup molasses

3 eggs–beaten

3 cups flour ·····················

1 teaspoon baking powder

1 teaspoon soda

1 teaspoon salt

1 1/2 teaspoons ginger

1 1/2 teaspoons cinnamon

Directions (Makes one 13x9x3-inch cake)

Pour water over shortening.

Add opposite ingredients to the above.

Sift together remaining ingredients and add to the mixture. Beat with an egg beater until smooth. Pour batter into a greased and floured 13x9x3-inch pan. Bake in 350° oven for 30 to 40 minutes.

The Duncan Hines Dessert Book

Sour Cream Gingerbread

Ingredients

1 cup flour ·······················
1/4 teaspoon salt
1/4 cup sugar
1/2 teaspoon soda
1 1/2 teaspoons ginger
1 teaspoon cinnamon
1/2 teaspoon cloves
2/3 cup thick sour cream
3 tablespoons butter
1/3 cup dark molasses
1 egg

Directions (Serves 6)

Mix and sift all dry ingredients in mixing bowl. Heat cream; remove from fire and add butter and stir until melted. Add molasses. Beat egg and pour into it the other ingredients gradually, beating constantly. Add this to dry ingredients, mixing only enough to make a smooth batter. Pour into a buttered 8-inch square cake pan, and bake in 350° oven for 25 to 30 minutes or until done. Serve hot with whipped cream or hot buttered rum sauce.

Sponge Cake

Ingredients

12 egg yolks–beaten ················
1/2 cup sugar
Juice of 1 lemon ················
1 cup flour–sift 4 times
12 egg whites–beaten ················
Pinch of salt
1/2 cup sugar
1 teaspoon vanilla ················

Directions (Makes one 10-inch tube cake)

Beat in sugar with egg yolks, a teaspoon at a time.

Add alternately to above until it becomes a smooth dough.

Slowly beat sugar and salt into the egg whites. Cut into the batter.

Add to mixture. Pour batter into an ungreased 10-inch tube pan. Bake in a 325° oven for 1 hour and 15 minutes. (We use this delicious sponge cake to make our famous "Ice Cream Sandwiches." One slice of cake, coffee ice cream with butterscotch sauce. It's "yummy.")

Sponge Cake

Ingredients

6 egg yolks ···············

1 cup sugar ···············

1 cup sifted cake flour ···············

1/4 cup cold water

1 teaspoon lemon extract

1 teaspoon vanilla extract

6 egg whites ···············

1/2 teaspoon cream of tartar

1/2 teaspoon salt

Directions (Makes one 10-inch tube cake)

Beat until very thick and lemon-colored.

Beat sugar into yolks very gradually.

Add flour gradually to the above mixture alternately with water. Beat until blended. Add flavorings.

Combine in large bowl and beat with wire whip or rotary egg beater until just stiff enough to hold a peak. Gradually and carefully fold the egg yolk mixture into the beaten egg whites. Pour batter into an ungreased 10-inch tube pan. Bake in slow oven 325° for 60 to 65 minutes. Invert and cool in pan, 1 to 2 hours. Loosen from sides and center tube with knife and gently pull out. Serve plain or frost with Butter Cream Frosting. Or serve a wedge of cake covered with ice cream topped with fresh berries, Fudge or Butterscotch Sauce.

Egg Yolk Sponge Cake

Ingredients

2 cups sifted cake flour ···············

2 teaspoons baking powder

1/2 teaspoon salt

11 egg yolks (3/4 cup) ···············

1 whole egg

1 3/4 cups sugar ···············

1/2 cup cold water ···············

1 tablespoon grated orange rind

1 tablespoon orange juice

Directions (Makes one 10-inch tube cake)

Sift together opposite ingredients. Set aside.

Beat together until thick and lemon-colored.

Beat into above very gradually.

Combine remaining ingredients. Add flour gradually to the above mixture alternately with water. Beat until well blended. Pour batter into an ungreased 10-inch tube pan. Bake in slow oven 325° for 60 to 65 minutes. Invert and cool 1 to 2 hours.

Chocolate Sponge Cake

Ingredients

1/4 lb. or 4 squares unsweetened chocolate

1 cup milk

5 eggs

2 cups sugar

1 1/4 cups flour

1 teaspoon baking powder

Pinch of salt

1 teaspoon vanilla

Directions (Makes three 8-inch or two 10-inch layers)

Shave chocolate and add to milk. Cook over slow fire, stirring constantly until thick. Let stand until cool.

Separate and put whites aside.

Cream egg yolks and sugar well. Add chocolate and milk mixture.

Sift together dry ingredients and add to above.

Add to above. Beat the egg whites and fold into cake mixture. Pour batter into three 8-inch layer pans or two 10-inch layer pans which have been greased and floured. Bake in 350° oven until a straw or cake tester pulls out clean. Do not over bake or cake will be dry. Ice with caramel or chocolate icing.

Daffodil Cake

Ingredients

1 1/4 cups sifted cake flour

1/2 cup sifted sugar

1 1/4 cups egg whites

1/4 teaspoon salt

1 1/2 teaspoons cream of tartar

3/4 teaspoon vanilla

1 cup sugar

Directions (Makes one 10-inch tube cake)

Sift together opposite ingredients three times. Set aside.

Combine opposite ingredients in large bowl. Beat with flat wire whip, egg beater, or at a high speed of electric mixer until whites are stiff enough to hold up in soft peaks, but still moist and glossy.

Add sugar to the egg whites, 4 tablespoons at a time, beating after each addition until blended. Sift about one fourth of the flour mixture over beaten egg whites. Fold in with 15 fold-over strokes, turning bowl often. Fold in remaining flour in same manner. Pour batter into ungreased 10-inch tube pan. Bake in slow oven 325° for 60 minutes.

Sunshine Cake

Ingredients

Directions (Makes one 10-inch tube cake)

5 egg yolks (1/3 cup) ·················· Beat until very thick and lemon-colored.

1/2 cup sugar ·························· Beat into yolks very gradually.

1 cup sifted cake flour ··············· Add flour gradually to the above mixture alternately with water. Beat until
2 tablespoons cold water   blended. Add flavoring.
1 teaspoon vanilla

8 egg whites (1 cup) ·················· Combine opposite ingredients in large bowl and beat with wire whip or rotary
1/2 teaspoon cream of tartar   egg beater until just stiff enough to hold a peak.
1/2 teaspoon salt

1 cup sugar ··························· Gradually beat sugar into stiffly beaten egg whites. Slowly and carefully fold the
egg yolk mixture into the beaten egg whites. Pour batter into an ungreased
10-inch tube pan. Bake in slow oven 325° for 60 to 65 minutes. Invert and cool in
pan 1 to 2 hours. Loosen from sides and center tube with knife and gently pull
out. Serve plain or frosted.

Sunshine Cake

Ingredients

Directions (Makes one 10-inch tube cake)

1 cup flour ··························· Sift together opposite ingredients three times.
1 teaspoon baking powder
1 1/2 teaspoons cornstarch
1/2 teaspoon salt

4 egg yolks–beaten ··················· Beat yolks and sugar together.
1/2 cup sugar

2 tablespoons flour ·················· Add opposite ingredients to egg mixture and stir into dry ingredients.
3 tablespoons cold water
1 teaspoon vanilla

4 egg whites–beaten ·················· Fold egg whites and sugar into mixture and pour into 10-inch tube pan. Bake in
1/2 cup sugar   300° oven for 45 minutes, then in 350° oven for 15 minutes. Invert pan until the
cake is cold.

The Duncan Hines Dessert Book

Angel Food Cake with Eggnog Filling

Mrs. Gordon Pilkington, St. Louis, Missouri

Ingredients

1 1/2 cups egg whites
1 teaspoon cream of tartar
Pinch of salt

1 cup sifted cake flour
1 1/2 cups less 2 tablespoons sifted sugar

1/2 teaspoon almond extract
1 teaspoon vanilla
1 tablespoon strained lemon juice

Directions (Serves 16)

Whip white with wire whisk until frothy; add cream of tartar and salt. Beat until stiff but not dry. Remove wire whisk.

Sift flour and sugar together several times and fold a small amount at a time into the egg whites.

Add flavorings and pour batter into a 9 to 10-inch tube pan. Bake at 325° for about an hour. Remove from oven and invert the pan. Let stand until cold. Remove from pan and slice crosswise into four layers.

Eggnog Filling

1/2 lb. butter
1 lb. powdered sugar–sifted

5 egg yolks

1/2 cup bourbon whiskey

1/4 lb. chopped toasted almonds

1/4 lb. crushed macaroon crumbs

1 pint whipping cream
2 tablespoons sugar
2 tablespoons whiskey

1/4 lb. chopped toasted almonds

1/4 lb. macaroon crumbs
Cherries and green leaves

Cream butter. Add sugar to butter and whip until creamy.

Add yolks to the above and mix well.

Fold in bourbon whiskey (rum may be substituted), chopped almonds, and macaroon crumbs. Fill layers of cake.

Whip cream and add sugar and whiskey. Coat outside of cake with whipped cream.

Cover whipped cream with almonds and macaroon crumbs mixed together.

Decorate with cherries and green leaves.

Ribbon Cake

Lowell Inn, Stillwater, Minnesota

LEMON AND CHOCOLATE LAYERS

Ingredients

Directions (Makes a 9-inch four layer cake)

1/2 cup shortening ·················· Cream together shortening and sugar thoroughly. Add eggs, one at a time, and
1 1/2 cups sugar beat until fluffy.
2 eggs

2 1/4 cups cake flour ················ Sift flour, measure, add other dry ingredients and sift together. Add to butter and
2 1/2 teaspoons baking sugar mixture, alternately with milk, and blend well. Divide batter into two equal
  powder portions.
1 teaspoon salt
1 cup plus 2 tablespoons milk

1/2 teaspoon lemon extract ········· Mix lemon flavor into one portion of batter.
1 1/2 squares unsweetened ·········· Melt chocolate in milk and let cool slightly. Then stir into other portion of cake
  chocolate batter. Pour each batter into a greased, paper lined 9-inch cake pan. Bake in
1 tablespoon milk moderate oven 375° for 25 minutes or until done.

SILVER AND PINK LAYERS

5 egg whites ··················· Beat egg whites until fairly stiff; gradually add sugar and beat until meringue
1/2 cup sugar stands up in peaks.
2/3 cup shortening ·············· Cream shortening until fluffy; add sugar gradually and vanilla. Beat until smooth
1 1/4 cups sugar and creamy.
1 teaspoon vanilla

2 2/3 cups cake flour ············ Sift flour, measure, add other dry ingredients and sift again. Add to creamed
3 teaspoons baking powder mixture alternately with milk. Mix well until smooth. Fold in beaten egg whites
1 teaspoon salt and blend well. Divide into two equal portions.
1 cup milk

1 teaspoon peppermint extract ····· Flavor 1 portion of batter with peppermint extract and add red coloring to make
A drop or two of red food a delicate pink. Pour each batter into a greased, paper lined 9-inch cake pan and
  coloring bake in 375° oven for 30 minutes or until done. Let all layers cool.

FROSTING

4 cups sugar .... Combine sugar, cream of tartar and water and let come to boil. Cook to 240°.
1 teaspoon cream of tartar
1 1/2 cups water

4 egg whites .... Beat egg whites until stiff. Pour syrup into whites, little by little, beating
2 teaspoons vanilla   constantly. Add vanilla and just enough coloring to give a delicate pink color.
Few drops red food coloring .... Beat until of spreading consistency. Place chocolate layer first on plate, frost; then
                                                           the lemon flavored layer, frost; then add the pink layer, frost; and last the silver
                                                           layer. Frost top and sides of cake.

Lane Cake

Dr. T. J. Leblanc, Cincinnati, Ohio

Ingredients   **Directions** (Makes two 10-inch layers or one tube cake)

1 cup butter .... Cream butter and sugar together until very light.
2 cups sugar

3 1/4 cups flour .... Sift dry ingredients together four times. Add milk to creamed mixture, alternately
3 teaspoons baking powder   with the flour.
1 cup milk

8 egg whites–beaten .... Add vanilla to egg whites and fold into mixture. Bake in two 10-inch layer pans
1 tablespoon vanilla   or one tube pan in 350° oven for 40 to 50 minutes, or until cake springs to touch.
                                                Test with straw.

LANE CAKE FILLING

1/2 cup butter .... Cream butter and sugar together.
1 cup sugar

7 egg yolks–beaten .... Add egg yolks and cook in double boiler, stirring constantly until smooth and
                                             thick. Remove from fire.

1 cup raisins–chopped .... Add opposite ingredients to mixture while it is still hot.
1 cup nut meats–chopped
1 teaspoon vanilla

1 wineglass brandy .... Add brandy to mixture and spread over the cake.

Fresh Coconut Angel Cake

The White Turkey Town House, New York, New York

Ingredients	Directions (Makes one 10-inch tube cake)
12 egg whites ·················	Beat together egg whites and salt until foamy.
1 teaspoon salt	
1 teaspoon cream of tartar ···········	Add cream of tartar to eggs and beat until stiff, but moist.
1 cup pastry flour	Sift together three or four times and carefully fold into the beaten eggs. Pour into
1 cup sugar	a 10-inch tube pan free of grease and bake in 300° oven for 50 minutes. Turn off oven and let cake remain for another ten minutes. Cool and frost with Boiled Frosting. Sprinkle top with fresh grated coconut.

Cakes should always be cooled thoroughly before frosting.

Cherry Sponge

Mrs. A. E. R. Peterka, Cleveland, Ohio

Ingredients	Directions (Serves 4)
3 egg yolks–beaten ··············	Beat sugar into yolks until smooth and lemon-colored.
3 tablespoons sugar	
3 egg whites–beaten ··············	Put whites on top of yolks.
3 teaspoons flour ···············	Sift flour over the egg whites. Fold in lightly. Put mixture in an 8-inch square or round cake pan, 1 ½ inches deep.
1 1/2 cups sweet black ·············· cherries	Wash and dry cherries. Drop into the egg batter so they are distributed evenly over the surface. Bake in 320° oven for 10 to 15 minutes or until lightly browned. Let cool; slice; and then dust with powdered sugar and serve.

If you do not have the proper pan size, do not fill the pan more than two-thirds full of batter.

Patio Ice Cream Cake

Ingredients

Directions (Serves 6 to 8)

2 eggs
1 cup sugar
1/2 cup milk
1 teaspoon butter

Beat eggs well and add sugar. (Use an electric mixer if possible.) Bring milk just to a boil; add butter and add to egg mixture.

1 cup flour
1 1/2 teaspoons baking powder
1/2 teaspoon salt
1/2 teaspoon vanilla

Sift dry ingredients together. Add to egg mixture gradually. Add vanilla. Pour batter into 8-inch greased and floured square pan. Bake in a 350° oven for 20 minutes or until done.

PATIO CARAMEL SAUCE

1 cup brown sugar
1 cup dark corn syrup

Boil sugar and syrup together for 5 minutes.

1/4 cup granulated sugar
1/4 cup butter

Caramelize sugar; add to syrup. Add butter and boil a few minutes longer.

1/2 cup coffee cream
Pinch of salt
1 teaspoon vanilla
Vanilla ice cream
Whipped cream
Slivered toasted almonds

Remove from fire and stir in cream, salt and vanilla. When ready to serve, cut cake in squares. Split each square and place vanilla ice cream between layers. Put whipped cream over top and drip Caramel Sauce over all. Sprinkle with toasted almonds.

It is best to wait until cakes cool before slicing.

De Luxe Coffee Cake

Mrs. Gordon Pilkington, St. Louis, Missouri

Ingredients

3/4 cup butter
1 1/2 cups sugar
3 eggs
3 cups flour
Pinch of salt
3 teaspoons baking powder
1 cup sweet milk
Grated rind of 1 lemon
2 tablespoons lemon juice
Chopped pecans
Powdered sugar

Directions (Makes one 10-inch tube cake)

Cream butter and sugar well.

Add eggs, one at a time, and beat well.

Sift flour and measure. Add salt and baking powder and sift again. Add to butter and sugar mixture, alternately with milk. Mix well.

Add lemon rind and juice. Grease deep 10-inch tube pan with butter. Sprinkle with flour and cover bottom thickly with pecans. Pour batter into pan and bake at 350° for 50 to 60 minutes, or until done. Turn out and cover nut covered top thickly with powdered sugar. If desired, a cup each of raisins and pecans can be added to batter. If so, flour with a little extra flour before stirring into batter.

Banana Dutch Coffee Cake

Home Economics Department, Fruit Dispatch Company, New York City

Ingredients

1 cup sifted flour
1 1/4 teaspoons baking
  powder
1/2 teaspoon salt
2 tablespoons sugar
1/4 cup shortening
1 egg–well beaten
3 tablespoons milk
3 bananas (firm)
2 tablespoons butter–melted
2 tablespoons sugar
1/4 teaspoon cinnamon
1 teaspoon grated orange rind

Directions (Serves 6 to 8)

Sift together dry ingredients.

Cut shortening into the above.

Mix together egg and milk and stir into flour mixture. The dough should be stiff. Turn into a well greased baking pan.

Peel and slice bananas into ½-inch diagonal pieces. Cover dough with bananas.

Brush butter over the bananas.

Mix together remaining ingredients and sprinkle over the bananas. Bake in 350° oven about 35 minutes. Serve hot for breakfast or as dessert with whipped cream or Lemon Hard Sauce (see Dessert Sauces Section.)

Chocolate Fudge Upside Down Cake

Cathryn's, Portland, Oregon

Ingredients

3/4 cup sugar ·························

1 tablespoon butter

1/2 cup milk ·························

1 cup flour ·························

1/4 teaspoon salt

1 teaspoon baking powder

1 1/2 tablespoons cocoa

1/2 cup walnuts–chopped ············

1/2 cup sugar

1/2 cup brown sugar ················

1/4 cup cocoa

1 1/4 cups boiling water ············

Directions (Makes one 9-inch square cake)

Cream butter and sugar together.

Add milk to the above and stir.

Sift together opposite ingredients and add to mixture. Stir well and put in 9-inch buttered, square pan.

Sprinkle with nuts.

Mix opposite ingredients well together and spread over top.

Pour water over the top of all. Bake in 350° oven for 30 minutes. Let cool in pan.

Apricot Coconut Upside Down Cake

Ingredients

1/4 lb. dried apricots ···············

1/4 lb. butter

1 cup brown sugar

1/2 cup butter ·····················

1 cup sugar

2 eggs ·····························

2 cups cake flour ··················

2 teaspoons baking powder

1/2 teaspoon salt

1 cup milk

Freshly grated coconut

Directions (Makes one large upside down cake)

Apricots should be simmered gently until tender but not mushy. In a heavy, large iron skillet melt butter; spread sugar evenly over butter and place a layer of apricot halves to cover the bottom.

Cream butter and sugar together.

Beat eggs into above mixture thoroughly.

Sift flour, measure, and add baking powder and salt and sift together twice. Add flour, alternately with milk to the creamed mixture. Pour batter over the apricots in the skillet and bake in a 350° oven for 35 minutes or until done. Turn out on large round platter and top with freshly grated coconut.

Torte

Ingredients	Directions (Serves 10-12)
6 egg whites	Beat egg whites stiff, adding sugar gradually.
1 1/2 cups sugar	
1 1/2 teaspoons vinegar	Add opposite ingredients to the above. Drop on brown paper placed on cookie
1 teaspoon vanilla	sheet, using a spoon that holds about 2 tablespoonfuls. After they are placed on
1/4 teaspoon almond extract	the sheet, make an indentation with the back of the spoon. Bake in 300° oven for
	45 minutes; then raise the temperature to 325° for 15 minutes. Remove from
	paper using a spatula. If they stick, reheat the sheet and try again.
1 quart strawberries	Do not crush the berries. Add sugar and fill each indentation with berries.
1/2 cup sugar–superfine	
1 cup whipping	Top each meringue with whipped cream. If berries are not used, peaches may be
cream–whipped	upturned and filled with a soft custard.

CUSTARD

3 cups milk and 1/2 cup sugar, ...	Scald.
or 2 cups milk and 1 cup	
peach juice and 1/3 cup	
sugar	
6 egg yolks–beaten	Put opposite ingredients in double boiler and pour hot milk over. Cook slowly
1/3 cup sugar	until mixture coats a spoon. Stir while cooking. Cool.
1 teaspoon salt	
1/8 teaspoon almond flavoring	

There are four basic principles that should not be overlooked in cooking any dish—
proper and accurate measurements, proper cooking temperature,
proper length of cooking time, and proper time of serving.

Baked Cherry Torte

Ingredients

1 egg

1 1/4 cups sugar

2 cups well drained cherries

1 cup pastry flour

1/4 teaspoon salt

1/2 teaspoon soda

1 teaspoon cinnamon

1 tablespoon melted butter

1 teaspoon almond extract

1/2 cup cut pecans

SAUCE

1 cup cold cherry juice (add water to make 1 cup)

1/4 cup sugar

1 tablespoon cornstarch

1/8 teaspoon salt

1 tablespoon butter

2 drops almond extract

1/2 cup whipped cream—sweetened

Directions (Serves 12)

Beat egg. Gradually add sugar and continue beating until sugar is dissolved in egg. Fold in cherries.

Sift dry ingredients. Fold into above mixture.

Add melted butter and flavoring. Turn batter into a greased pan.

Scatter cut pecans over top of batter. Bake in 350° oven about 45 minutes. Cool. Prepare sauce.

Combine dry ingredients with several tablespoons of the cold liquid. Heat remaining liquid. Add first mixture to the hot cherry juice and cook until thick and no starch taste remains. Taste for sweetness and add more sugar if needed.

Add and cool.

Serve torte cold topped with whipped cream and then add cherry sauce on top of whipped cream.

Blitz Torte

Ingredients

1 3/4 cups sifted cake flour ·········
2 1/4 teaspoons baking powder
3/4 teaspoon salt
1 cup plus 2 tablespoons sugar

4 egg whites ·········
1 cup sugar

1/2 cup butter ·········
2/3 cup milk ·········
1 teaspoon vanilla
2 eggs ·········

1/3 cup slivered blanched almonds ·········

Directions (Makes two 9-inch layers)

Sift together opposite ingredients. Set aside.

Beat egg whites until frothy throughout. Add sugar, 2 tablespoons at a time, beating after each addition until blended. Continue beating until stiff peaks are formed. Set aside.

Stir butter just to soften. Sift in dry ingredients.
Add milk and vanilla to above mixture and mix until all flour is dampened.
Beat 2 minutes at a low speed of electric mixer or 300 vigorous strokes by hand.
Add eggs and beat 1 minute longer in mixer or 150 strokes by hand. Pour batter into two round 9-inch layer pans which have been lined on bottoms with paper. Spread egg white meringue over batter.
Sprinkle almonds over top. Bake in moderate oven 350° for 35 to 40 minutes, or until the meringue is lightly browned and cake is done when cake tester is inserted. Cool and spread Pineapple Filling between layers and whipped cream on sides.

L. S. Ayers Tea Room, Indianapolis, Indiana

Date Nut Torte

Ingredients

1/2 cup egg whites ·········
1 1/2 teaspoons water
5/8 cup sugar ·········
1 cup cake crumbs ·········
1/4 teaspoon baking powder
1/2 cup walnuts or pecans
1 cup chopped dates

Directions (Serves 9)

Whip egg whites until stiff; add water gradually.

Add sugar to egg whites beating during the addition.
Combine cake crumbs with baking powder, nuts, and dates and add to above mixture. Pour into an ungreased 9-inch square cake pan. Bake at 325° for 30 minutes.

Fruit Cake

Virginia McDonald's Tea Room, Gallatin, Missouri

Ingredients	Directions
4 lbs. seeded raisins	Soak raisins in brandy overnight.
2 cups peach brandy	
2 cups butter	Cream butter and sugar until light and fluffy. Add beaten egg yolks.
2 cups sugar	
10 egg yolks–beaten until thick	Fold beaten egg whites into the above. Sift flour and baking powder together. Add to the above mixture.
10 egg whites–stiffly beaten	
2 cups sifted flour	
1 teaspoon baking powder	
1/2 teaspoon soda	Combine soda and molasses and add to mixture.
1 cup molasses	
1 teaspoon allspice	Combine opposite ingredients and add to mixture.
1 teaspoon cloves	
1 teaspoon cinnamon	
3 cups candied citron–cut	Add remaining ingredients and the raisins to the batter. Mix together thoroughly. Pour batter into load pans which have been greased and lined with waxed paper or heavy brown paper. Fill pans about three-fourths full. Or bake fruit cake in an old-fashioned corset box if you have one. Line box with greased brown paper. After pouring in the batter cover with greased brown paper, and then put on the box lid. Bake in slow oven 300° for 3 to 4 hours or until done. Cover fruit cakes with brown paper about halfway through baking to prevent it from browning too much.
1 cup figs–cut	
1 cup dates–cut	
1 cup candied lemon peel–cut	
1 cup candied orange peel–cut	
2 cups almonds–finely chopped	
2 cups pecans–finely chopped	

Have you ever eaten a cold baked apple? Then try one with a little cinnamon, nutmeg, and warm milk. You may bake these while using the oven for something else, letting them cool and then storing them in the refrigerator for later use. Stale bread may be toasted at the same time and will add flavor as well as proteins along with your baked apple and warm milk.

Gumdrop Fruit Cake

Dolores Restaurant and Drive-In, Oklahoma City, Oklahoma

Ingredients

1 cup butter

2 cups sugar

2 eggs–beaten

4 cups flour

1 teaspoon cinnamon

1/4 teaspoon nutmeg

1/4 teaspoon cloves

1/4 teaspoon salt

1 1/2 cups sieved applesauce

1 teaspoon soda

1 tablespoon hot water

1 teaspoon vanilla

1 to 2 lbs. gumdrops

1 lb. white raisins

1 cup pecans

Directions (Makes 2 or 3 small loaf cakes)

Cream butter and sugar together.

Add eggs to the above.

Sift together dry ingredients. Put a little aside to mix with raisins, nuts and gumdrops. Add the remainder to the above alternately with the applesauce.

Dissolve soda in hot water and stir into mixture.

Add vanilla to mixture.
(Do not use any black gumdrops.) Cut in pieces with scissors.

Fry pecans in a little butter and add to gumdrops and raisins. Mix in the flour and add to the mixture. Line two or three small load pans with greased parchment or heavy paper and bake in 300° to 325° oven for 2 hours. If oven glass or casseroles are used, do not line with paper but bake at a lower temperature of 275° to 300°.

Dark Fruit Cake

Ingredients

3/4 lb. butter

2 cups sugar

8 egg yolks

4 cups flour

1 tablespoon cinnamon

1/2 teaspoon cloves

1 teaspoon nutmeg

3 teaspoons soda

Directions (Makes about 12 lbs.)

Cream butter and sugar together.

Add yolks to above.

Hold out a little flour to mix later with fruits. Sift dry ingredients together and add to mixture.

Mix soda and water together and stir into mixture.

1/2 cup cold water

8 egg whites–beaten ·················· Fold beaten egg whites into mixture.

2 lbs. moist raisins ···················· Mix fruits and nuts with the flour held out. Stir into mixture.

2 lbs. currants

1/4 lb. candied orange
 peel–cut

1/4 lb. candied lemon peel–cut

1/2 lb. citron–cut

1/4 lb. candied cherries–cut

1/4 lb. candied pineapple–cut

1/4 lb. candied fruit mix

3/4 lb. walnuts–broken

1/2 lb. pecans–broken ··················· Stir in the wine. Bake in 350° oven for about 75 minutes; then turn oven down to

1 cup sherry wine   300° and bake another 75 minutes, or about 3 hours. Be careful not to bake too
                           fast, or it will burn.

Christmas Nut Cake

Ingredients

Directions (Makes one 10-inch tube cake)

1/2 lb. butter ··························· Cream butter and sugar together in electric mixer.

1/2 lb. sugar

5 egg yolks ···························· Add yolks to above, one at a time. Remove from beater.

1/4 cup sour cream

1/4 teaspoon soda ···················· Dissolve soda in cream and add to above, stirring lightly.

1/2 lb. flour ·························· Sift flour and nutmeg together. Add to above alternately with whiskey.

1/2 whole nutmeg–grated

1/3 cup whiskey

3/4 lb. raisins ························ Chop fruit and nuts and flour well with extra flour. Add to above folding in gently.

1/2 lb. hickory nuts or pecans

1 pkg. candied red cherries ··········· Beat egg whites stiff and fold into above. Pour in greased 10-inch tube pan with

1/8 lb. citron   paper in bottom. Place in 300° oven. Put pan of water on lower level and bake for

5 egg whites   2 hours or until done. This cake cannot be kept for any length of time, but must
                      be eaten within a week.

Christmas Wine Cake

Dupul's Tavern, Port Angeles, Washington

Ingredients

2 cups sugar
1 cup butter
2 eggs

3 1/2 cups flour
1/2 teaspoon salt
1 teaspoon soda
1 teaspoon cinnamon
1 teaspoon cloves

2 cups unsweetened
  applesauce

1 cup chopped mixed
  candied fruit
1 cup raisins
1 cup nuts

Directions (Makes about 30 cup cakes)

Cream butter and sugar until fluffy. Add eggs and beat well.

Sift flour and measure. Retain ½ cup to flour fruits and nuts. To remaining flour add other ingredients and sift again. Stir into creamed mixture.

Heat applesauce to the boiling point and add to batter.

Combine opposite ingredients and flour well with the ½ cup reserved flour. Stir into batter and mix well. Spoon batter into paper lined muffin pans filling ⅔ full. Bake for 30 minutes in a 350° oven. Serve warm with wine sauce.

WINE SAUCE

3 cups sugar
1/2 teaspoon salt
6 tablespoons cornstarch
6 cups currant or claret wine
Few drops red coloring

Mix together sugar, salt and cornstarch. Stir in wine; mix well and cook over slow fire until thick and clear. Add a few drops of red coloring to make ruby red. Serve hot over cakes.

Jam Cake

Ingredients

1 cup shortening
1 1/4 cups sugar
5 eggs
2 cups blackberry jam

Directions (Makes two 9-inch square layers)

Cream shortening and beat in sugar.

Add eggs one at a time and blend well. Stir in jam until well mixed.

2 1/2 cups flour ································	Sift flour, measure and add cocoa and spices. Sift again.
1 tablespoon cocoa	
1 teaspoon cinnamon	
1/2 teaspoon allspice	
1/2 teaspoon nutmeg	
1 teaspoon cloves	
1/2 teaspoon mace	
Pinch of salt ································	Dissolve soda in buttermilk and add to creamed mixture alternately with flour
1 teaspoon soda	and spices. Blend well and pour batter into two 9-inch square cake pans which
1 cup buttermilk	have been greased and lined on bottoms with paper. Bake in 350° oven for about 30 minutes or until done. Ice with Caramel Fudge Icing.

Blackberry Jam Cake

Ingredients	**Directions** (Serves 15 to 20)
3 cups sifted flour ····················	Sift together opposite ingredients three times.
1 teaspoon soda	
2 teaspoons cinnamon	
1 teaspoon nutmeg	
1 teaspoon cloves	
1 teaspoon allspice	
1 cup soft butter ·······················	Cream butter; add sugar gradually, and cream together until light and fluffy.
2 cups sugar	
4 egg yolks ·······························	Add yolks, one at a time, beating well after each addition.
1 cup buttermilk or sour milk ········	Add flour, alternately with milk, in small amounts, beating after each addition until smooth.
1 teaspoon vanilla ····················	Add vanilla and jam to mixture and mix well.
1 cup blackberry jam	
4 egg whites–stiffly beaten ··········	Fold in beaten egg whites. Pour batter into a 9 to 10-inch tube pan which has been greased and floured on the bottom. Bake in slow oven 325° for 30 minutes. Increase heat to 350° and continue baking for about 55 minutes or until done. Cool. Frost top and sides with Boiled Frosting (using 3 egg whites) or Quick Brown Sugar Icing.

Jelly Roll

Ingredients

Directions (Makes one jelly roll)

3/4 cup sifted cake flour ·············· Sift together opposite ingredients. Set aside.
3/4 teaspoon baking powder
1/4 teaspoon salt

4 eggs ······································· Beat eggs in small bowl. Add sugar gradually, and beat until thick and lemon-
3/4 cup sugar   colored. Gradually fold in flour.

1 teaspoon vanilla ···················· Fold in vanilla. Spread batter in a 15x10-inch jelly roll pan which has been lined
on bottom with paper. Bake in hot oven 400° for 13 minutes. Immediately turn
cake out onto cloth sprinkled lightly with confectioners' sugar. Quickly remove
paper and cut off crisp edges of cake. Roll up cake. Place on rack to cool. When
cool spread with 1 cup tart jelly and re-roll. Sprinkle with more confectioners'
sugar.

Chocolate Roll

Old English Inn, Omaha, Nebraska

Ingredients

Directions (Serves 9)

6 eggs ······································· Separate eggs and beat yolks and whites separately. Fold the yolks into the whites.

1 cup powdered sugar ··················· Sift dry ingredients and fold into egg mixture. Line a greased flat cake pan, 12x18
3 tablespoons cocoa   inches with heavy waxed paper. Grease the waxed paper and pour in the batter.

1 tablespoon flour ···················· Bake in a 375° oven until done, approximately 25 to 30 minutes. Turn cake pan
over onto a dampened tea towel. Remove the waxed paper and roll lengthwise in
the towel. Let cool.

1 pint whipping ······················· Unroll the cooled cake and spread with whipped cream. Reroll and frost with
cream—whipped   Mocha Icing.

Chocolate Roll

Ingredients

5 egg yolks ....
1 cup confectioners' sugar
1/4 cup flour
1/2 teaspoon salt
5 tablespoons cocoa
1 teaspoon vanilla extract
5 egg whites-stiffly beaten

Directions (Serves 8)

Beat egg yolks until thick and lemon-colored. Add sifted dry ingredients and beat until well blended. Add vanilla and fold in egg whites. Spread in greased, paper lined 10 ½x15-inch jelly roll pan. Bake in moderate hot oven 375° for 15 to 20 minutes. Turn out onto towel sprinkled with confectioners' sugar. Remove paper; cut off crisp edges; roll up. Cool. Unroll and spread with sweetened, whipped cream. Roll like jelly roll and dust with confectioners' sugar.

Refrigerator Cake

Ingredients

3 tablespoons butter ·····················
3/4 cup powdered sugar
3 egg yolks–beaten ·····················
1/2 cup strong cold coffee ·············
2 tablespoons brandy ·····················
3 egg whites–beaten ·····················
24 ladyfingers ·····················
1/2 cup sherry wine
1 pint whipping ·····················
   cream–whipped

Directions (Serves 6 to 8)

Cream butter and sugar together.

Add yolks to above mixture.

Add coffee to mixture, drop by drop, constantly stirring.

Add brandy to mixture, drop by drop, constantly stirring.

Fold egg whites into mixture.

Dip ladyfingers in sherry. Line the bottom and sides of a mold. Cover with half the mixture.

Cover the coffee mixture with whipped cream and on top of the cream put the rest of the mixture. Top that with nuts and fruit (candied orange peel, candied lemon peel, candied cherries, and pistachio nuts), if desired. Place in refrigerator and chill until firm.

CHOCOLATE SAUCE

1 1/2 cups sugar ·····················
1/2 cup water
4 squares unsweetened ·····················
   chocolate
1/2 teaspoon vanilla ·····················
1/4 cup cream ·····················

Boil sugar and water together five minutes.

Melt chocolate over hot water and when the syrup is partially cooled add to above.

Add vanilla to mixture and put in double boiler to keep warm until ready to serve.

Add cream to sauce just before serving.

Mocha Refrigerator Cake

Mrs. E. H. Salter, Vernon Manor, Cincinnati, Ohio

Ingredients

1/2 cup butter
1 cup powdered sugar
2 egg yolks–beaten
1/3 cup very strong
  coffee–cooled
1 cup whipping
  cream–whipped
1 teaspoon vanilla

Sponge cake or ladyfingers

Directions

Cream butter and sugar; add beaten yolks. Then add the cooled coffee very slowly, a little at a time, beating constantly until smooth. Add whipped cream and vanilla.

Line a mold with waxed paper, then with sponge cake or ladyfingers. Pour into this the above mixture. Cover with sponge cake and place in refrigerator 12 to 24 hours. Or make the alternate layers of sponge cake and filling as preferred.

Pineapple Refrigerator Cake

Colony House, Trevor, Wisconsin

Ingredients

1/2 lb. vanilla wafers or
  butter cookies
1/2 cup butter
1 1/2 cups powdered sugar
2 eggs
1/2 pint whipping cream
1 can (9oz.) crushed
  pineapple–drained

Directions (Makes one 12x8x2-inch cake)

Grind the wafers or roll them into crumbs and put half of them in the bottom of a buttered 12x8x2-inch pan. Cream butter and sugar. Add eggs, one at a time, and beat until smooth and creamy. Pour this mixture over the crumbs.

Whip cream; add the pineapple and pour over the first mixture. Cover with the rest of the crumbs and put in the refrigerator overnight.

Chocolate Chip Cake

Duncan Hines Division, Nebraska Consolidated Mills Company, Omaha, Nebraska

(Using White Cake Mix) Use recipe as directed on package of White Cake Mix. Just before turning batter into cake pans, fold in ½ cup semi-sweet chocolate pieces or coarsely grated unsweetened chocolate. Bake as directed on package.

Banana Nut Cake

Duncan Hines Division, Nebraska Consolidated Mills Company, Omaha, Nebraska

(Using Devil's Food Cake Mix) Use recipe on package of Devil's Food Cake Mix substituting 1 cup mashed bananas for ⅓ cup liquid. Add 2 tablespoons soft shortening and fold in ⅔ cup chopped nuts. Bake five minutes longer than directed on package.

Orange Cake

Duncan Hines Division, Nebraska Consolidated Mills Company, Omaha, Nebraska

(Using Yellow Cake Mix) Use recipe as directed on package of Yellow Cake Mix, substituting fresh or frozen orange juice for liquid. Bake as directed on package. Frost with orange frosting.

Cherry Coconut Angelfood Cake

Duncan Hines Division, Nebraska Consolidated Mills Company, Omaha, Nebraska

(Using Angelfood Cake Mix) Use recipe as directed on package of Angelfood Cake Mix adding ¾ teaspoon almond extract. Just before pouring batter into pan, fold in ½ cup well-drained, chopped maraschino cherries and ½ cup finely shredded coconut. Bake as directed on package.

Whipped Cream Cake

Ingredients

Directions (Makes two 9-inch layers)

2 1/4 cups sifted cake flour ·········· Sift together opposite ingredients. Set aside.

1 1/2 cups sugar

2 teaspoons baking powder

1/2 teaspoon salt

1 1/2 cups heavy cream— ············· Whip cream until stiff.
  30° to 35° butterfat

3 eggs-very well beaten ················ Fold well beaten eggs into whipped cream. Then fold in flour mixture.

1 1/2 teaspoons vanilla

Blend in vanilla. Pour batter into two round 9-inch layer pans which have been lined on bottoms with paper. Bake in moderate oven 350° for 30 to 35 minutes. Serve unfrosted.

Mazarin Cake

Ingredients

1/2 cup soft butter ·····················
1/4 cup confectioners' sugar
1 egg yolk ····································
1 cup flour ····································

FILLING

1/2 cup sugar ····························
1/3 cup soft butter
2/3 cup blanched almonds ···········
   finely ground
2 eggs
1/2 teaspoon almond extract

Directions (Serve 10)

Work together butter and sugar with pastry blender or fingers until well blended.

Add yolk and flour to above mixture and stir until smooth. Chill about 1 hour.
Roll dough on lightly floured board to fit a 9-inch buttered pie pan.

Work together butter and sugar until smooth.

Add remaining ingredients and mix together until well blended. Pour into prepared pie pan. Bake in slow oven 300° about 45 minutes. Cool. Sprinkle top with confectioners' sugar.

Orange Tea Cakes

Chalet Suzanne, Lake Wales, Florida

Ingredients

1 1/4 cups almonds–chopped ·······
   about the size of rice kernels
1/2 lb. orange peel–chopped
2 cups cake flour
2 1/2 cups powdered sugar
1 pint heavy cream ····················
A few drops orange coloring

Directions

Place opposite ingredients in a mixing bowl. Blend.

Mix heavy cream and coloring into ingredients and put into pastry bag with a No. 5 or No. 6 tube. Lay out in little mounds on a heavily greased pan. Bake in 340° oven. Do not allow to get brown, as they should retain their orange color. Ice the bottoms with temperate sweet chocolate.

The Duncan Hines Dessert Book

Baba au Rhum

The Toll House, Whitman, Massachusetts

Ingredients

Directions (Serves 6)

2 egg whites ·································· Beat egg whites stiff. Beat egg yolks until light; add to whites and beat together.
2 egg yolks ··································· Add sugar slowly and beat with spoon for 5 minutes.
1 cup sugar
1 cup flour ··································· Sift dry ingredients together and add to egg mixture. Melt butter in hot milk and
1 teaspoon baking powder   beat into mixture. Add flavoring. Pour into Mary Ann pan and bake in 360° oven
Pinch of salt   for 25 to 30 minutes. Makes 6 Mary Anns.
1/2 cup hot milk
1 tablespoon butter
1/2 teaspoon lemon extract
1/2 teaspoon vanilla

BUTTERED RUM SAUCE

2 cups sugar ································· Boil sugar and water for 2 minutes. Remove from heat and add butter. Cool and
1 cup cold water   add rum. Soak the cake in rum sauce; then place in serving dish. Fill center with
1 tablespoon butter   vanilla ice cream and garnish with whipped cream. Serve at once.
1/3 cup rum

Orange Cupcakes

Mission Inn, Riverside, California

Ingredients

Directions (Makes 12)

2 tablespoons shortening ············· Cream together shortening and sugar.
1 cup sugar
2 eggs–slightly beaten ·················· Add eggs and orange juice to mixture.
Juice of 2 oranges
3 cups flour ·································· Sift dry ingredients together and stir into the above mixture. Leave a little of the
1 tablespoon baking powder   flour to stir in later.
1/2 teaspoon salt
1/2 cup milk ································· Add milk to mixture.
Rind of 2 oranges–grated ············ Add orange rind to mixture with the balance of the flour. Pour batter into
                                                    greased muffin pans and bake in 350° oven for 30 minutes.

Little Apple Cakes

Ingredients

1/2 cup lard
1 cup sugar
1 egg–beaten
2 cups flour
1/2 teaspoon soda
1 teaspoon salt
2 teaspoons baking powder
1/2 teaspoon cinnamon
1/2 teaspoon cloves
1/2 teaspoon nutmeg
1/2 cup nuts–broken
1 cup chopped apples
1/2 cup chopped dates
1 teaspoon vanilla
1/2 cup cold coffee

Directions (Makes 12 large or 18 small cakes)

Cream lard and sugar together. Add beaten egg. Stir remaining ingredients into the mixture, in the order listed, and bake in Gem tins in a 350° oven for 30 to 40 minutes.

Mrs. Mathew Jackson,
Chicago, Illinois

Iced Brandied Cupcakes

Ingredients

ICING

8 tablespoons powdered sugar ·····
2 tablespoons brandy
1 tablespoon currant jelly

Directions (Makes 18)

Mix together until smooth; place in refrigerator to set while making cakes.

CUPCAKES

3 cups flour ··························
1/2 cup sugar
1 tablespoon baking powder
1/2 lb. butter
1 tablespoon brandy

Sift flour once; mix with sugar and baking powder. Work in butter. Last add brandy. Put in Mary Ann pans; prick with fork; bake in 350° oven for 5 to 10 minutes or until slightly brown. Remove from oven and allow to cool while filling is being prepared.

FILLING

1 cup powdered sugar
1/4 lb. butter ··························
1 teaspoon vanilla
1 cup heavy cream ··················

Cream butter, sugar and vanilla together.

Whip cream lightly and add to above. Remove cakes from Mary Ann pans and fill with above mixture. Spread with prepared icing and top with half pecan. Set in refrigerator for a few hours.

Frostings and Fillings

A GOOD CAKE DESERVES A LUSCIOUS FROSTING. TO SOME PEOPLE THE FROSTING IS MORE important than the cake itself. It is this final touch that adds flavor, color, moistness and glamour. Most frostings will suit any number of cakes. However, the cake specialist knows when and how to use them to best advantage. A rich butter type frosting glamourizes the plain cake; a light fluffy frosting or a cooked fondant type best suits the rich cake; and a simple glaze or icing enhances the angel food or chiffon.

Choosing and preparing the frosting are only the first steps. They must be followed by careful workmanship to insure the best success. If you want to add raisins, nutmeats, or pineapple to the icing, wait until the last minute to do so. The natural acid or oil in fruits and nuts is apt to thin the icing if added too soon.

First, allow the cake to cool thoroughly before icing it. If the cake is too warm it will cause the frosting to run which will spoil the effect you want. ▶

After brushing all the crumbs from the sides of the cake, place the first layer top-side down on the cake plate. Then spread the frosting or filling almost to the edge of the cake. Allow the filling to set slightly before adding another layer. Place the top layer on the filling, bottom-side down. Frost the sides first, using a wide flexible spatula. Spread with an easy upward stroke and keep the sides of the cake straight. Finally spread the frosting on top, making deep graceful swirls with a spatula, back of a spoon or knife handle.

Once the cake has been frosted you can further glamourize it by adding special decoration. A plain cake can be transformed into one for a festive occasion by garnishing with tinted or toasted coconut, chopped or sliced nuts, grated or melted chocolate, tiny fresh flowers, candied or fresh fruits and small candies such as gum drops, peppermints, cinnamon candies, small chocolate patties or chocolate covered nuts.

Many remarkable creations can be squeezed out of your pastry bag or cake decorator. If your cake is a seasonal one, you may want to decorate it in a pattern, such as a Christmas tree, a peppermint candy cane, or a Valentine heart shaped from cinnamon candies. Whatever you use to decorate your cake, here is your chance to express your individuality. Perhaps you'll come up with a brand new idea.

A special filling different from the frosting will enhance the flavor of your cake. It can give a plain cake a new taste appeal or make a rich cake more appetizing.

A custard filling, or perhaps a fruit, whipped cream or raisin and nut filling will give variety. By a simple variation of your cream filling you can have caramel, mocha or chocolate, orange, lemon, coconut or banana.

Sometimes you may want to tie in your filling and frosting to create the same mood: some grated orange rind in your icing to match an orange filling, or pineapple to go with a pineapple cream filling. The same idea can be carried through with coconut, banana, nuts and many other ingredients.

Here is a nice idea for a dessert surprise; cut angelfood or sponge cake horizontally through the middle and fill with whipped cream and fruit. Then frost with whipped cream. Strawberries, raspberries and blackberries all lend themselves to this combination. Such a cake should be refrigerated or served immediately.

Boiled Frosting

The White Turkey Town House, New York, New York

Ingredients

Directions (Frosts 10-inch tube cake)

2 cups sugar ·
1 cup water

Boil sugar and water until it forms a soft ball when dropped in cold water.

3 egg whites ·

Whip egg whites until stiff. Slowly add the sugar syrup and whip until cold. Spread over cake.

1 coconut–grated ·

Sprinkle top generously with fresh grated coconut.

Caramel Frosting

Ingredients

Directions (Frosts 9-inch layer cake)

1/4 lb. butter ·
1 cup brown sugar–firmly packed

Melt butter; add brown sugar; stir and let come to a boil. Cook for 1 minute or until slightly thick. Cool slightly.

1/4 cup cream ·
4 cups sifted confectioners' sugar

When sugar and butter mixture has cooled, add cream and beat smooth. Stir in confectioners' sugar and beat until of spreading consistency. May have to add a little extra cream if too thick.

Creamy Orange Frosting

Ingredients

Directions (Frosts 9-inch layer cake)

1/2 cup butter ·
1/8 teaspoon salt
1 box (I lb.) sifted
  confectioners' sugar

Cream butter until soft. Add salt and part of sugar gradually, beating well after each addition.

1 egg or 2 egg yolks · · · · · · · · · · · · · · · · ·
1 1/2 teaspoons grated
  orange rind

Add egg and rind to above mixture and blend well.

2 tablespoons milk (about) · · · · · · · · · · ·

Add remaining sugar, alternately with the milk until frosting is of right consistency to spread. Beat after each addition of sugar. Add a little orange food coloring, if desired.

Creamy Butter Frosting

Directions (Frosts 9-inch layer cake) Use recipe for Creamy Orange Frosting substituting 1 teaspoon vanilla for the orange rind.

Creamy Lemon Frosting

Directions (Frosts 9-inch layer cake) Use recipe for Creamy Orange Frosting substituting 1 ½ teaspoons grated lemon rind for the orange rind.

Date Nut Frosting

Ingredients

1 cup sour cream
2 cups brown sugar
1 cup dates–chopped
1 teaspoon vanilla
1 cup walnuts–chopped

Directions (Frosts 8-inch layer cake)

Beat cream; add sugar and cook over slow fire. Add chopped dates and vanilla. Remove from fire. Add nuts. Spread on cake while warm.

Festive Frosting

Ingredients

4 egg whites
2 teaspoons vanilla
1 cup granulated sugar
1 cup light corn syrup
1/2 cup water
1/4 cup broken walnut meats
1/4 cup seedless raisins
1/4 cup candied
  cherries–chopped
3/4 cup grated coconut

Directions (Frosts 8-inch layer cake)

Beat egg whites until stiff. Add vanilla.

Boil sugar, syrup, and water in covered saucepan to 240° F. (spin thread stage). Pour slowly over egg whites, beating constantly.

Divide mixture in half. To one half add walnut meats, raisins, cherries, and ¼ cup coconut. Color mixture delicately pink. Spread filling between cake layers. Spread top with remaining half of frosting and cover with remaining grated coconut.

Seven Minute Frosting

Ingredients

2 egg whites ....
1 1/2 cups sugar
Pinch of salt
1/2 cup cold water
2 teaspoons light corn syrup
1/4 teaspoon cream of tartar ....
1 teaspoon vanilla

Directions (Frosts a two or three 8-inch layer cake)

Combine opposite ingredients in top of double boiler. Beat at medium speed of electric mixer 1 minute. Place over boiling water and beat at high speed of mixer 7 minutes.

Turn into bowl and add cream of tartar and vanilla. Beat for 1 minute longer. Spread on cake.

Chocolate Seven Minute Frosting

Directions (Frosts a two or three 8-inch layer cake)
Use recipe for Seven Minute Frosting folding in 3 squares unsweetened chocolate, melted and cooled, to the frosting just before spreading on the cake.

Chocolate Frosting

Ingredients

2 eggs ....
2 lbs. powdered sugar–sifted
1/2 lb. butter ....
4 squares unsweetened
   chocolate
2 teaspoons lemon juice
2 teaspoons vanilla
2 cups chopped nuts
3 tablespoons cream

Directions (Frosts 9-inch layer cake)

Beat the eggs well and gradually work in the sugar.

Melt together butter and chocolate. Add to above. Add lemon juice and vanilla and mix well. Add cream and mix. Fold in nuts and spread on cake.

Chocolate Confectioners' Frosting

Ingredients

2 cups sifted confectioners' ··········
  sugar
2 tablespoons hot milk (about)
1 teaspoon vanilla
1 square unsweetened
  chocolate–melted

Directions (Makes about 2 cups)

Combine all ingredients. Beat until smooth and of good spreading consistency.

Creamy Soft Chocolate Frosting

The Derings, Green Lake, Wisconsin

Ingredients

1 cup sugar ·······························
1/8 teaspoon salt ·······················
1/4 cup cornstarch
1 1/2 cups water
3 squares unsweetened
  chocolate
1/2 cup milk
1 teaspoon butter
1 teaspoon vanilla

Directions (Frosts 8-inch layer cake)

Mix together dry ingredients. Stir in water. Cook and stir until thick and clear.
Combine chocolate and milk in top of double boiler. Cook over boiling water until chocolate melts. Add to the above mixture.
Add butter and vanilla to above mixture. Cool and spread.

Caramel Fudge Frosting

Ingredients

1 1/2 cups firmly packed ··············
  brown sugar
1 cup milk
2 tablespoons butter ····················
Pinch of salt
1/2 teaspoon vanilla

Directions (Frosts 8-inch layer cake)

Combine sugar and milk together in saucepan. Bring to a boil, stirring constantly. Boil, covered 3 minutes and then uncovered until the soft ball stage is reached or to a temperature of 236° F ., stirring occasionally. Remove from heat.
Add opposite ingredients to the above mixture. Cool frosting until it is lukewarm or has reached 110° F. Beat until thick and creamy. Spread on cake.

The Duncan Hines Dessert Book

Fudge Frosting

Ingredients

2 cups confectioners' sugar ··········
1/3 cup butter
2 squares unsweetened
    chocolate
Pinch of salt
1 teaspoon vanilla
1/3 cup milk

Directions (Frosts 8- inch layer cake)

Place all ingredients in a saucepan and cook over very low heat for about 3 minutes. Spread on cooled cake. (Marshmallows may be cut in pieces and placed over top of cake and frosting poured over them.)

Praline Fudge Frosting

Ingredients

2 1/2 cups sugar ·····················
1 cup maple syrup
1 cup light cream

Pinch of salt ··························
1 teaspoon vanilla

Directions (Frosts 8-inch layer cake)

Combine opposite ingredients in large saucepan. Bring to a boil, stirring constantly; boil covered for 3 minutes. Then boil uncovered until mixture reaches the soft ball stage or to a temperature of 236° F., stirring occasionally. Remove from heat.

Add to the above mixture. Cool frosting until it is lukewarm or has reached 110°F. Beat until thick and creamy. Spread on cake.

Chocolate Marshmallow Frosting

Ingredients

1 1/2 boxes powdered sugar ··········
1/8 teaspoon salt
3 squares unsweetened
    chocolate
3 tablespoons butter
1/2 cup cream
1 teaspoon vanilla
18 marshmallows ·····················
1/2 cup chopped pecans

Directions (Frosts 9-inch layer cake)

Sift together sugar and salt. Melt chocolate and butter in double boiler. To the sugar add cream and vanilla and bland. Stir in hot chocolate mixture and beat well.

Cut marshmallows in small pieces. Stir into frosting along with nuts. Let stand, stirring occasionally until of spreading consistency.

Maple Frosting

Ingredients

2 tablespoons butter ·······

1 lb. confectioners' ·······
  sugar–sifted

1 teaspoon maple flavor

Cream

1/2 cup pecan halves

Directions (Frosts 10-inch square layer cake)

Cream butter and work in sifted sugar.

Add maple flavor and sufficient cream to make it of spreading consistency. Spread on cooled cake. Top with pecan halves.

Mocha Frosting

Ingredients

1 1/2 boxes (1 1/2 lbs.) ·······
  powdered sugar

3 squares unsweetened
  chocolate

3 tablespoons butter–melted

1/2 cup strong cold coffee

1/4 cup plus 1 tablespoon ·······
  cream

Directions (Frosts 9-inch layer cake)

Sift sugar. Melt together butter and chocolate. Stir into sugar along with coffee.

Add cream and stir to blend well. If the cream is not enough, add just a bit more to make of spreading consistency.

Rum Butter Frosting

Ingredients

1/2 lb. butter ·······

2 lbs. powdered sugar

4 tablespoons rum

1 tablespoon cream

Directions (Frosts 10-inch tube cake)

Cream butter at high speed in electric mixer. Gradually add all of the sugar. Scrape down bowl and add rum a tablespoon at a time. Add cream and if still too stiff, add a little more until of good spreading consistency. This will make nice thick icing between the layers, on top and on all sides.

Mocha Butter Cream Frosting

Ingredients

1 box (1 lb.) sifted ·························
  confectioners' sugar

1/4 cup cocoa

Pinch of salt ······································

1/2 cup butter

5 tablespoons cold coffee ···········
  (about)

1/2 teaspoon vanilla ·····················

Directions (Frosts 9-inch layer cake)

Sift together opposite ingredients.

Cream butter and gradually add part of the sugar mixture. Beat after each addition until light and fluffy.

Add the remaining sugar alternately with coffee until of right consistency to spread. Beat after each addition until smooth.

Add vanilla.

Seafoam Frosting

Williamsburg Inn, Williamsburg, Virginia

Ingredients

1 1/2 cups brown sugar ················

1/2 cup water

1/4 teaspoon cream of tartar

2 egg whites–beaten ····················

Directions (Frosts 8-inch layer cake)

Boil together opposite ingredients until it spins a thread.

Slowly add the above syrup to eggs, beating all the time. Spread on cooled cake.

Sour Cream Frosting

Old Tyme Coffee House, Moose Lake, Minnesota

Ingredients

1 cup heavy sour cream ···············

1 1/2 cups granulated sugar

1/2 teaspoon soda ·························

1 teaspoon vanilla ·······················

Pinch of salt

1 tablespoon butter

2 tablespoons fresh cream

Directions (Frosts a loaf cake)

Boil sour cream and sugar slowly over low heat, stirring occasionally. Cook until the soft ball stage has been reached. His will take about half an hour. Remove from heat.

Add soda. Cook over high heat, stirring rapidly all the time, for one minute or until it turns a nice caramel color. Remove from stove.

Add vanilla, salt, and butter. Cool slightly; then beat adding cream until the frosting is the right consistency to spread. Should spread like butter.

Spiced Sour Cream Frosting

Ingredients

Directions (Frosts 9-inch layer cake)

1 cup sugar ·········· Combine sugar and sour cream and boil for 1 minute, stirring constantly.

1/2 cup sour cream

1/8 teaspoon nutmeg ·········· Add nutmeg to the above mixture and cool slightly. Beat until thickened and white in color (about 20 minutes).

White Mountain Frosting

Ingredients

Directions (Frosts one 10-inch tube cake)

1/2 cup sugar ·········· Boil opposite ingredients together until a candy thermometer registers 242° or mixture will spin a 6 to 8-inch thread.

1/4 cup light corn syrup

1/4 cup egg whites ·········· Beat egg whites until stiff. Pour above mixture into egg whites beating constantly.

1/2 teaspoon vanilla ·········· Add vanilla and enough red coloring to get a deep pink frosting.

Red vegetable coloring

1 pint fresh strawberries– halved or 1 box frozen thawed strawberries–halved

Frost cake and decorate top and sides with strawberries.

White Icing

Lake Breeze Resort, Three Lakes, Wisconsin

Ingredients

Directions (Frosts a 9-inch layer cake)

2 egg whites ·········· Mix together opposite ingredients and cook in double boiler until thick. Beat constantly with an egg beater while cooking. Put on cake while hot.

1 cup sugar

4 tablespoons cold water

The Duncan Hines Dessert Book

Boiled White Icing

Ingredients

2 3/4 cups sugar ·······················

2 tablespoons corn syrup

1 teaspoon vinegar

Dash of salt

1 cup water

3/4 cup egg whites ·······················

1/4 cup sugar

1/4 teaspoon cream of tartar

Directions (Frosts one 9-inch cake)

Combine opposite ingredients and bring to a boil. Cook to 238° F. on a candy thermometer.

Beat together opposite ingredients until frothy. Add ⅓ of above syrup to egg whites mixture, beating all the time. Return syrup to range and let come to a boil. Again add ⅓ of the syrup to egg white mixture and beat well. Bring remaining syrup to a boil and let cook two minutes. Fold into mixture and beat icing until cold and ready to spread.

Caramel Icing

Ingredients

2 cups brown sugar ·······················

1 cup light cream

3 tablespoons butter ·······················

1 teaspoon vanilla

Directions (Frosts 9-inch layer cake)

Combine brown sugar and cream in saucepan. Stir until the sugar is dissolved. Then cook, without stirring, to the soft ball stage, 238° F.

Add butter. Remove from heat and cool. Then add vanilla. Beat icing until thick and creamy. Add a little cream if too thick.

Orange Butter Cream Icing

Damon's, Cleveland, Ohio

Ingredients

1/4 cup butter ·······················

2 cups confectioners' sugar

1 egg–beaten

1 cup orange marmalade

1/4 teaspoon salt

Directions (Frosts a 9- inch layer cake)

Cream together butter and sugar. Stir in egg. Fold in marmalade and salt. If the marmalade is thin, reduce amount to ¾ cup and it may be necessary to add a little more sugar.

Fluffy Orange Icing

Ingredients

2 cups sifted confectioners' ·············
   sugar
1 tablespoon melted butter
1 1/2 tablespoons grated
   orange rind
1/4 cup orange juice

Directions (Frosts 9-inch layer cake)

Place all ingredients in top of double boiler. Cook and stir over hot water for 10 minutes. Beat icing until cool and of right spreading consistency.

Maple Sugar Icing

Ingredients

2 cups maple sugar ·····················
1 cup light cream
Pinch of salt
1/2 cup chopped walnuts ············

Directions (Frosts 8-inch layer cake)

Combine opposite ingredients in a saucepan. Cook and stir until mixture reaches the soft ball stage or 234° F. Remove from heat. Cool slightly. Beat until creamy.

Add nuts. Spread on cooled cake.

Caramel Whip Icing

Cromer's Restaurant, Flint, Michigan

Ingredients

2 cups brown sugar ·····················
6 tablespoons butter
1 1/3 cups water ·························
5 tablespoons cornstarch
1 1/3 cups whipping ···················
   cream–whipped

Directions (Makes about 3 cups)

Combine brown sugar and butter in heavy skillet. Cook and stir until mixture bubbles and the sugar darkens.

Mix a little of the water with the cornstarch. Add this with remaining water to the above mixture. Cook and stir until thickened. Chill.

Fold into caramel mixture. Spread between cake layers.

      The Duncan Hines Dessert Book

Mocha Icing

Old English Inn, Omaha, Nebraska

Ingredients

1/2 cup hot coffee

3 tablespoons butter

4 tablespoons cocoa

3 cups powdered sugar

Directions (Frosts one jelly roll)

Pour hot coffee over the butter and add the cocoa and powdered sugar. Stir well. Ice the roll and keep in refrigerator until ready to serve.

Quick Brown Sugar Icing

Ingredients

1 1/2 cups brown sugar

5 tablespoons cream

3 teaspoons butter

Pinch of salt

1/2 teaspoon vanilla

Directions (Frosts 8-inch layer cake)

Combine in saucepan the opposite ingredients. Cook and stir until mixture comes to a boil. Remove from heat. Cool slightly.

Add vanilla and beat until frosting is of spreading consistency.

Chocolate Filling

Ingredients

2 eggs

1/2 cup sugar

1 cup milk

1 tablespoon butter

1 square unsweetened
  chocolate–grated

Pinch of salt

1 teaspoon vanilla

Directions (Makes about 1 cup)

Beat eggs until thick and lemon-colored. Gradually add sugar and continue beating until smooth and well blended.

Add milk slowly to the above mixture. Then add remaining ingredients. Cook in double boiler until thick, stirring frequently. Cool.

Add vanilla and spread between cake layers.

Clear Orange Filling

Francis Fowler, Jr., Los Angeles, California

Ingredients

2 tablespoons butter ·················
4 tablespoons cornstarch
2 tablespoons grated
  orange rind
1 cup sugar
1/2 teaspoon salt
1 1/2 teaspoons lemon juice
1 cup orange juice and pulp

Directions (Makes enough for 9-inch layer cake)

Mix all together and cook in double boiler 5 minutes. Spread between layers and on top and sides of cake.

Lemon Filling

Lake Breeze Resort, Three Lakes, Wisconsin

Ingredients

2 egg yolks ··························
Juice of 1 lemon
2 tablespoons cornstarch
1 cup scalding water
Pinch of salt
1/2 cup chopped nuts ·················

Directions (Makes about 1 ½ cups)

Cook opposite ingredients until thick. Spread lemon filling between cake layers.

Sprinkle with nuts and top with icing.

Almond Custard Filling

Ingredients

1 cup sugar ·······················
1 cup sour cream
1 tablespoon flour
1 egg–beaten ·····················
1 cup blanched,
  ground almonds ·················
1/2 teaspoon vanilla

Directions (Makes about 2 cups)

Combine opposite ingredients in top of double boiler. Cook over low heat, but do not let the mixture boil.

Pour above mixture over the beaten egg. Place over boiling water and cook and stir until custard is thick.

Add nuts to the above mixture. Cool custard and then add vanilla.

Pineapple Filling

Ingredients

1/4 cup sugar
1 tablespoon flour
Pinch of salt

2/3 cup milk
2 egg yolks-slightly beaten

1 1/2 tablespoons butter

1 cup canned crushed
  pineapple—well drained

Directions (Makes about 2 cups)

Combine opposite ingredients in top of double boiler.

Mix milk with egg yolks and add to above mixture. Cook and stir over boiling water for 15 minutes or until thickened. Remove from heat.

Add remaining ingredients. Cool. Spread.

Cream Filling

Ingredients

2/3 cup sugar
5 tablespoons flour
1/8 teaspoon salt
2 cups milk
2 eggs–slightly beaten

1 teaspoon vanilla

Directions (Makes about 2 cups)

Combine dry ingredients in top of double boiler. Stir in milk gradually. Cook over boiling water until mixture thickens, stirring constantly. Cover and cook for 10 minutes longer, stirring occasionally.

Stir a little of the hot mixture into the slightly beaten eggs. Slowly add to the above mixture. Cook over hot water for 2 minutes, stirring constantly. Chill.

Add flavoring. Makes enough filling for 3-layer cake or use in cream puffs or éclairs.

Rum Cream Filling

(Makes about 2 cups) Use recipe for Cream Filling omitting the vanilla and substituting 1 tablespoon rum flavoring.

To make a good uncooked icing, thorough beating is necessary.
Too much sugar and too little beating makes a brittle hard frosting.

Cocoa Whipped Cream

Ingredients

2 tablespoons sugar ·····················

2 tablespoons cocoa

Pinch of salt

1 cup heavy cream

Directions (Makes about 1 ½ cups)

Mix sugar, cocoa, and salt together. Add to heavy cream. Chill 1 hour. Whip until stiff.

Coffee Glaze

Ingredients

2 1/2 tablespoons water ··············

1 tablespoon butter ··················

1 1/3 cups sifted confectioners' sugar

Pinch of salt

2 teaspoons instant coffee powder

Directions (Makes about 1 cup)

Heat water and butter together.

Combine opposite ingredients in bowl and add hot liquid. Stir until smooth. Pour over the top of a tube angel food cake.

For best results with cooked frostings, use an accurate candy and icing thermometer.

Biscuit Desserts

(Shortcakes, dumplings, cobblers)

COBBLERS, FOR WHICH THERE ARE SOME WONDERFUL RECIPES IN THIS SECTION, ARE A CONCOCTION from New England. A cobbler is a deep-dish fruit pie with a biscuit mixture usually on top. This quick fruit pie gets its name from the phrase "cobble up" meaning put together in a hurry. The familiar apple pan dowdy is an early version of the apple cobbler. But cherries, peaches, blackberries, apricots and huckleberries make excellent cobblers too. Whipped cream or rich heavy cream are marvelous over this dessert, and you have to go a long way to find something as quick and easy for a family meal or for that unexpected company. Other sauces may be used too, depending on the occasion and your particular taste. Custard sauce goes well with blueberry and peach cobblers and hot lemon sauce with apple cobbler.

Still another dessert which can be made as a biscuit or as a cake is shortcake. This is made of a biscuit mixture and baked as either a large cake or as individual cakes. When ready to be served, shortcakes are ▶

split in half and fruit is spooned between the layers and on top. Perhaps strawberries, raspberries and peaches are the best known fruits used for shortcake. Shortcakes may be served plain, with heavy cream or, for a really special dessert, with whipped cream.

Today with the modern food processing of canned and frozen fruits and the plentiful selection on your grocer's shelves, shortcakes are no longer limited to the summer season.

Still another type of biscuit dessert I cover in this section is fruit dumplings which get their name from their irregular shape. Originally all dumplings were steamed. However, some recipes today call for baking. This results in a more uniform shape. Apples, peaches, cherries, blueberries and apricots can be used for delicious fruit dumplings.

Dumplings are made by rolling a biscuit mixture until it is 1/4-inch thick and then cutting the dough into 4-inch squares. Fruit which has been pared or cored, as the need may be, is then placed in the center of a square of dough, and the four corners are drawn up around the fruit. The ends are then pinched together and the dumplings are ready to bake. Dumplings are usually served with a sauce of some type. A lemon or foamy sauce is good with them, or in some cases a hard sauce.

Biscuit desserts in their many forms can be adapted to any fruit and suited to every taste. Fruit, whether fresh, frozen, crushed, mashed, sliced or whole, is good when used in a biscuit dessert. Don't forget you can make a really wonderful treat by just using a simple sauce.

Serve steamed puddings piping hot.

Make your sauce with care. It can make or break the pudding.

Put the steamed pudding in the oven for a minute or two to dry out the top.

Hard sauce flavored with rum or brandy is delicious with steamed puddings.

Peach Cobbler

Ingredients

Directions (Serves 6)

1 cup sugar .... Combine sugar and cornstarch in saucepan.

1 tablespoon cornstarch

1 cup boiling water ···················· Add boiling water gradually. Boil 1 minute, stirring constantly.

3 cups fresh, sliced, ···················· Add peaches to syrup. Pour into a 10x6x2-inch baking dish.
   peeled peaches

1 tablespoon butter ···················· Dot mixture with butter. Sprinkle with cinnamon.

1/2 teaspoon cinnamon

1 cup sifted flour ···················· Sift together opposite ingredients.

1 tablespoon sugar

1 1/2 teaspoons baking
   powder

1/2 teaspoon salt ···················· Cut shortening into flour mixture with pastry blender.

3 tablespoons shortening

1/2 cup milk (about) ···················· Stir milk into above mixture to make a soft dough. Drop mixture by spoonfuls onto fruit mixture in baking dish. Bake in hot oven 400° about 30 minutes. Serve warm with cream.

Cherry Cobbler

Use recipe for Peach Cobbler substituting 3 cups sweet pitted cherries for the peaches. (If desired add 2 drops almond extract.) Bake as directed for Peach Cobbler.

Blackberry Cobbler

(Serves 6) Use recipe for Peach Cobbler substituting 3 cups blackberries for the peaches and reducing the sugar from 1 cup to ¾ cup. Bake as directed for Peach Cobbler.

Apple Dumplings

Richards Treat Cafeteria, Minneapolis, Minnesota

Ingredients

Directions (Serve 6)

2 cups cake flour .... Mix and sift dry ingredients.

2 teaspoons baking powder

1/2 teaspoon salt

2/3 cup shortening .... Work shortening into flour mixture lightly with the tips of fingers.

1/3 cup milk, or .... Make hole in flour and add milk gradually while mixing lightly. Knead lightly
   perhaps 1/2 cup into a ball and roll into a rectangular-shaped piece of dough about ¼-inch thick
and cut into six pieces.

6 to 8 tart apples .... Peel and slice apples and divide between six squares of dough.

1/2 teaspoon cinnamon .... Mix these ingredients and add to the apples.

1/4 teaspoon nutmeg

3/4 cup brown sugar

6 tablespoons butter .... Dot each square with a tablespoon of butter and bring up the corners of the
dough and pinch together to make dumpling.

1/2 cup brown sugar .... Make a syrup of these ingredients and while hot set in dumplings, and bake in
1/2 cup granulated sugar 350° to 375° oven for 1 hour, or until apples are done. Dumplings are best when
2 cups water made of quick cooking apples, though winter apples may be used if slowly
1/2 cup butter cooked.

Strawberry and Rhubarb Shortcake

Ingredients

Directions (Serves 4)

1 lb. fresh rhubarb

1/2 cup water

1 cup sugar

1 package frozen
   strawberries–defrosted

Cut rhubarb in ½-inch slices. Simmer in water until tender and while hot add
sugar and strawberries. Serve over your favorite shortcake. Top with whipped
cream.

Strawberry Shortcake

Ingredients

1 1/2 quarts fresh, stemmed, ·········
slightly crushed strawberries

1 cup sugar

2 cups sifted flour ·······················

2 tablespoons sugar

3 teaspoons baking powder

1 teaspoon salt

6 tablespoons shortening ············

2/3 cup milk (about) ····················

Directions (Serves 6)

Combine strawberries and sugar and let stand while preparing the shortcake.

Sift together opposite ingredients into a bowl.

Cut shortening into the flour mixture with pastry blender until fine crumbs are formed.

Add milk to the above and stir until a soft dough is formed. Knead lightly on lightly floured board. Spread half of the dough into a well greased 8-inch round layer pan. Dot with butter. Spread remaining dough on top. Bake in hot oven 450° for 12 to 15 minutes. Separate layers. Spoon sweetened berries between the layers and on top. Serve with whipped cream.

Raspberry Shortcake

(Serves 6) Use recipe for Strawberry Shortcake substituting raspberries for the strawberries.

Peach Shortcake

(Serves 6) Use recipe for Strawberry Shortcake substituting 1 quart fresh, peeled, sliced peaches for the strawberries.

Banana Gingerbread Shortcake

Ingredients

Directions (Serves 16)

3/4 cup shortening (1/2 butter ······ Cream shortening with 1 cup sugar. Add eggs.
and 1/2 shortening or 6
tablespoons of each)

1 cup sugar

2 eggs–slightly beaten

1 cup molasses ······················· Add opposite ingredients to the creamed mixture.

1 teaspoon ginger

1 teaspoon cinnamon

1/2 teaspoon salt

1 teaspoon soda ························· Put soda into warm coffee. Add to above mixture.

1 cup warm coffee

2 1/2 cups sifted flour ·················· Add to the above and stir well. Pour into an 8X12-inch pan and bake in a 350°
oven for 40 to 50 minutes or until done, depending upon the size of the pan used
and the thickness of the dough.

Sliced bananas ························· When ready to serve, split each serving and put sliced bananas between and on
Whipped cream   top. Serve with whipped cream.

Dutch Apple Cake

Ingredients

Directions (Serves 6 to 8)

1 1/2 cups sifted flour ················· Sift together opposite ingredients into a bowl.

2 1/2 teaspoons baking
powder

1/2 teaspoon salt

4 tablespoons sugar

1/4 cup shortening ····················· Cut shortening into flour mixture with pastry blender or two forks until coarse
crumbs are formed.

1 teaspoon vanilla	Add vanilla and milk to above mixture. Stir until a soft dough is formed. Roll out dough on lightly floured board and line a 9-inch pie pan.
1/2 cup milk (about)	
4 1/2 cups sliced tart apples	Press apple slices into dough.
3 tablespoons butter	Cream butter and gradually add the remaining ingredients. Spread on top of apples. Bake in hot oven 400° for 40 to 50 minutes. Serve warm with cream.
2/3 cup sugar	
1 tablespoon flour	
1 teaspoon cinnamon	
1 tablespoon lemon juice	

Dutch Peach Cake

(Serves 6 to 8) Use recipe for Dutch Apple Cake substituting fresh sliced peaches for the apples. Bake as directed.

Blueberry Shortcake au Kirsch

Ingredients **Directions** (Serves 4)

2 cups blueberries	Wash blueberries; place in saucepan; cover with sugar; stir and heat. Bring to quick boil.
1 cup sugar	
2 teaspoons arrowroot	Dissolve arrowroot in water and stir into blueberries. Cook for a few minutes to thicken. Let cool.
3 teaspoons water	
2 liqueur glasses Kirschwasser	When cool, add Kirschwasser; cover tightly and let stand in cool place for several hours.
4 slices sponge cake	Serve on slices of sponge cake, and top with vanilla ice cream.
Vanilla ice cream	

Blueberry Slump

Ingredients

Directions (Serves 8)

1 quart blueberries ·······················

1 cup sugar ··································

4 tablespoons arrowroot
  or cornstarch

Juice of 1 lemon

1/2 cup sugar

4 tablespoons butter

1/4 teaspoon salt

1 egg

1/2 cup milk

1 1/2 cups sifted cake flour

2 teaspoons baking powder

Wash berries and drain. Mix sugar and arrowroot and add to berries. Place in greased casserole and sprinkle with lemon juice.

Cream together butter and sugar. Add salt. Beat the egg and add to creamed mixture. Add milk and mix well. Stir in flour and baking powder briskly and spoon over berries. Bake in 425° oven for 20 to 25 minutes. Serve warm with vanilla ice cream. Note: If fresh blueberries are not available, frozen ones may be used. In that case, use two packages and let defrost slightly.

Plum Rolls

Ingredients

Directions (Serves 8 to 10)

1 No. 2 1/2 can prune plums ·········
  or 1 quart canned damsons

4 tablespoons sugar ·····················

2 tablespoons butter

1 teaspoon Angostura bitters

2 cups flour ·······························

1/2 teaspoon salt

3 teaspoons baking powder

2 tablespoons sugar

4 tablespoons butter ····················

Drain plums thoroughly; remove pits, and cut into coarse pieces.

Add opposite ingredients to juice strained from plums; place in baking pan and bring to boil on high heat.

Sift dry ingredients together.

Cut butter into dry ingredients as in any pastry.

The Duncan Hines Dessert Book

1 egg .... Beat egg thoroughly; combine with milk, and add pastry to make soft dough.

1/2 cup milk

Place on floured board and roll to ½-inch thickness. Spread with chopped plums and roll up. Slice roll crosswise into 1 ½-inch lengths and place cut side down, in hot syrup. Bake in 350° oven for about 30 minutes or until pastry is done.

Peach Pinwheels

Ingredients

Directions (Serves 8)

2 tablespoons cornstarch .... Combine opposite ingredients in an 11x7x2-inch baking dish.

1 cup sugar

1/4 teaspoon salt

1/2 teaspoon cinnamon

4 cups sliced, fresh peaches

1 tablespoon lemon juice

1 cup water

1 cup biscuit mix

2 tablespoons butter–melted .... Add melted butter and milk to biscuit mix. Stir until a soft dough is formed. Turn

1/4 cup milk

onto lightly floured board and knead 10 times. Roll out into a 6-inch square about ¼-inch thick.

2 tablespoons butter–melted .... Spread dough with melted butter. Combine sugar and cinnamon and sprinkle

1/4 teaspoon cinnamon

over the dough. Top with chopped pecans. Roll up as for jelly roll. Moisten edge

2 tablespoons sugar

and press against roll to seal. Cut with sharp knife into 8 slices about ¾ inch

1/4 cup chopped pecans

thick. Place cut side up on peach mixture. Bake in hot oven 425° for 25 minutes or until lightly browned. Serve warm with cream.

Apple Pudding

Ingredients

4 lbs. winesap apples ·················
2 cups granulated sugar
2 cups brown sugar
3/4 lb. butter ·······················
2 cups flour

Directions (Serves 12 to 14)

Peel apples and slice thin. Place in bottom of buttered 8x14-inch baking pan. Sprinkle with sugar.

Cream butter and sugar together in mixer. Stir in flour. Pat out dough and cut in cookie shapes. Place close together all over top of apples. Bake until golden brown in preheated oven, 350° for 45 to 50 minutes. Serve warm with cream or ice cream.

Apple Betty Pudding

Ingredients

6 cups sliced apples ················
1/3 cup granulated sugar
3/4 cup hot water
4 tablespoons vegetable ···········
  shortening
2 tablespoons butter
1/2 cup brown sugar
1/2 teaspoon ground ··············
  cinnamon
1 cup sifted flour
1 teaspoon baking powder
1/4 teaspoon salt

Directions (Serves 6)

Combine opposite ingredients and simmer, covered, in saucepan for 10 minutes. Put into greased 9-inch pan.

Blend shortening and butter until soft. Add brown sugar and work until creamy.

Sift together and add to shortening mixture, blending thoroughly. Sprinkle over top of apples. Bake 40 minutes in 350° oven. Serve with rich cream or with vanilla ice cream.

Sally Lunn

Althaea, Lewisburg, West Virginia

Ingredients

1/2 cup butter

1 tablespoon sugar

1/2 teaspoon salt

2 eggs

1 yeast cake

1 cup milk

3 cups flour

Directions

Cream together opposite ingredients.

Beat eggs and add to above and beat well.

Heat milk to lukewarm and dissolve yeast in it. Add to above. Add flour, mix thoroughly; pour into buttered tube pan. Let rise 1 ½ hours or until doubled in bulk. Bake in 350° oven 45 to 50 minutes. Serve hot with butter.

Maple Rag-a-Muffin Dessert

Twist-o' Hill Lodge, Williston, Vermont

Ingredients

1 1/2 cups flour

1/2 teaspoon salt

3 teaspoons baking powder

1/4 teaspoon cream of tartar

4 tablespoons shortening

1/3 to 1/2 cup milk

Butter

1 1/2 cups maple syrup

1/4 cup chopped nuts

1/2 cup whipping cream—
  whipped or 1 pint vanilla
  ice cream

Directions (Serve 6)

Sift dry ingredients. Cut in shortening and add milk to make a soft dough. Roll out on lightly floured board and cut 12 small biscuits. Place in well greased pan and dot generously with butter. Heat syrup and pour over biscuits. Bake 15 minutes in a 450° oven.

Serve warm with whipped cream or a small scoop of ice cream. Garnish with nuts.

Custards

IN PLAIN OR DRESSED-UP FASHION, THE CUSTARD DESSERT, LIKE THE EGG, IS A FOUNDATION TO good eating.

Composed of eggs, milk, and sugar, custards contain ingredients necessary in our daily diet. The plain custard may be varied with chocolate, coffee, maple syrup, wine, or heavy cream. To perk up the flavor of a plain custard, drop fruit, candied cherries, jelly, or nuts into the bottom of the custard cup.

The two most common faults in making custards are cooking too long or cooking at too high a temperature. Custard sauces and puddings must not boil because high heat destroys the flavor, and causes the egg to cook, giving the dessert a curdled appearance. If soft custard shows signs of curdling, remove from the boiling water at once and set in a bowl of ice water to cool quickly. ▶

In custard making do not hesitate to use left over yolks. The whites do not improve the custard. If you want a rich brown crust on your custard, beat the eggs until thick and lemon-colored. For a crunchy crust, try spreading left over cake, cookie, or macaroon crumbs over the custard before baking.

Yes, in plain dress or "glad rags," custard desserts can become a favorite in any season with almost any type of menu.

Baked Custard

Ingredients	Directions (Serves 6)
2 large eggs or 4 egg yolks–slightly beaten	Mix opposite ingredients together in bowl.
1/3 cup sugar	
1/4 teaspoon salt	
1/2 teaspoon vanilla	
2 cups milk–scalded	Add to egg mixture gradually. Strain into custard cups or a 1 ½-quart baking dish. Place baking dish in pan of hot water. Sprinkle with nutmeg, if desired. Bake in moderate oven 350° for 30 to 35 minutes or until silver knife inserted into custard comes out clean. Remove from hot water immediately. Serve cool or chilled.

To preserve yolks of eggs for a day, slide them into a bowl
without breaking and cover them with cold water.

Baked Chocolate Custard

Ingredients

Directions (Serves 8 to 10)

2 squares unsweetened chocolate ·············· Combine chocolate and milk in top of double boiler. Cook and stir over boiling water until chocolate melts. Beat with rotary egg beater until blended.

4 cups milk

4 eggs–slightly beaten ·············· Combine eggs, sugar, and salt in bowl. Add above mixture gradually, stirring until sugar is dissolved.

1/3 cup sugar

1/4 teaspoon salt ·············· Add to the mixture. Pour into custard cups. Place cups in pan of hot water and bake in slow oven 325° for 45 minutes or until knife inserted comes out clean. Chill, Top with cream and a dash of cinnamon, or unmold and serve with cream.

1 teaspoon vanilla

Baked Caramel Custard

(Serves 6) In small frying pan melt over low heat, stirring constantly, ½ cup sugar. Divide caramelized sugar syrup among the custard cups, turning cups around so that the caramel will coat the insides. Allow to harden. Meanwhile prepare recipe for Molded Custard.

Baked Maple Custard

(Serves 6) Place 1 tablespoon maple syrup into the bottom of each custard cup. Then prepare recipe for Molded Custard.

Caramel Custard

Ingredients   **Directions** (Serves 4)

1/2 cup sugar ························· Place in small heavy skillet. Melt over low heat, stirring constantly.

1 tablespoon hot water ················ Add water to the melted sugar. Stir until sugar is dissolved.

2 cups scalded milk ·················· Add above mixture to the scalded milk.

3 egg yolks–well beaten ·············· Pour milk gradually over eggs.

1/2 teaspoon vanilla ················· Add to the above mixture. Beat custard until blended. Pour into 1-quart baking

Pinch of salt   dish. Place baking dish in pan of hot water. Bake in slow oven 325° about 1 hour

                                      or until silver knife comes out clean when inserted.

Coconut Custard

(Serves 6) Use recipe for Baked Custard adding ¾ cup shredded cut coconut to the custard mixture.

Molded Custard

(Serves 6) Use recipe for Baked Custard except use 3 eggs or 6 egg yolks. Pour into greased molds. Unmold on serving dish.

Pecan Custard

(Serves 6) Use recipe for Baked Custard adding ⅔ cup finely chopped pecans to custard mixture.

Ivory Cream Custard

Ingredients   **Directions** (Serves 6)

6 egg whites ······················· Beat slightly with fork.

1/3 cup sugar ······················ Add remaining ingredients to egg whites and stir until thoroughly mixed. Pour

1/2 teaspoon salt   into custard cups. Place cups in pan of hot water. Bake in moderate oven 350° for

1 1/2 cups cold water   40 to 50 minutes or until silver knife comes out clean when inserted in the center.

1 1/2 cups heavy cream   Remove from water to cool. Chill.

Whipped Cream Custard

Ingredients

4 egg yolks ··························
3/4 cup sugar
2 tablespoons cornstarch
1 pint light cream–scalded ···········
2 tablespoons butter
Pinch of salt
1 1/2 teaspoons vanilla ···············
1 cup heavy cream–whipped

Directions (Serves 6)

Combine in top of double boiler and beat together until blended.

Stir into above mixture gradually.
Add to mixture. Cook over boiling water, stirring frequently, until thick. Cool

Fold vanilla and whipped cream into cooled mixture. Pour into serving dishes or individual dessert glasses. Chill.

Lemon Sponge Custard

Ingredients

3/4 cup sugar ·····················
2 tablespoons butter
2 teaspoons grated lemon rind
3 egg yolks ·····················
1 cup milk ·····················
1/4 cup lemon juice
3 tablespoons flour ·················
3 egg whites ·····················
1/8 teaspoon salt

Directions (Serves 4 to 6)

Cream together until well blended.

Add yolks to the above mixture, one at a time, beating well after each addition.
Combine opposite ingredients together.

Add flour, alternately with liquid, to creamed mixture.
Beat together until stiff peaks are formed. Fold into egg yolk mixture. Pour into greased custard cups. Place cups in pan of hot water and bake in moderate oven 350° about 45 minutes. Serve hot or cold with heavy cream.

Orange Sponge Custard

(Serves 4 to 6) Use recipe for Lemon Sponge Custard substituting 1 tablespoon grated orange rind for the lemon rind and ⅓ cup orange juice for the lemon juice.

Floating Island

Ingredients

Directions (Serves 4)

1 pint milk ·································· Scald milk in double boiler.

2 tablespoons sugar ·············· Stir together until smooth and add scalded milk. Return to double boiler and stir
1 teaspoon cornstarch   until smooth. Cool.
2 egg yolks

Nutmeg ································· Pour custard into sherbet dishes and sprinkle top with nutmeg.

2 egg whites–beaten ············ Beat egg whites until stiff and add sugar; then beat again. Drop from spoon in
2 tablespoons sugar   pan with small amount of water. Bake in slow oven 325° about 15 minutes or
    until brown. Life from pan with fork and top custard with meringue.

Cabinet Pudding

Ingredients

Directions (serves 6)

2 cups milk ························· Combine in saucepan. Cook over low heat until milk reaches the scalding point.
2 tablespoons butter   Cool slightly.
2 tablespoons sugar

2 cups cake or bread crumbs ······· Add to the milk mixture.

2 eggs–slightly beaten ············ Combine opposite ingredients and stir slowly into the milk. Pour into greased
1/4 teaspoon salt   1-quart casserole and place casserole in pan of hot water. Bake in moderate oven
1/2 teaspoon vanilla   375° about 1 hour.

Grapenut Pudding

(Serves 6) Use recipe for Cabinet Pudding substituting 1 cup grapenuts for cake crumbs. Heat grapenuts with the milk.

Old-Fashioned Bread Pudding

Ingredients	Directions (Serves 4 to 6)
2 cups stale bread cubes (1/4 to 1/2-inch cubes)	Place in greased 1-quart casserole.
2 cups milk 1/4 cup butter 1/4 cup sugar	Combine opposite ingredients in saucepan. Cook over low heat until milk reaches the scalding point.
2 eggs Pinch of salt 3/4 teaspoon vanilla	Beat eggs slightly. Add salt. Stir in warm milk. Add vanilla. Pour over bread cubes. Place casserole in pan of hot water. Bake in moderate oven 350° about 1 hour or until silver knife comes out clean when inserted in center of pudding. Serve hot or cold with plain cream, currant jelly, or hot Caramel, Lemon, Chocolate, or Clear Sauce. (See Dessert Sauces Section.)

Chocolate Bread Pudding

(Serves 4 to 6) Use recipe for Old-Fashioned Bread Pudding adding 1 square unsweetened chocolate to the milk-butter-sugar mixture before heating.

Fruit Bread Pudding

(Serves 4 to 6) Prepare Old-Fashioned Bread Pudding adding ½ cup chopped raisins, dates, figs, or nuts before baking.

Store cooked custards or custard puddings, pies, éclairs, sauces in a cool or refrigerated place (50° F. or lower) to prevent them from spoiling and to prevent possible growth of bacteria (staphylococcus) which, although rarely fatal, can make you "deathly sick."

Old-Fashioned Lemon Pudding

Ingredients

Directions (Serves 6)

1/2 cup bread, zwieback, ·············· Soak crumbs and milk together; set aside.
  or cake crumbs
2 cups milk

1/3 cup soft butter ····················· Cream butter and sugar together until well blended.
1/2 cup sugar

3 egg yolks–beaten ···················· Add yolks to creamed mixture and mix well.

3 tablespoons lemon juice ··········· Add juice and rind of lemon with milk mixture to the creamed butter, sugar, and
2 teaspoons grated lemon rind   egg yolks.

3 egg whites ····························· Beat until stiff but not dry. Fold into mixture. Pour into greased 1-quart casserole. Bake in slow oven 325° about 45 minutes.

Crème Brûlée

Mrs. Virginia Safford, The Minneapolis Star, Minneapolis, Minnesota

Ingredients

Directions (Serves 8)

1 quart light cream ····················· Scald cream. Beat egg yolks and sugar together. Remove cream from heat and
8 egg yolks   pour very slowly into egg mixture, stirring constantly. Add vanilla; set mixture in
5 tablespoons granulated   baking dish and place in pan of hot water. Bake in moderate oven 350° about one
  sugar   hour or until silver knife inserted in center comes out clean.
2 teaspoons vanilla

2 tablespoons brown sugar ·········· When above is done sprinkle with brown sugar. Place under broiler until sugar
melts and forms a glaze. Serve cold as an ice cube. (Many times the Crème Brûlée
is served with fruit or assorted brandied fruit. The Brûlée is placed in a glass
pudding dish; this centered on a large platter encircled with fruit–pears, peaches,
black cherries, or green gage plums. Canned fruit which is brandied in a hurry
may also be used. Follow this simple process: Drain off syrup, cover fruit with
brandy or kirsch and let stand 12 hours covered in the refrigerator.)

The Duncan Hines Dessert Book

Trifle

Ingredients

1 dozen ladyfingers

1/2 cup jam (apricot, strawberry, raspberry, etc.)

6 large macaroons

1/3 cup sherry or brandy

1 1/2 recipes Soft Custard–chilled

1/2 cup heavy cream–whipped

1/3 cup blanched, slivered, toasted almonds

Candied cherries

Directions (Serves 8)

Line sides of dessert bowl with ladyfingers which have been split in half and spread on one side with jam. Place macaroons on the bottom of the bowl.

Pour over the macaroons and let stand until absorbed.

Pour over the soaked macaroons and chill.

Garnish with whipped cream, almonds, and cherries.

Soft Custard

Ingredients

2 eggs or 4 egg yolks–slightly beaten

3 tablespoons sugar

Pinch of salt

1 1/2 cups scalded milk

1/2 teaspoon vanilla

Directions (Makes 2 cups)

Combine opposite ingredients.

Add milk slowly to egg mixture. Strain into the top of a double boiler. Cook over hot water (about 5 minutes) stirring constantly or until mixture thickens and coats a metal spoon. Remove pan immediately from hot water and place in pan of cold water to cool quickly.
Add to the above mixture and chill.

Sabayon

Ingredients

8 egg yolks ··················

1 cup confectioners' sugar

1/8 teaspoon salt

1/2 cup Madeira ··················

8 egg whites–stiffly beaten ··········

Directions (Serves 6)

Beat together until very light. Place in top of double boiler. Cook over hot water, beating constantly, until foamy. (Do not allow water to touch the bottom of the top section of the double boiler.)

Add to the above mixture gradually. Continue to beat until it doubles in bulk. Remove from heat.

Fold in hot custard gradually. Serve at once in sherbet glasses. This may also be served as a sauce.

Vanessi's Zabaglione

Vanessi's Restaurant, San Francisco, California

Ingredients

8 egg yolks ··················

5 tablespoons sugar

10 oz. dry sauterne

1/4 teaspoon lemon
  rind–chopped fine

1 oz. anisette

Directions (Serves 4)

Put eggs in round saucepan. Add sugar, lemon rind, and wine. Beat rapidly with wire whip over fire. Do not let boil. Whip until thick, then add anisette.

Zabaglione

Marguerite Vollmer, New York, New York

Ingredients

6 egg yolks ··················

1/3 cup sugar

1/3 cup Marsala or sherry

Directions

Put yolks in top of double boiler. Beat until thick and add sugar. Put over hot water (not boiling). Cook over low heat, beat constantly. In about 5 minutes slowly add Marsala. Cook and beat until thick. Serve hot or chilled.
Note: Use Dry Sack (Williams & Humber), Florio's or a medium sweet sherry.

Fruit Desserts

FRUITS: FRESH, FROZEN, OR CANNED, RAW OR COOKED, PLAIN OR FANCY, ARE A WELCOME TREAT any season of the year.

For a light refreshing dessert after a heavy meal (and for those of you who are low calorie conscious) fruits are a popular choice. As a homemaker you can easily display your skill by transforming the simple fruit into a glamorous dish. Defrost frozen fruits only about half way. If they are completely defrosted they will become soft and flabby and lose some of their flavor. If peeled fresh fruits are to be used, wait until the last minute before peeling. Otherwise, they will become spotted and discolored. If you must pare ahead of time, sprinkle lemon juice over the fruit to keep it fresh looking.

A good rule of thumb in buying fruits is to look first at those that are in season. Produce in season tastes better because it is fresher. It is also less expensive at that time. But do not buy the cheapest fruit on the market just because it is the cheapest. Fruit in this category usually turns out to be an expensive bargain. Freshness is your best buy. ▶

Apple Sauce

The House by the Road, Ashburn, Georgia

Ingredients

Directions (Serves 8)

8 medium apples–tart ···················· Peel, core, and cut in large pieces. Cook and drain and put in bowl.

1/4 cup water

1/2 cup sugar ······························· Add opposite ingredients to apples.

1 teaspoon butter

1 teaspoon nutmeg

1 dozen marshmallows ···················· Put apples in baking dish and cover with marshmallows. Stick in oven until brown.

Arabian Nights Baked Apples

Charles H. Baker, Jr., Coconut Grove, Florida

Ingredients

Directions (Serves 8)

8 large red tart apples ···················· Core and remove peeling down ¼ way from stem end. Place in kettle on rack and

3/4 cup brown sugar   add ¾ cup hot water. Stuff cavities with sugar and color peeled part with a drop

Red color   or two of red color. Put orange peel in water; put on lid and cook slowly until

Large piece of orange peel   tender. Remove and let cool.

1/2 cup finely chopped dates ·········· Mix all well together. Stuff cavities of apples; place in greased baking dish. Dust

1/2 cup finely chopped figs   heavily with brown sugar which has been mixed with cinnamon and cloves.

1/4 teaspoon cloves   Brown in 375° oven until sugar caramelizes.

1/2 teaspoon cinnamon

2 teaspoons Jamaica rum

Brown sugar

Baked Apple Sunshine

Ingredients

Directions (Serves 12)

12 red cooking apples ·················· Wash and core apples. Peel half way down from top. Cut mincemeat into 12 equal
1 (8 oz.) pkg. dry mincemeat   portions or blocks. Fill centers with mincemeat. Place in baking pan.
1 1/2 cups sugar ························· Mix together and boil for 5 minutes. Pour over apples and bake in 400° oven for
2 cups water   45 minutes, basting occasionally with this liquid.
1/2 cup sugar ····························· Sprinkle over apples and glaze quickly under broiler. Lift into serving dishes.
1 1/2 cups orange juice ················ Drain juice from apples, add orange juice and rind and boil 10 minutes. Pour
Little grated orange rind   over apples, chill and serve with cream.
  (cranberry juice or lemon
  juice is also good)

Cherries Jubilee

Cameo Restaurant, Chicago, Illinois

Ingredients

Directions (Serves 6)

1 pint fresh black cherries ············· Put into covered pot and cook slowly for 10 minutes. Canned black cherries may
1 pint water   be used, providing they are whole, sweet, and have the pits in them. Drain the
3/4 cup sugar   cherries from the syrup. Put cherries in a chafing dish.
4 teaspoons sugar ····················· Place in chafing dish with cherries and bring to a boil.
1 lemon peel—whole
1/2 cup cherry syrup
6 oz. brandy ···························· Pour over cherries and set aflame.
2 oz. Grand Marnier liqueur
6 (3 oz.) scoops of ice cream ········ Put cake in individual dishes, cover with ice cream and pour blazing cherries over
6 slices of plain cake   all. Serve immediately.

This dish was created for the Jubilee of Queen Victoria of England.

Killarney Cherries

Ingredients

Directions (Serves 6)

1 lb. ox-heart or Bing cherries ········ Let come to boil, cover, then reduce heat and simmer 12 to 15 minutes. Drain the cherries and chill. Cook juice until it reduces to about one-third to make the sauce.

1 pint claret

1 cup sugar

1 stick cinnamon bark

12 whole cloves

2 tablespoons red currant jelly ······ Add to sauce, melt and chill.

3 tablespoons cherry brandy ·········· Put in sauce just before serving.

1 1/2 cups whipped cream ·········· Serve cherries in silver dishes, set in bed of ice. Pour over sauce and top with whipped cream. Should be very cold.

1 tablespoon Kirschwasser

1 tablespoon sugar

Grapefruit Burgundy

Ingredients

Directions (Serves 6)

1 cup fruit juice ···················· Simmer fruit juice and sugar until it becomes of medium thickness.

1/2 cup sugar

1/4 cup wine (either red ············· After syrup has cooled, add the wine.
  or white)

6 grapefruit halves ·················· Cover top of half grapefruit with syrup and decorate with half cherry or mint leaves.

Peaches Supreme

Ingredients

Directions (Serves 8 to 10)

8 to 10 peaches–halved ············· Cook just enough to tenderize peaches. Set aside to chill.

1 vanilla bean

1/2 cup sugar

1/2 cup water

1 quart raspberries–fresh ············· Mash into a puree. Chill

Peaches Flambée Royale

Ingredients

Directions (Serves 4)

4 peaches ·········· Cook peaches in this mixture with skins on. Let water come to boiling point and
1 pint cold water   boil for 15 minutes, keeping the pot covered all the time. Take out the peaches,
1/2 cup sugar   skin, cut them in half and remove pits. Place them in a chafing dish.
1/4 stick cinnamon
1 lemon peel–whole
1/2 cup strawberries ·········· Put in chafing dish with the peaches and let get hot.
  or raspberries–crushed
1/2 cup syrup (that the peaches
  were cooked in)
4 oz. brandy ·········· Add to the above, and set aflame.
2 oz. of curacao
3 or 4 small pieces of orange peel
4 scoops of vanilla ice cream ·········· Put in individual dishes and pour the flaming ingredients over all.

Black Currant Mousse

1 cup black currant jam or ·········· Put jam or fresh currants through a strainer or colander. Combine with
  fresh currants   powdered sugar.
1/2 cup powdered sugar
2 cups whipping ·········· Fold into mixture and freeze in refrigerator trays, 2 hours.
  cream–whipped
1 teaspoon vanilla
2 tablespoons Cassis liqueur ·········· Just before serving, blend this mixture. Put the mousse on a platter, cover with
1 pint whipping   brandy mixture. Put peaches on top and all around and pour puree over all.
  cream–whipped
3 tablespoons currant jam
1/2 lb. almonds–chopped ·········· Top with nuts. Serve at once and have all mixtures ice cold.

Pineapple Delight

Mrs. Wallace Rigby, Larchmont, New York

Ingredients

Directions (Serves 6)

1 large ripe pineapple ···············
1 pint fresh strawberries
1 large banana ·····························
1/2 cup crème de menthe

Cut off the top of the pineapple, retaining the top to use as a lid. Scoop out the meat of the pineapple, leaving only the rind with a thin inside layer of pineapple. Cut the scooped out fruit into small cubes. Put into a bowl with the strawberries which have been capped and washed. Chill. Just before serving, quarter the banana lengthwise and cube. Mix with other fruits and put all the fruit into the pineapple shell. Pour the crème de menthe over the fruit in the shell. Replace top. Serve from the pineapple into dessert dishes. (Pineapple and strawberries may be sprinkled with sugar before chilling if desired.)

Brandied Grapefruit

Waldorf-Astoria, New York City

Ingredients

Directions (Serves 6)

6 grapefruit halves ····················
12 tablespoons light brown ··········
   sugar
6 tablespoons brandy ·················

Selected grapefruits. Remove core and seeds.

Spread 2 tablespoons of light brown sugar on top of each.

Pour 1 tablespoon of brandy over each and allow to marinate for half an hour. Bake in oven, 325°, until hot and bubbling. Serve very hot.

Golden Grapefruit

Old Spinning Wheel Tea Room, Hinsdale, Illinois

Ingredients

Directions (Serves 1)

1/2 grapefruit ····························
1 tablespoon brown sugar
1 tablespoon sherry

Core grapefruit and fill center with sugar and wine. Heat in 350° oven until sugar is melted. Repeat for as many servings as desired.

The Duncan Hines Dessert Book

Fried Peaches

Fred Waring, New York City

Ingredients

Directions (Serves 6 to 8)

1 tablespoon butter	Place in frying pan and let melt.
6 to 8 peaches–peeled	Place whole peaches in pan.
1 cup brown sugar	Put over peaches and let simmer for 30 minutes. Keep turning the peaches.
1/2 cup cream	Just before serving, pour over peaches and let it boil up. Serve hot.

Baked Pineapple Hawaiian

Charles H. Baker, Jr., Coconut Grove, Florida

Ingredients

Directions

1 large pineapple	Cut off the top down the fruit 1 ½ inches. Reserve this for use later. Cut out the heart with a curved grapefruit knife, but do not dig through the shell. Dice the fruit, discarding the pithy center.
1/2 cup sugar	Coat the fruit and put back in the shell. Add the juice of the pineapple.
4 tablespoons Cognac	Pour over the fruit.
1 teaspoon cinnamon	Dust the fruit. Put the top back on and skewer in place. Bake in 350° oven 30 to 40 minutes until the fruit is tender. Remove top and serve on a silver platter.
1 tablespoon brandy	Light and bring to the table blazing.

Pineapple Flambée à la Marie

Arnaud's Restaurant, New Orleans, Louisiana

Ingredients

Directions

1 fresh pineapple–sliced 1/2-inch thick	Roll sliced pineapple in flour; then dip in milk; then roll in flour again. Fry pineapple in oil or shortening until golden brown. Place cherry in center of pineapple and cover freely with sugar. Bake in oven five minutes or until sugar is bubbly and golden brown; our cognac over it. Heat until cognac is warm. Light with match; then serve, and add sherry wine.
Flour	
Milk	
Cherries	
Sugar	
Cognac	
Sherry wine	

Strawberries Biltmore

Biltmore Hotel, Los Angeles, California

Ingredients

1 quart strawberries ·················

Rum–enough to cover berries ········

1/4 lb. powdered sugar

SAUCE

1 pint vanilla ice cream ···············

2 oz. Kirschwasser

1 cup whipping ·····················

   cream–whipped

1/2 cup sugar

Directions (Serves 4 to 6)

Stem and wash thoroughly. Drain. Place on napkin to further drain off water.

Add to berries and let stand for 2 hours before serving. Not too long, however, as the berries will become soggy. Drain. Add sauce and serve very cold.

Mix and stir well.

Fold into the above mixture and chill. Serve over the strawberries in glass compote.

Strawberry Lindomar

Ingredients

15 marshmallows ···················

1/2 pt. crushed strawberries

1 cup cream ·······················

1/2 pt. sliced strawberries ···········

2 oz. sauterne

Directions (Serves 8 to 10)

Quarter marshmallows and melt in double boiler with the crushed strawberries. Cool.

Whip cream and combine with above mixture. Put in refrigerator tray and let freeze.

Pour sauterne over sliced strawberries. Just before serving put over frozen mixture as a sundae.

Ambrosia

Ingredients

3 oranges–peeled ··················

2 bananas

1/2 cup grated coconut ··············

4 Maraschino cherries

Directions (Serves 4)

Section oranges and slice bananas in rounds. Chill together for 1 hour.

Serve in chilled sherbet glasses topped with coconut and a maraschino cherry.

128   The Duncan Hines Dessert Book

Strawberries à la Tsarina

Charles H. Baker, Jr., Coconut Grove, Florida

Ingredients

2 cups stemmed strawberries

2 tablespoons powdered sugar

2 tablespoons port wine

2 tablespoons orange curacao

2 tablespoons cognac

1 teaspoon curacao

1 cup whipped cream

Directions (Serves 2)

Toss strawberries and sugar and put in bowl. Chill.

Blend and pour over berries.

Add curacao to whipped cream. Place berries in individual dishes, cover with whipped cream and serve

Strawberry Fruit Cup

The Birches on Moosehead Lake, Rockwood, Maine

Ingredients

1 pint strawberries

3 large oranges–peeled

2 cups fresh squeezed orange juice

1/2 cup grated fresh coconut

2 bananas

Light honey

Directions (Serves 4-6)

Wash before capping. Cut in half. Put into large bowl.

Slice with sharp knife; then dice.

Add to other ingredients in bowl.

Add grated coconut.

Sliced round not too thin. Put immediately into bowl.

Sweeten to taste. Chill until icy cold. Serve in cold sherbet glasses.

Raspberry Royal

Royal Savage Inn, Plattsburg, New York

Ingredients

1 pint fresh raspberries or 1 box frozen raspberries defrosted and drained

12 graham crackers–crushed

1/2 pint whipped cream

Directions (Serves 4)

In sherbet glasses, alternate whipped cream, raspberries, crushed graham crackers–repeating this twice. Place whipped cream on top. Serve at once. (Blackberries are equally as good.)

Pineapple Trifle

Ingredients

Directions (Serves 6 to 8)

1 cup canned crushed ···················· Combine ingredients in bowl.
  pineapple–drained
10 marshmallows-cut
1 cup macaroon crumbs
1 cup chopped dates
3/4 cup heavy cream–whipped ······ Fold whipped cream into above ingredients. Chill.

Fresh Fruit Trifle

Ingredients

Directions (Serves 8)

24 almond macaroons ···················· Dip macaroons in wine and place in a flat serving dish.
3/4 cup sherry wine
6 egg yolks–beaten ···················· Beat eggs 5 minutes in electric mixer or with rotary beater for 15 minutes, adding
1 cup sugar   sugar and beating a little longer. Add the balance of sherry and salt. Place in
1/8 teaspoon salt   double boiler and cook until it thickens, stirring constantly. Pour this mixture
                                        over the macaroons and allow to cool.
Any fresh fruit, or whipped ··········· Just before serving cover with fresh sliced peaches, figs, or strawberries. Or with
  cream and almonds   whipped cream and blanched almonds.

Cherry-Nut Trifle

Use recipe for Pineapple Trifle substituting ⅔ cup maraschino cherries, cut in pieces, for the pineapple. Substitute 1 cup chopped nuts for the macaroons.

Macédoine of Fruits

Waldorf-Astoria, New York, New York

Ingredients	Directions
Take some fresh fruit of the season (bananas, pineapple, orange, grapefruit)	Peel and slice. Mix together and set bowl on ice. Add some syrup (Kirsch or Maraschino), and let them macerate for two hours.

The Wonder Dessert

O. B. Wright, Long Beach, California

Ingredients

Directions (serves 5)

1 cup oranges — Cut in small pieces and squeeze out some of the juice. This is important or the dessert will be soft and run.

1 cup walnuts — Break in pieces not too small.

1 cup fresh marshmallows — Cut marshmallows with scissors and add sugar to present them from sticking
1/4 cup sugar — together.

1 pint whipping cream–whipped — If possible whip with an electric whipper to make stiff. Add vanilla and mix in other ingredients. Serve in fruit cup, piled high. Will keep for a few hours in
1/4 teaspoon vanilla — refrigerator, but is better if served at once.

Hedelmakeitto (Cold Fruit Soup)

Ingredients

Directions (Serves 6)

1/2 lb. prunes — Wash opposite ingredients in warm water and let soak overnight with the sugar
1/2 lb. apricots and pears (dried) — added to 1 ½ quarts water.

1/2 cup sugar — Add to the above and boil. Strain.
3 fresh apples–cored and sliced 1/8-inch thick

1 cinnamon bark — Mix with 1 ½ tablespoons of cold water and thicken the fruit juice. Boil again for
1 to 2 tablespoons potato starch — a few minutes and add the fruit. Serve cold.

Cheese Desserts

ONE OF THE MOST ROMANTIC OF ALL FOODS IS CHEESE. NO MAN CAN SAY HOW LONG CHEESE HAS been a staple food of mankind, but we can safely assume that people have been eating cheese for at least 2,000 years.

There is a legend about the first cheese. According to the tale, an ancient Arabian trader poured milk into his sheepskin canteen before starting out on a long journey. All day the bag swung and jostled at his saddle-bows. At night when he stopped to make camp and to eat, he opened the bag of milk and found that it had become a curious mass of white curd. The action of certain enzymes under ideal conditions had curdled the milk, and the world had its first cheese.

The ancient Greeks believed that cheese was of divine origin and offered it as a fitting sacrifice to the gods on Mount Olympus. The Bible tells us that the boy David carried ten cheeses to his captain. ▶

We also know that cheese was used as money by the nomads of Asia centuries ago. During the Crusades, when Christian knights fought the Mohammedans, cheese was regarded as a desirable booty of war, and when captured was divided like jewelry and other valuable spoils.

But cheese is as American as any food on our tables. It can boast of a wonderful ancestry. It came over on the Mayflower along with some of our first citizens. The first cheese factory in the United States was built in Rome, New York, in 1851, where today a bronze plaque stands on the site to commemorate this important event.

Today, cheese is an important part of our meals, and the American housewife can choose from literally hundreds of different kinds. The cheese dessert may range from cream cheese on crackers to the elegant cheese cake, but whatever the choice, serving cheese will surely enhance your reputation as a hostess.

For the unexpected guests here are a few suggestions for a quick, last minute cheese dessert:

A cheese and cracker tray consisting of crackers, an assortment of cheeses, and served along with a large bowl of fresh polished fruit. Serving can be simple: individual dessert plates, and knives for cutting the fruit and for spreading or slicing the cheese. Finger bowls are appropriate to save your linen napkins from fruit stains.

A tray of lightly toasted flaky crackers spread with cream cheese and a choice of preserves or jams (currant, guava, elderberry, or cranberry) and a bowl of salted nuts also makes a delightful "passing" tray.

Use your imagination and serve any combination you desire.

Another "quicky" cheese dessert is to sieve 1 cup cottage cheese and thin to desired consistency with milk or cream. Sweeten to taste with sugar and vanilla. Place in bowl and sprinkle with cinnamon. Chill. Serve with crushed sweetened strawberries, raspberries, peaches, or any fresh fruit in season.

Pineapple Cheese Pudding

The Clark Restaurant Company, Test Kitchen, Cleveland, Ohio

Ingredients

1 #2 can pineapple–crushed ·········
2 tablespoons cornstarch
1/4 cup water
1 cup creamy cottage cheese ·········
1 cup granulated sugar
1/4 cup butter–softened ·············
1/2 cup cake flour–unsifted ·········
2 eggs ·································
3/4 cup milk ·························
1 teaspoon vanilla

Directions (Serves 8)

Heat pineapple in pan over direct heat. Dissolve cornstarch in a little cold water and add to pineapple. Cook until clear. Spread evenly in bottom of 10-inch pyrex pie plate and set aside to cool.

Mix cottage cheese and sugar together.

Add to the above and mix.

Add to butter–cottage cheese mixture and blend well.

Add eggs, one at a time, and mix well after each addition.

Mix milk and vanilla together and slowly add to the batter. Pour batter over pineapple and bake in 450° oven for 10 minutes. Then turn oven down to 350° and bake for 30 minutes or until silver knife inserted in center comes out clean. Serve cold.

Note: All ingredients for this pudding should be at room temperature before using.

For the lunch box or picnic, cheese cake makes an excellent dessert.
It is filling and not messy to eat.

Strawberries and Cottage Cheese

Ingredients

Strawberries ·······················
Sugar
Cottage cheese

Directions

Wash strawberries and remove stems. Place into individual serving dishes and sprinkle with sugar. Serve with cottage cheese.

Cottage Cheese Currant Jelly Whip

Ingredients

3 egg whites ·······················
1/4 cup sugar
Pinch of salt
1/2 cup currant jelly ·················
1 cup cottage cheese

Directions (Serves 4 to 5)

Beat egg whites until foamy. Add sugar gradually and salt; continue beating until stiff.

Combine and fold into above. Serve with Plain Custard Sauce (see Dessert Sauces Section), if desired.

Cottage Cheese Parfait

Ingredients

1 cup cottage cheese ················
1 egg white ·······················
2 tablespoons sugar
1/2 teaspoon salt
1 cup heavy cream ··················
1/2 teaspoon almond extract
1 box frozen ·······················
   strawberries–defrosted or
   fresh strawberries–crushed
   and sweetened

Directions (Serves 6)

Beat until smooth.
Combine and beat until stiff. Fold into cottage cheese.

Whip cream adding extract. Fold into mixture.

Alternate spoonfuls of cottage cheese mixture and fruit into individual serving dishes.

Fromage à la Crème

Ingredients

1 cup heavy cream ·····················

3 (3 oz.) packages cream ···············
cheese

2 tablespoons heavy cream

1 box frozen strawberries ···············
defrosted or sweetened fresh
strawberries–crushed

Directions (Serves 3 to 4)

Beat until stiff.

Combine and beat until soft. Fold into above whipped cream. Pour into individual molds and chill.

Unmold and serve with strawberries over the top.

Molded Cream Cheese with Fruit

Ingredients

2 (3 oz) packages cream ·················
cheese

1 tablespoon confectioners'
sugar

1 tablespoon milk

1 box frozen strawberries or ··········
raspberries–defrosted or
crushed, sweetened, fresh
strawberries or raspberries

Directions (Serves 4)

Beat cheese until smooth. Add sugar and blend. Thin to a smooth consistency with milk. Pour into individual molds and chill.

Unmold and serve with fruit over the top.

Pear à la Fromage

Ingredients

Fresh pears ····························

Cottage cheese

Sugar ·································

Cinnamon

Directions

Pare and slice thinly.

Sweeten cottage cheese with sugar and cinnamon. Serve over the pears.

Cheese Cakes

Cheese cakes, one of my favorite desserts, is a superlative ending to any light meal. In the following section I have chosen some of my best liked cheese cake recipes. The ingredients in all are very much alike, but with some slight changes a different cake results.

In general, there are two kinds–baked cheese cakes and refrigerator cheese cakes. Refrigerator cheese cakes are made with gelatin and require no baking because when the mixture is chilled it becomes firm. Cheese cakes are made with cottage cheese or cream cheese or both kinds of cheese. They are made in various shapes, sizes, flavors and textures depending upon the recipe.

Contrary to the opinion of most people, cheese cake is easy to make. It is deluxe and "gourmet," yet, it can be made in your own kitchen with little trouble and not have to be bought at the neighborhood pastry shop. By following one of my recipes you will surprise yourself with perfect results—and how easy!

Lindy's Cheese Cake
Lindy's, New York, New York

Ingredients

1 cup sifted flour
1/2 cup sugar
1 teaspoon grated lemon rind
1 egg yolk
1/4 cup butter–melted
1/4 teaspoon vanilla

Directions

Combine dry ingredients including lemon rind in bowl. Make a well in center. Add egg, butter and vanilla; work together quickly until well blended. Add a little cold water if necessary to make hold together. Wrap in waxed paper and chill thoroughly in refrigerator for about 1 hour. Roll out ⅛-inch thick and place over greased bottom of 9-inch spring form pan.

Trim off extra dough. Bake in hot oven, 400° for 15 to 20 minutes or until a light gold color. Cool. Butter sides of pan and place over base. Roll remaining dough ⅛-inch thick and line sides of pan. Fill with following mixture.

2 1/2 lbs. cream cheese ·············· Put cheese in electric mixer and beat at second speed. Add sugar gradually then
1 3/4 cups sugar   remainder of ingredients in order given. Eggs should be added one at a time.
3 tablespoons flour   When thoroughly blended and smooth, pour into lined pan above and place in
1 1/2 teaspoons grated orange   preheated oven 550° and bake from 12 to 15 minutes. Reduce heat to 200° and
  rind   continue baking for 1 hour. Cool before cutting.
1 1/2 teaspoons grated lemon
  rind
1/4 teaspoon vanilla
5 eggs
2 egg yolks
1/4 cup heavy cream

Cheese Cake

Hody's, Los Angeles, California

Ingredients

Directions (Serves 6 to 8 people)

1/4 lb. graham crackers ·············· Roll crackers very fine. Add other ingredients, mixing well. Line 10-inch spring
2 tablespoons sugar   form pan.
1 1/2 teaspoons cinnamon
6 tablespoons melted butter
1 1/2 lbs. cream cheese ·············· Place cheese in electric beater and beat well. Add sugar gradually and then eggs
1 cup sugar   one at a time. Vanilla last. Pour into pan and bake 20 minutes at 375°.
3 eggs
1/2 teaspoon vanilla
1 pt. sour cream ·················· Whip cream lightly, add sugar and vanilla. Pour carefully over baked pie. Bake in
3 tablespoons sugar   500° oven for 5 minutes. Cool and place in refrigerator.
1/2 teaspoon vanilla

Refrigerator Cheese Cake

Ingredients

Directions (Serves 8 to 9)

1/2 cup graham cracker ·············· Reserve ¼ cup crumbs. Sprinkle remaining crumbs into bottom of a 1 ½-quart
crumbs   greased spring form pan.

1 package lemon-flavored ············ Dissolve gelatin and sugar in boiling water. Add gradually to egg yolks. Add
gelatin   remaining ingredients.

1/2 cup sugar

1 1/4 cups boiling water

2 egg yolks, slightly beaten

1/4 cup concentrate lemonade

1/2 cup heavy cream

12 oz. cream cheese ·················· Beat until smooth. Add gelatin mixture. Chill until slightly thickened.

2 egg whites ··························· Beat until stiff. Fold into slightly thickened gelatin mixture. Pour into pan.
                                                 Sprinkle with remaining crumbs. Chill until firm (about 2 hours). To serve,
                                                 loosen sides carefully with spatula and remove from pan.

Cottage Cheese Cake

Ingredients

Directions (Serves 12)

1 3/4 cups zwieback ·················· Combine. Reserve ½ cup of the mixture. Press remaining crumbs with fingers (or
pieces–finely crushed   use bottom of cup) into the bottom and sides of a greased 9-inch spring form
                                                 pan.
1/2 cup butter–melted

1/2 cup sugar

24 oz. cottage cheese ··············· Sieve.

4 eggs ··································· Beat eggs. Add sugar gradually and beat until thick and creamy. Add remaining
                                                 ingredients and cottage cheese. Beat well. Turn into pan and sprinkle with
1 cup sugar   remaining crumbs. Bake in slow oven 325° for 1 hour. Turn off heat and leave in
                                                 oven 1 hour longer. Cool and chill 5 to 6 hours or overnight.
1/2 cup heavy cream

1/2 teaspoon salt

1/4 cup flour

2 tablespoons lemon juice

2 teaspoons grated lemon rind

Creamy Cottage Cheese Cake

Ingredients

12 zwieback pieces–finely ·········· crushed
2 tablespoons sugar
1/4 cup butter–melted

24 oz. cottage cheese ················
2 eggs
2/3 cup sugar
1/8 teaspoon salt
1 teaspoon vanilla

1/2 pint sour cream ·····················
1/4 cup sugar
2 teaspoons vanilla

Directions (Serves 10)

Combine. Press mixture with fingers into the bottom and sides of loose-bottom 9-inch cake pan. Chill.

Beat cottage cheese in blender at high speed until consistency of very heavy cream (about 3 minutes). Add remaining ingredients and beat at high speed for about 5 minutes. Pour mixture into prepared pan and bake in moderate oven 350° for 30 minutes.

Mix well. Spread carefully over cheese cake. Return to oven and bake 8 to 10 minutes. (Topping does not brown.) Cool and chill.

Graham Cracker Cheese Pie

Pals Cabin, West Orange, New Jersey

Ingredients

1 lb. cream cheese ·······················
1 lb. cottage cheese
1 pint sour cream
1 lemon–rind and juice ···············
Vanilla flavor
Salt to taste
5 egg yolks
1 cup sugar
20 graham crackers–finely ···········
crushed
1/2 cup butter–melted

Directions (Makes two 9-inch pies)

Cream cottage cheese, sour cream and cream cheese.

Add lemon, vanilla, and salt; beat yolks and sugar well; and fold together.

Line pie tins with crushed graham crackers mixed with melted butter. Pour in cheese mixture. Bake in 375° oven for 30 minutes. Chill in refrigerator before cutting.

Fort Hayes Cheese Cake

Hotel Fort Hayes, Columbus, Ohio

Ingredients

Directions (Makes 1 spring form cake pan)

1/4 lb. butter–melted
24 graham crackers

Combine butter with crackers that have been crushed fine and line spring form cake pan. (Hold back ½ cup cracker crumbs for top of cake.) Bake 10 to 15 minutes.

1 lb. cottage cheese
1/4 cup sugar
1/2 teaspoon vanilla
Juice and rind of 1 lemon

Mash cottage cheese through strainer and combine with sugar, vanilla, grated rind, and lemon juice.

2 egg yolks
1/2 teaspoon salt
1/4 cup sugar
1/4 cup milk

Combine these ingredients and make a cooked custard.

1 envelope (1 tablespoon) unflavored gelatin
1/4 cup cold water

Soak gelatin in cold water. Beat into custard while still hot. Cool custard.

1/2 pt. cream
2 egg whites

Beat together and fold in above mixture.

1/2 cup cracker crumbs

Pour above mixture into baked spring form. Sprinkle crumbs on top and leave in refrigerator overnight.

A simple cheese and fruit dessert is wonderful for those watching their "spread."

Pie without cheese is like a kiss without a squeeze!

Cheese with pie is not new but you may be surprised to find how good it tastes with fresh peaches, apples, or other fruit.

The Duncan Hines Dessert Book

Pennsylvania Dutch Cheese Pie

Ingredients

Directions (Makes one 10-inch pie)

4 eggs ···································· Separate egg yolks and whites.

1/2 lb. cottage cheese ················ Press through a sieve.

1/2 lb. sugar ····························· Cream together the cottage cheese, sugar, egg yolks, flour, salt and flavoring. Beat

1 tablespoon flour   the egg whites until stiff and fold into mixture.

Pinch of salt

A little lemon and vanilla
  flavoring

1 10-inch unbaked pie shell ·········· Bake in unbaked pie shell in 400° oven for 25-30 minutes.

Cheese cake is best the second day because it mellows in flavor.

Gelatin Desserts

THE PURPOSE OF GELATIN IS TO SET UP COLORFUL AND DELICIOUSLY FLAVORED MIXTURES SO THAT they can be molded into attractive shapes. Gelatin is the base for those familiar sponge, jelly, whip, cream, and other refrigerator desserts. These desserts will lend sparkle and color to your meals.

In the early days women made their own gelatin by following a long and tedious recipe. Today both flavored and unflavored gelatins are available for quick and easy use.

To be good, a gelatin dessert should be firm without being too stiff. The flavors used should blend well with the other ingredients (and even with the meal itself) to furnish just the right "finishing touch."

Gelatin desserts also offer the hostess an opportunity for a special holiday touch. A bright green lime flavor is appropriate for St. Patrick's Day, something in cherry flavor for Father Washington's Birthday, or an orange flavor for Halloween. Possibilities for creative adventures are unlimited. ▶

Above all do not get into a "flavor rut." If you use a variety of flavors, different recipes, and some of your own ideas your family will never tire of a gelatin treat for dessert.

Bavarian Cream

Ingredients	Directions (Serves 6)
1 envelope (1 tablespoon) unflavored gelatin 2 tablespoons cold water	Soak gelatin in cold water about 5 minutes.
1 1/3 cups milk 1/2 cup sugar 1/4 teaspoon salt	Scald milk in top of double boiler. Add sugar, salt, and gelatin to the scalded milk. Stir until dissolved.
2 egg yolks–slightly beaten	Stir a little of the hot milk mixture into the egg yolks; then stir into the remaining hot milk. Cook over hot water until slightly thickened, stirring constantly. Chill until almost set.
2 egg whites–stiffly beaten 1 cup heavy cream–whipped 1 teaspoon vanilla	Fold into the above mixture. Pour into individual molds and chill until firm.

To hasten the thickening of a gelatin mixture, place the bowl of gelatin mixture
in a larger bowl filled with ice and water. (It is best to use metal bowls.)
Stir occasionally to prevent a stiff layer forming on the bottom.

Berry Bavarian Cream

Ingredients

1 package raspberry or strawberry–flavored gelatin
1 cup boiling water
1/4 cup sugar
1 cup crushed raspberries or
  strawberries

1/2 cup heavy cream–whipped

Directions (Serves 10 to 12)

Pour boiling water over gelatin and stir until dissolved.

Sprinkle sugar over fruit in bowl and let stand 20 minutes. Drain off juice into cup and add water to make 1 cup. Reserve fruit. Add juice to dissolved gelatin mixture. Chill until slightly thickened. Set the bowl of slightly thickened gelatin mixture in a larger bowl partly filled with ice and water. Whip gelatin mixture with a rotary egg beater or at a high speed of electric mixer until thick and fluffy like whipped cream.

Fold fruit and whipped cream into the gelatin mixture. Pour into serving dish or individual molds. Chill until firm. Garnish with whole berries.

Coconut Bavarian Cream

Dolores Stephens Boyle, Oklahoma City, Oklahoma

Ingredients

1 pint coffee cream
2 envelopes (2 tablespoons)
  unflavored gelatin
1 cup sugar
Pinch of salt
1 teaspoon almond flavor
2 cups shredded coconut
1 1/2 pints whipped cream

Directions (Serves 8)

Let come to a boil.

Dissolve gelatin in small amount of cold water. Add sugar, salt, and gelatin to cream and let cool.

Add to above and chill in ring mold. When ready to serve, turn out on platter; top with more shredded coconut and serve with Caramel Sauce.

▶

CARAMEL SAUCE

1 tablespoon butter ··················	Combine butter and sugar in double boiler. Add beaten egg yolks, cream and salt.
1 lb. brown sugar	
1 cup coffee cream	
2 egg yolks	
Pinch of salt	
1 teaspoon vanilla ····················	When smooth and thick, let cool. Add vanilla.

Grenadine Bavarian Cream

Ingredients	**Directions** (serves 6)
1 envelope (1 tablespoon) ··········· unflavored gelatin	Soak gelatin in cold milk about 5 minutes.
1/4 cup cold milk ····················	Scald milk in top of double boiler. Add opposite ingredients and gelatin. Stir until all is dissolved.
1 1/2 cups light cream	
1 cup milk	
1/3 cup sugar	
1/4 teaspoon salt	
4 egg yolks–slightly beaten ···········	Stir a little of the above mixture into the eggs. Stir into remaining hot milk mixture. Cook over hot water, stirring constantly, until mixture coats a metal spoon. Remove from heat.
1 to 2 tablespoons Jamaica rum ···········	Stir into the above mixture. Pour into serving dish and chill until firm.
Grenadine syrup ····················	Serve with Grenadine syrup.

Strawberry Bavarian Cream

Ingredients

1 envelope (1 tablespoon) unflavored gelatin

2 tablespoons cold water

1 1/2 cups crushed strawberries

1 tablespoon lemon juice

1/2 cup sugar

Pinch of salt

1 cup heavy cream–whipped

Directions (Serves 6)

Soak gelatin in cold water about 5 minutes. Place over boiling water and stir until dissolved.

Add the opposite ingredients to the above mixture and stir until blended. Chill until almost set.

Fold into the gelatin mixture. Pour into mold and chill until firm. Serve plain or with whipped cream and top with fresh berries, if desired.

Chocolate Marshmallow Cream

Ingredients

1 envelope (1 tablespoon) unflavored gelatin

1/4 cup milk

2 cups milk

1/2 cup sugar

1 square unsweetened chocolate

1/4 lb. marshmallows– quartered

1/4 cup finely chopped walnuts

2 egg whites–stiffly beaten

1 cup heavy cream–whipped

Directions (Serves 8)

Soak gelatin in milk about 5 minutes.

Combine opposite ingredients in saucepan. Cook and stir over low heat until mixture just comes to a boil. Beat with rotary egg beater. Remove from Fire. Add above gelatin mixture and beat until smooth. Chill until slightly thickened.

Stir marshmallows and nuts into the above mixture.

Fold in. Pour into sherbet glasses. Chill until firm.

Maple Cream

Ingredients

Directions (Serves 6)

1 envelope (1 tablespoon) unflavored gelatin
2 tablespoons cold water

Soak gelatin in cold water about 5 minutes.

2 1/2 cups milk
1/4 teaspoon salt

Scald milk in top of double boiler. Add above gelatin mixture and salt and stir until dissolved.

3 egg yolks–slightly beaten

Stir a little of the above hot milk mixture into eggs. Stir this into remaining hot milk mixture. Cook in double boiler until slightly thickened, stirring constantly. Cool.

2/3 cup maple syrup
1 teaspoon vanilla

Stir slowly into the cooled custard mixture.

3 egg whites–stiffly beaten

Fold in. Pour into mold or individual molds. Chill until firm. Serve with whipped cream.

Rum Cream

Ingredients

Directions (serves 6)

1 envelope (1 tablespoon) unflavored gelatin
1/4 cup cold milk

Soak gelatin in cold milk about 5 minutes.

1 1/2 cups milk
1/3 cup sugar
1/8 teaspoon salt

Scald milk in top of double boiler. Add opposite ingredients and above gelatin mixture. Stir until dissolved.

2 egg yolks–slightly beaten

Stir a little of the above hot milk mixture into eggs. Stir this into remaining hot milk. Cook in double boiler until slightly thickened, stirring constantly. Chill until almost set.

2 egg whites–stiffly beaten
1 teaspoon rum or vanilla extract (1 to 2 tablespoons Jamaica rum may be substituted)

Fold into the above mixture. Pour into serving dish. Chill until firm. Serve with crushed fruit.

Spanish Cream

Ingredients

Directions (Serves 6 to 8)

1/2 cup sugar ························
1 envelope (1 tablespoon) unflavored gelatin
Pinch of salt

Combine in top of double boiler. Mix well.

2 1/2 cups scalded milk ··············

Add to the above mixture. Cook directly over medium heat, stirring until gelatin dissolves. Remove from heat.

3 egg yolks–slightly beaten ··········

Slowly stir into the hot milk mixture. Return to top of double boiler and cook over hot water until mixture coats a metal spoon. Remove from hot water.

1 teaspoon vanilla ··················

Add to the above mixture.

3 egg whites–stiffly beaten ··········

Fold hot custard mixture very gradually into beaten egg whites. Pour into individual molds. Chill until firm. Serve with whipped cream.

Macaroon Spanish Cream

(Serves 6 to 8) Use recipe for Spanish Cream folding in ¾ cup macaroon crumbs with the egg whites and vanilla.

Chocolate Spanish Cream

(Serves 6 to 8) Use recipe for Spanish Cream adding 2 squares unsweetened, shaved chocolate to the milk before scalding. When chocolate is melted beat with rotary egg beater until blended. Increase sugar to ¾ cup.

Turkish Cream

Ingredients

Directions (Serves 8 to 10)

1 envelope (1 tablespoon) ············
unflavored gelatin ··················

Pour hot sherry wine over gelatin and stir until dissolved.

1/4 cup hot dry sherry wine
1 pint heavy cream–whipped
3 tablespoons sugar
12 nut macaroons–crushed

Combine remaining ingredients. Add above gelatin mixture and mix well. Pour into sherbet glasses and chill. Serve with whipped cream.

Festive Jellied Dessert

Ingredients

Directions (Serves 8)

2 envelopes (2 tablespoons) ·········· Soak gelatin in cold water about 5 minutes.
  unflavored gelatin
1/2 cup cold water

1/2 cup boiling water ···················· Add to the above mixture. Stir until dissolved. Cool to room temperature.
3/4 cup sugar
1/4 teaspoon salt

1/2 cup orange juice ····················· Add to gelatin mixture and stir. Chill until slightly thickened.
2 tablespoons lemon juice
1 1/2 cups dry sherry

1 cup pitted dates–finely ·············· Fold into gelatin mixture. Pour into mold and chill until firm. Unmold and serve
  chopped   with whipped cream on top.
2/3 cup walnuts–broken

Coffee Rum Jelly

Ingredients

Directions (Serves 4)

1 envelope (1 tablespoon) ·············· Soak gelatin in cold water about 5 minutes. Add hot coffee and rum and stir until
  unflavored gelatin   gelatin is dissolved. Add sugar and stir until well mixed and dissolved. Pour into
1/2 cup cold water   serving dish. Chill until firm. Serve with sour cream on top, if desired.
1 1/2 cups strong hot coffee
1 tablespoon Jamaica rum
1/4 cup sugar

Fresh pineapple and its juice must be scaled before using in gelatin
otherwise the gelatin will not thicken.

The Duncan Hines Dessert Book

Strawberry Charlotte

(Serves 10) Use recipe for Strawberry Bavarian Cream. Pour mixture into a 1 ½-quart mold which has been lined on the bottom and sides with about 2 dozen ladyfingers, split in half. Chill until firm.

Charlotte Russe

Ingredients

Directions (Serves 10 to 12)

2 envelopes (2 tablespoons) ·········· Soak gelatin in cold water about 5 minutes.
   unflavored gelatin
1/4 cup cold water

2 cups milk ································· Scald milk in top of double boiler. Add remaining opposite ingredients and above
1/2 cup sugar   gelatin. Stir until all is dissolved.
1/8 teaspoon salt

4 egg yolks–slightly beaten ·········· Stir a little of the hot milk mixture into eggs. Then stir this into remaining hot
                                           milk. Cook in double boiler until slightly thickened, stirring constantly. Chill
4 egg whites–stiffly beaten   until almost set.
1 pint heavy cream–whipped ········ Fold in beaten egg whites, whipped cream, and flavoring.
1 teaspoon vanilla or 1 table-
   spoon brandy

Ladyfingers–split ···························· Line mold with ladyfingers. Turn in gelatin mixture. Chill until firm. Serve with
                                           whipped cream on top.

Fruit Whip

Ingredients

Directions (Serves 8 to 10)

1 package flavored gelatin ··········· Pour boiling water over gelatin and stir until dissolved.
1 cup boiling water

1 cup cold water or fruit juice ······· Add to the above mixture. Chill until slightly thickened.
   and water

▶

Fruit Whip continued

2 egg whites ································· Add egg whites to gelatin mixture. Set the bowl of slightly thickened gelatin in a larger bowl partly filled with ice and water. Whip gelatin mixture with rotary egg beater or at high speed of electric mixer until fluffy and thick like whipped cream.

1 cup fruit–drained (crushed ········· Fold into gelatin mixture. Pour into mold or individual serving dishes. Chill until firm.
strawberries, raspberries,
diced peaches, sliced
bananas, cherries, etc.)

Fruited Lime Sour Cream Whip

Ingredients

Directions (Serves 4 to 6)

1 package lime-flavored ················ Dissolve gelatin in hot water. Add remaining opposite ingredients and blend well with rotary beater. Pour into refrigerator tray and chill 15 to 20 minutes or until firm about one inch from edge but soft in center. Pour mixture into a bowl. Place in a larger bowl filled with ice water. Whip above gelatin mixture with rotary beater until fluffy.
gelatin
1 cup hot water
1/4 cup cold water
2 tablespoons lemon juice
1 cup sour cream ······················· Fold into gelatin mixture. Pour into 1-quart mold or individual serving dishes and chill until firm.
1/2 teaspoon salt
1 1/2 cups drained, crushed
pineapple tidbits

If the gelatin mixture gets too stiff before you add the fruit, whipped cream, or egg whites, soften over a very low flame and start again using an ice bath.

Lemon Fluff Dessert

Ingredients

2 teaspoons unflavored gelatin ⋯⋯
3 tablespoons cold water ⋯⋯⋯⋯
4 egg yolks
1/3 cup lemon juice ⋯⋯⋯⋯⋯⋯
2/3 cup sugar
4 egg whites ⋯⋯⋯⋯⋯⋯⋯⋯⋯
1/8 teaspoon salt
1/4 cup sugar

Directions (Serves 4 to 6)

Soak gelatin in cold water about 5 minutes.

Combine opposite ingredients in top of double boiler. Beat with rotary egg beater or with electric mixer until light in color.

Beat sugar into above mixture gradually. Add gelatin. Continue beating over boiling water until mixture thickens. Cool.

Beat egg whites and salt together until foamy throughout the mixture. Add sugar gradually and continue beating until peaks are formed. Fold into custard. Pour into serving dish or sherbet glasses. Chill until firm.

Bavarian Date Loaf

Hotel Florence, Missoula, Montana

Ingredients

1 envelope (1 tablespoon) ⋯⋯⋯⋯
   unflavored gelatin
1/4 cup cold water
1/4 cup boiling water
4 eggs ⋯⋯⋯⋯⋯⋯⋯⋯⋯⋯⋯⋯
3 tablespoons sugar
Few grains salt
5 drops vanilla
3 drops almond extract
1/2 pint whipping cream ⋯⋯⋯⋯
20 dates (remove pits)
Sponge cake

Directions (Serves 4 to 6)

Soak gelatin in cold water, and add boiling water to dissolve. Let get cold.

Beat eggs, add other ingredients and cook over boiling water until set. Remove and beat until cold.

Whip cream; mix with egg mixture; add gelatin and dates. Mix well. Line loaf pan with slices of sponge cake; pour in the date mixture. Place in refrigerator to set for 6 hours. Serve with whipped cream.

Chocolate Sponge

Ingredients

2 envelopes (2 tablespoons) ·········
  unflavored gelatin
1/2 cup cold water
3 squares unsweetened ················
  chocolate
1/2 cup boiling water
1 cup sugar
1/8 teaspoon salt
3 cups scalded milk ·····················

1 teaspoon vanilla ······················
2 egg whites–stiffly beaten

Directions (Serves 6)

Soak gelatin in cold water about 5 minutes.

Combine opposite ingredients in saucepan and bring to a boil. Cool slightly.

Add soaked gelatin to milk and stir until dissolved. Then stir in chocolate mixture. Cool.

Fold in. Pour into ring mold. Chill until firm. Unmold and fill center with whipped cream and garnish with chopped nuts.

Lemon Bisque

Blosser's Restaurant, Logan, Ohio

Ingredients

1 package lemon-flavored ············
  gelatin
2 cups hot water
3/4 cup heavy cream–whipped ·······
Grated rind of 1 lemon
1 tablespoon lemon juice
1/2 cup sugar
1/8 teaspoon salt
1 cup rolled vanilla wafers ············

Directions (Serves 6 to 8)

Dissolve in water and chill until thickened but not firm. Beat until fluffy.

Fold into above.

Cover bottom of 9-inch square pan with half of wafers; pour in filling and sprinkle remaining wafers on top. Chill until firm.

Macaroon Pudding

Miss Katharine L. Little, Chicago, Illinois

Ingredients

Directions (Serves 6 to 8)

4 egg yolks–beaten ·················· Mix together.
1/2 cup sugar

1 envelope (1 tablespoon) ············ Dissolve gelatin in milk and add to the above. Let come to a boil–just to the
  unflavored gelatin   boiling point.
1 cup milk

4 egg whites–beaten ················· Stir into mixture and put in a large or individual molds.
Vanilla to taste

12 almond macaroons ················· Break into small pieces and fill the molds.

1 cup whipped cream ················· Put in refrigerator until it sets. Serve with whipped cream. Sprinkle with glazed
                                  cherries and chopped nuts. If a circle mold is used, fill the center with whipped
                                  cream.

Snow Pudding

Ingredients

Directions (Serves 6)

1 envelope (1 tablespoon) ············· Soak gelatin in cold water about 5 minutes. Pour over boiling water and stir until
  unflavored gelatin   gelatin is dissolved.
1/4 cup cold water
1 cup boiling water

3/4 cup sugar ························· Add opposite ingredients and stir until blended thoroughly. Chill until slightly
1/4 cup lemon juice   thickened.
1/4 teaspoon salt
1 1/4 teaspoons grated lemon
  rind

2 egg whites–stiffly beaten ··········· Fold into slightly thickened gelatin. Whip together until mixture is fluffy and
                                  holds its shape when the beater is raised. Pour into individual serving dishes and
                                  chill. Serve with Plain Custard Sauce. (See Dessert Sauces Section.)

Cabinet Pudding

Ingredients

1 1/2 tablespoons unflavored gelatin

1/3 cup cold water

6 egg yolks

1/3 cup sugar

1/8 teaspoon salt

6 egg whites–stiffly beaten

1 teaspoon vanilla

18 macaroons

1/2 cup Jamaica rum or sherry wine

Cherries

Directions (Serves 8)

Soak gelatin in water about 5 minutes. Dissolve over hot water to melt gelatin.

Combine yolks, sugar, and salt and beat until thick and lemon-colored. Add above gelatin mixture and beat until blended.

Fold into the above mixture.

Soak macaroons in rum. Line mold with macaroons. Alternate layers of custard and macaroons, topping with custard. Chill until firm. Unmold and garnish with cherries. Serve with whipped cream on top.

Rice Pudding with Whipped Cream

Ingredients

2 teaspoons unflavored gelatin

1/4 cup cold water

1 cup cooked rice

1/3 cup sugar

1/2 cup blanched, slivered almonds (optional)

1 pint heavy cream–whipped

2 teaspoons vanilla

Directions (Serves 10)

Soak gelatin in cold water about 5 minutes. Heat to dissolve gelatin. (Heating the gelatin after it has soaked helps to gel the final mixture.)

Add to above mixture and blend well. Chill.

Fold in. Pour into wet mold and thoroughly chill. Unmold and serve with crushed, sweetened strawberries or raspberries, or Butterscotch Sauce. (See Dessert Sauces Section.)

To unmold gelatin molds put them in hot water for a second
and then cut around the inside of the mold with a sharp knife. Shake out over serving dish.

Sherry Pudding

Chef, Hotel Florence, Missoula, Montana

Ingredients

2 cups milk

2 egg yolks

1/2 cup sugar

2 envelopes (2 tablespoons)
  unflavored gelatin

1/2 cup cold milk

2 egg whites

3 tablespoons powdered sugar

1/2 pint whipping cream

1 jigger whiskey

1/2 cup sherry wine

Almond macaroons–crumbled

Candied cherries–sliced

Directions (Serves 8)

Scald milk in double boiler. Beat egg yolks and ½ cup sugar. Add to hot milk; cook until it coats a spoon.

Mix gelatin in cold milk; add to hot custard, mixing well. Let set in cool place until slightly thickened.

Beat egg whites stiff; add powdered sugar. Beat cream. Mix all together.

Add to egg whites and cream, and fold into custard mixture, stirring well.

Combine crumbled macaroons and sliced cherries. Place alternately in pudding mold with custard mixture. Let stand in refrigerator until firm. Serve with whipped cream sauce to which has been added 3 tablespoons powdered sugar and 1 tablespoon sherry wine.

Stephanie Pudding

Marjorie Mills, Boston, Massachusetts

Ingredients

1 envelope (1 tablespoon)
  unflavored gelatin

1/4 cup cold water

1 cup grape or loganberry
  juice–hot

1/2 cup sugar

1/4 cup lemon juice

3 egg whites–beaten

Directions (Serves 4)

Soak.

Dissolve gelatin with hot juice.

Add to dissolved gelatin and strain. Set in a cool place. Stir mixture occasionally and when thick whisk until frothy.

Add to above mixture and beat until stiff enough to hold its own shape. Serve cold with Boiled Custard Sauce.

Keep unmolded gelatin desserts in the refrigerator until you serve them.

Syllabub

Ingredients

Directions (Serves 4)

2 egg yolks ·································· Beat egg yolks thoroughly; add sugar and salt and beat well.
1/2 cup sugar
1/4 teaspoon salt

1 cup milk ·································· Add to above and cook in top of double boiler over boiling water until of thin custard consistency. Stir constantly while cooking.

1 envelope (1 tablespoon) ·············· Soften unflavored gelatin in cold water and stir into hot custard until dissolved.
  unflavored gelatin ····················· Allow mixture to cool until it just begins to set.
1/4 cup cold water

1/2 pint whipping cream ·············· Whip cream until stiff. Chop cherries and fold into whipped cream along with rum. Fold in.
2 tablespoons rum
2 tablespoons cherries

Peppermint-Chocolate Dessert

Chateau Hutter, Sturgeon Bay, Wisconsin

Ingredients

Directions (Serves 9)

1/2 lb. peppermint stick candy ······· Crush candy; add cream and heat until candy dissolves.
1/2 cup light cream

1 envelope (1 tablespoon) ············· Dissolve gelatin in cold water and add to the above. Chill until partially set.
  unflavored gelatin
2 tablespoons cold water

1 1/2 cups heavy ························· Fold in whipped cream. Crush cookies and place ½ of the crumbs into the bottom of pan; then add layer of peppermint mixture. Repeat. Chill 12 hours.
  cream–whipped
1/2 lb. chocolate sandwich
  cookies.

Egg whites beat best at room temperature.

Chocolate Ice Box Cake

Ingredients

Directions (Serves 8 to 10)

3 squares unsweetened ·············· Melt chocolate in top of double boiler. Add remaining opposite ingredients. Stir
  chocolate until sugar is dissolved and mixture blended.

1/2 cup sugar

Pinch of salt

1/4 cup hot water

1 1/2 teaspoons unflavored ··········· Soak gelatin in water about 5 minutes. Add to hot chocolate mixture and stir
  gelatin until gelatin is dissolved. Cook in double boiler until mixture is smooth and well

1 tablespoon cold water thickened. Remove top section from boiling water.

4 egg yolks ······································ Add yolks to the above mixture, one at a time, beating thoroughly after each

1 teaspoon vanilla addition. Place top section over boiling water and cook 2 minutes, stirring
  constantly. Add vanilla and cool.

4 egg whites–stiffly beaten ·········· Fold chocolate mixture into egg whites. Chill.

1/2 cup heavy cream– ················· Fold into chocolate mixture.
  whipped

24 ladyfingers ······························· Line bottom and sides of mold with waxed paper. Arrange ladyfingers on bottom
  and sides of mold. Add a small amount of the chocolate mixture, then add
  ladyfingers and chocolate mixture in alternate layers, topping with chocolate. Cut
  off ladyfingers around sides of mold and arrange cut pieces on chocolate
  mixture. Chill 12 to 24 hours. Unmold. Serve with whipped cream, if desired.

Save the juices from canned pineapple, peaches and other fruits. Put them
in glass bottles; set them away in the refrigerator and use these juices in your
breakfast fruit cup or add a little lemon to make some refreshing hot weather "ades."

Chocolate Ice Box Cake

Ingredients

4 1/2 squares chocolate
3/4 cup sugar
6 tablespoons hot water
Pinch of salt

1 1/2 tablespoons cold water
1 1/2 teaspoons unflavored
  gelatin

6 egg yolks
1 teaspoon vanilla
6 egg whites
3/4 cup whipping cream
16 ladyfingers–split

Directions (Serves about 14)

Melt chocolate in top of double boiler; then add sugar, salt, and hot water, stirring until sugar is dissolved.

Dissolve gelatin in cold water and add to hot chocolate mixture. Cook in double boiler until smooth and thick. Remove from heat.

Add egg yolks, one at a time, beating mixture after adding each egg. Return to boiling water and cook 2 minutes, stirring constantly. Add vanilla and let cool.

Fold in beaten egg whites and whipped cream. Chill. Line bottom and sides of angel cake pan with waxed paper and arrange split ladyfingers on bottom and sides of pan. Add alternate layers of chocolate mixture and ladyfingers. Chill 12 to 24 hours.

Orange Ice Box Cake

Ingredients

2 cups milk
2 tablespoons cornstarch
1 cup sugar
2 eggs or 4 yolks
1 envelope (1 tablespoon)
  unflavored gelatin
2 tablespoons cold water
3/4 cup orange juice
1 teaspoon grated orange rind
1 pint whipping cream

Directions (Serves 4 to 6)

Heat milk in double boiler.

Mix cornstarch, sugar, and eggs thoroughly. Pour the hot milk over the egg mixture and return to double boiler and continue to cook 10 minutes or until thickened.

Soak gelatin in the cold water and add orange juice and rind. Place this mixture in refrigerator until cool and slightly thickened.

Beat cream until stiff and fold into orange mixture.

| 1 1/2 dozen ladyfingers .... | Split the ladyfingers and cut about ¼ inch from end of each half. Stand these around edge of a spring form pan and line the bottom with the small pieces of ladyfingers. Pour the whipped cream mixture into the lined mold and let stand several hours until thickened. |
| 1/2 pint whipping cream .... | Just before serving, cover top with whipped cream, using a pastry decorator. Garnish with maraschino cherries. Serve. |

Angel Food Mold

Mrs. Voijt Frank Mashek, Chicago, Illinois

Ingredients

Directions (Serves 6 to 8)

1 envelope (1 tablespoon) .... unflavored gelatin	Soak gelatin in cold milk.
1/2 cup cold milk	
2 cups milk	Cook in double boiler; pour over gelatin and milk; stir to dissolve. Let cool
2 egg yolks–slightly beaten	
1 cup sugar	
1 teaspoon vanilla	Add to cooled mixture.
2 egg whites–beaten	
1 pint whipping cream–whipped	
Bits of angel food cake	Put bits of angel food in mold and pour mixture over them. Serve with whipped cream into which cut and sugared strawberries have been added.

For satisfying results in anything you cook, take precautions from beginning to end.
Follow recipes carefully, use exact level measurements, and know your oven temperature.
Don't proceed by guess.

Almond Cream Mold

Ingredients

6 tablespoons sugar ·····················
3 tablespoons cornstarch
2 whole eggs
1 quart milk
1 envelope (1 tablespoon) ···········
  unflavored gelatin
1/4 cup cold water
2 teaspoons almond extract ··········
1 pint whipped cream
3 tablespoons sugar ·····················
14 graham crackers

Directions (Serves 12)

Stir together sugar, cornstarch, and eggs in double boiler into a smooth mixture and add to milk. Cook until smooth.

Soak gelatin in water for 5 minutes. Add to hot mixture and stir until thoroughly dissolved. Cool.

Add to custard.

Add sugar to whipped cream. Stir part of whipped cream into custard, leaving only enough to cover top. Pour into 9x12-inch pan and line top with crackers. Smooth rest of whipped cream on top. Chill until set and cut into squares.

One of the common faults in American cooking is the too generous use of sugar; thus the delicate flavor of many dishes is overshadowed by too sweet a taste.

Pastry

ALTHOUGH PIE HAS OFTEN BEEN CALLED "THE GREAT AMERICAN DESSERT," ESPECIALLY APPLE PIE, it has been known since the days of Chaucer in the fourteenth century. Originally in England "pie" meant a substantial entree of meat or fish with a top crust.

The French, on the other hand, specialized in pies or tarts with the crust on the bottom and the filling on top. For a long time there was a great deal of controversy in Europe as to whether the crust should go on the bottom or the top of a pie. In America the problem ended, for the early settlers put a crust on the bottom as well as on the top. That was America's contribution, and that is how "pie" (referring to dessert pie) earned the title "the great American dessert."

When the pioneers came to America, they found that apples, pumpkin, and squash would grow in abundance. Displaying Yankee ingenuity they put them in pies. To this day in New England, pumpkin and squash pies are as traditional as corn on the cob and baked beans.

I have not the slightest idea how the saying "as easy as pie" came about. However, if one follows a few basic rules, making a pie is easy. Here are some rules to keep in mind:

Measure ingredients accurately, use as little water as possible, handle dough quickly and lightly and bake in a preheated oven.

If your crust should break, make a small patch of dough, moisten the edges lightly, and place the patch over the broken area; run over lightly with the rolling pin. If you need more crust for a fluted edge, this also can be done by moistening the edges slightly and adding a new piece of dough.

You can make a nice trimming around your pie by fluting the crust with your thumb and forefinger, or pressing the edges down firmly with a fork. For a more elaborate pie trim, braid three strips of crust together and arrange neatly around edge of pie.

Be sure to cut vents for a two crust pie, especially in the case of fruit pies. Bake fruit pies in a hot oven 425° for fifteen minutes and then lower heat to 325°. This will help seal the crust and keep the pies from running over.

Follow these simple rules and with a little experience you too will be a good pastry baker.

Pastry Shells

Lowell Inn, Stillwater, Minnesota

Ingredients

1/2 cup lightly salted butter

1 cup sifted pastry or all purpose flour

5 teaspoons cold water

Directions (Makes 6 individual shells)

Cream butter as for cake. (Do not melt by heat.) Next add flour and cold water. Mix lightly. Roll out as pie crust. Cut to fit individual pastry shell pans. Bake at 450° 8 to 10 minutes.

To get a clean division between the white and the yolk use very cold eggs.

Pie Crust for Two 9-Inch Double Crust Pies

Lowell Inn, Stillwater, Minnesota

(Three to One Formula) Three parts of flour to one of shortening by volume.

Ingredients	Directions
1 1/3 cups (2/3 lbs) shortening	Carefully combine, using pastry blender, one half of the shortening with the flour to a corn meal consistency. Add remaining shortening and blend to the size of large peas. All flour must be completely absorbed in the shortening.
4 cups (1 qt.) all purpose flour (sifted)	If pastry flour is used, either the shortening may be slightly reduced, or the flour increased. This blended shortening and flour may be prepared the day before and set in the refrigerator.
To 12 tablespoons cold water, ... add 2 teaspoons salt	Add cold water, a little at a time while stirring, until dough forms a loose ball in the bowl. Cut dough in four equal parts for our crusts. We use pastry canvas and rolling pin cover which have been permeated with the same type of flour used in the dough. Lightly roll out dough to ⅛-inch thickness. Use trimmings in lower crust only which can be rolled a little thicker than the top crust. Place pie tin on dough and trim allowing ½-inch around the tin. Fit dough into pie tin and fold edge to form a rim; flute. Prick bottom and sides well with a fork. Bake in 450° oven till brown. Check oven temperature often with oven thermometer. Well browned pie tins or Pyrex give good results. Do not use new pie tins.

Graham Cracker Crust

Ingredients	Directions (Makes one 9-inch shell)
20 graham crackers–1 1/2 .... cups crumbs	Mix butter and sugar with crumbs and line the inside of a pie tin. Press it firmly into place and bake in a hot oven 8 to 10 minutes. This can be made the day before using.
1/2 cup melted butter	
1 tablespoon sugar	

Coconut Crust

Ingredients

2 tablespoons soft butter ············

1 1/2 cups shredded ·····················
coconut–cut

Directions (Makes one 8-inch pie shell)

Spread butter evenly in an 8-inch pie pan.

Press coconut into the bottom and sides of the buttered pie pan. Bake in a slow oven 300° for 15 to 20 minutes or until golden brown. Cool before filling. Fill with ice cream, a cream filling, or a chiffon filling.

Chocolate Coconut Pie Crust

Ingredients

2 squares unsweetened ················
chocolate

2 tablespoons butter ····················

2 tablespoons hot milk

2/3 cup sifted confectioners'
sugar

1 1/2 cups shredded ·····················
coconut–cut

Directions (Makes one 9-inch pie shell)

Melt chocolate and butter in the top of a double boiler, stirring until blended.

Combine opposite ingredients and add to chocolate mixture, stirring until blended.

Add coconut to the above mixture and mix well. Press mixture into the bottom and sides of a well-buttered 9-inch pie pan. Chill until firm. Fill with ice cream or a chiffon filling.

Meringue Pie Crust

Ingredients

2 egg whites ······························

1/4 teaspoon salt

1/4 teaspoon cream of tartar

1/2 cup sugar

Directions (Makes one 9-inch shell)

Beat egg whites until foamy; add salt and cream of tartar and beat until stiff but not dry peaks are formed. Gradually add sugar, 2 tablespoons at a time, beating after each addition. Continue beating until meringue will stand in stiff peaks and is smooth and glossy. Spread in bottom and sides of a greased 9-inch pie plate. Bake in slow oven 250° for about 60 minutes or until lightly browned. Cool and fill with fresh sweetened berries or ice cream.

Macaroon Pie Crust

Ingredients

1 egg white

2 tablespoons sugar

1 tablespoon light corn syrup

1/2 teaspoon vanilla

2 cups coconut–finely cut

Directions (Makes one 9-inch pie shell)

Beat egg white until foamy. Add sugar and beat until mixture will stand in soft peaks. Add corn syrup and flavoring. Fold in coconut. Using the back of a spoon, press macaroon mixture firmly into the bottom and sides of a greased 9-inch pie pan. Bake in moderate oven 350° for 15 minutes or until lightly browned. Cool. Fill with ice cream, cream filling, or sweetened fresh berries.

Apricot and Peach Turnovers

Ingredients

1/2 lb. dried apricots

1/2 lb. dried peaches

1 1/2 cups water

1 cup sugar

1/3 cup butter

1/2 grated nutmeg

1 tablespoon flour

1 recipe of pastry

Directions (Makes 8)

Cook opposite ingredients until the consistency of mush.
Add remaining ingredients to the above.
Cut pastry into saucer-shaped rounds and put in ample filling. Fold over and seal the edges. With a fork, prick the top so the steam can escape. Place on a baking sheet and bake in 350° oven for 15 minutes, then lower to 300° and bake until a golden brown and the crust seems crisp on both sides.

Raspberry Tart

Alcona Beach, Harrisville, Michigan

Ingredients

1 quart raspberries–fresh or frozen

1 cup sugar

1/4 teaspoon salt

1 tablespoon cornstarch

1 baked 9-inch pie shell or 8 baked tart shells

Directions (Serves 8)

Combine sugar and raspberries; let stand until they make a cup of juice. Drain, reserving the berries. Thicken the one cup of juice with cornstarch and cook until clear; add salt then pour over berries. Pour into baked pie shell or baked tart shells. Serve with whipped cream or ice cream.

Apple Tart, French Style

Ingredients

2 cups sifted flour ·············

1/2 teaspoon salt

2 tablespoons sugar

1/2 cup soft butter

1 egg–well beaten ··················

2 tablespoons cold water
  (about)

3 tablespoons cornstarch ···········

3/4 cup sugar

Pinch of salt

3/4 teaspoon cinnamon

1/4 teaspoon nutmeg

5 cups peeled, sliced tart
  apples

Directions (Makes one 9-inch)

Sift together dry ingredients. Cut in the butter until the mixture is like coarse crumbs.

Stir in the egg and water to make a pie dough. Take two-thirds of the dough and roll about ⅛-inch thick and fit into a 9-inch cake pan.

Combine remaining ingredients in a bowl. Then arrange the apple mixture in the shell. Roll remaining dough cut out to fit the top, making a slit in the center. Fit over the apple mixture. Bake in a hot oven 425° for 40 minutes or until brown. While warm spread with confectioners' sugar icing. Remove warm tart from cake pan by inverting on a wire rack. Serve warm.

Filling for Small Pastries, Tarts, etc.

Ingredients

1/4 lb. butter ····························

3/4 lb. lump sugar

2 lemons–grated rind only ··········

All juice from above

6 egg yolks–beaten ·····················

4 egg whites–beaten

Directions

Melt together.

Add rind and juice to above.

Add beaten yolks and whites to mixture and stir until it thickens. Pour into tart shells.

Apple Pie Deluxe

Ingredients

FILLING

1 1/2 tablespoons cornstarch ·········
3/4 cup sugar
Pinch of salt
3/4 teaspoon cinnamon
1/4 teaspoon nutmeg
3 1/2 cups peeled and thinly
  sliced, fresh, tart apples
1 tablespoon lemon juice
1 cup heavy cream
1 unbaked 9-inch pie shell

Directions (Makes one 9-inch pie)

Combine the opposite ingredients in a large bowl. Then turn into unbaked pie shell. Bake in hot oven 425° for 30 minutes. Then sprinkle the Walnut Crumb Topping over the top of the pie. Spoon ⅓ cup melted butter over the crumb topping. Bake 20 to 25 minutes longer or until done.

WALNUT CRUMB TOPPING

1/2 cup sugar ·······························
1/2 cup fine graham cracker
  crumbs
1/4 cup flour
1/4 cup chopped walnuts
1 teaspoon cinnamon
1/8 teaspoon nutmeg

Combine opposite ingredients.

When an unbaked pie crust is to be filled with a very moist filling, it is best to brush its surface with a small amount of lightly beaten egg white, and then to chill the crust. This precaution will prevent the moisture of the filling from penetrating into the lower crust.

Dutch Apple Pie

Elizabeth Parker's Restaurant, Richmond, Indiana

Ingredients

Directions (Makes one 10-inch pie)

1 unbaked 10-inch pie shell ········· Prepare.

Winesap apples ···························· Peel, core and cut in eighths and fill shell.

1/2 cup sugar ······························· Mix opposite ingredients and blend through apples.

1 tablespoon cornstarch

1/4 teaspoon nutmeg

1/4 teaspoon cinnamon

2/3 cup coffee cream ···················· Pour cream over apples.

1 tablespoon butter ······················ Dot butter over top. Preheat oven. Bake 30 minutes at 375° and then cover and reduce heat to 350°. Bake until apples are tender.

English Apple Pie

Daven Haven Lodges, Grand Lake, Colorado

Ingredients

Directions (Makes one 8-inch pie)

1 egg ·· Beat together.

3/4 cup sugar ····························· Add remaining ingredients to the above. Mix well. Put in Pyrex pie pan. Bake at

1/2 cup flour   350° for 25 to 30 minutes. Serve with cream or ice cream.

1 teaspoon baking powder

1/4 teaspoon salt

1 cup finely chopped apples

1/3 cup nut meats

Apple Pie

Ingredients

Directions (Makes one 9-inch pie)

1 1/4 cups flour ·························· Sift flour and salt. Cut in butter and poultry fat; add ice water and mix gently.

2 tablespoons poultry fat or ·········· Roll out thin and line pie pan which has been heavily buttered. Leftover pastry
   shortening   used for strips to cover top of pie. (If poultry fat is not available, use shortening.)

2 tablespoons butter

3 3/4 tablespoons ice water
Pinch of salt
1 stick butter ·································· Slice half of the stick of butter over the crust in the pie tin. Mix together sugar
1 cup sugar   and flour and put half over butter. Peel and chop enough apples to fill pie tin
1 heaping tablespoon flour   heaped up. Cover with remainder of sugar and flour mixture. Top with strips of
Winesap apples   crust and slice remainder of butter over top. Place in 450° preheated oven for
                                             10 minutes, lower heat to 350° and bake for 25 to 30 minutes or until done and
                                             pastry is brown on top.

Apple Pie

Ingredients   **Directions**

1 cup sugar ··························· Mix opposite ingredients all together.
2 tablespoons flour
1/2 grated nutmeg
1/2 cup orange juice
3 tablespoons light corn syrup
1/3 cup melted butter
Winesap apples cut into thin ········ Add to the above and thoroughly mix together. Butter a pie pan heavily before
  slices (enough to fill a pie   putting in the pastry, then fill with the apple mixture and make strips for the top.
  pan)   Preheat oven. Bake at 400° for 15 minutes, then reduce oven to 250° and bake for
                                       35 to 40 minutes.

Strawberry Pie

Ingredients   **Directions** (Makes one 9-inch pie)

1 baked 9-inch pie shell ·············· Place best berries points up, around edge of shell. Mix other berries with sugar
1 1/2 quarts fresh strawberries   and cornstarch, and cook in double boiler until thick.
1 cup sugar
6 tablespoons cornstarch
3/4 cup whipping ····················· When cool, place strawberry mixture in pie shell and cover with whipped cream
  cream–whipped   sweetened with sugar, and serve.
1 tablespoon sugar

Fried Apple Pie

The Park View Inn, Berkeley Springs, West Virginia

Ingredients

2 cups sifted flour ··················

3 teaspoons baking powder

1 teaspoon salt

1/4 cup shortening ··················

1/3 cup of milk approximately ·······

1 1/2 cups thick, sieved ··············
   apple sauce

1 cup sugar ·······················

3 teaspoons ground cinnamon

Directions (Makes 8 to 10 individual pies)

Mix and sift flour, baking powder, and salt.

Cut in shortening until well mixed.

Add milk gradually to make a soft dough. Put on lightly floured board and knead with a light touch. Roll very thin. Lay on saucer and cut eight or ten circles with a sharp knife.

Place on one side of each circle three tablespoons of thick apple sauce. Fold in half, moisten and seal edges with a fork. Fry in 1 ½ inches hot fat 350° in heavy bottom frying pan. When brown on one side, turn and brown the other.

Have ready a flat pan, the bottom covered with sugar and cinnamon. Lift pie from fat, drain and then place in sugar. Turn, giving both sides a good sugar coating. Serve while hot with ice cream or plain cream.

Fresh Apple Crumb Cake

Ingredients

1/2 cup soft butter ··················

1/2 cup sugar

1 1/2 cups sifted flour

Pinch of salt

5 cups peeled, sliced, tart ············
   apples

2 tablespoons cornstarch

1/2 cup sugar

3/4 teaspoon cinnamon

Directions (Makes one 9-inch cake)

Crumb together the opposite ingredients with pastry blender, fork or fingers until well mixed. Set aside ¾ cup of the crumbs. Press remaining crumbs into the bottom of a 9-inch spring form pan and about ¾ inch up the sides.

Combine opposite ingredients in bowl and mix well. Then arrange apple mixture in crumb shell. Bake in hot oven 425° for 20 minutes. Remove from oven and sprinkle the top with the reserved crumbs. Return to oven and continue baking 20 to 30 minutes longer or until shell is brown.

Riverside Lodge Fresh Strawberry Pie

Riverside Lodge and Ranch, Lyons, Colorado

Ingredients

CRUST

1 cup flour
1/4 teaspoon salt
1/4 teaspoon baking powder
1/6 cup lard
1/6 cup butter
2 tablespoons ice water –
  (about)

Directions (Makes one 9-inch pie)

Mix flour, salt, baking powder by sifting together. Work in lard and butter then add water drop by drop until mixture is right consistency to roll. Roll ¼-inch thick. Place 9-inch tin on pastry, cut one inch larger than tin; place in tin; flute and prick. Bake 12 to 15 minutes in 450° oven.

FILLING

1 quart fresh strawberries
1/2 cup sugar
2 tablespoons sugar
1/2 pint whipping cream
4 drops vanilla

Wash, stem, and quarter strawberries. Sprinkle with ½ cup sugar and let stand in refrigerator for 1 hour. Shortly before time to serve put in baked pit shell.

Whip cream with vanilla; add 2 tablespoons sugar and top pie with sweetened whipped cream.

Open Fresh Strawberry Pie

Lowell Inn, Stillwater, Minnesota

Ingredients

PIE SHELL

1 cup flour
1/2 cup shortening
1/2 teaspoon salt
1 tablespoon cold water

Directions

Cut shortening into flour. Mix salt and cold water together and stir into the flour-shortening mixture. Form into a ball. Roll out on lightly floured board. Fit into 9-inch pie pan. Bake in 425° oven for 15 minutes.

Open Fresh Strawberry Pie continued

FILLING

1 cup crushed fresh strawberries ·················· Boil opposite ingredients together until transparent.

1 cup sugar

1 tablespoon cornstarch

Fresh strawberries–enough to fill the pie shell ·········· Put strawberries in pie shell and pour over the hot berry syrup and chill.

Blueberry Pie

Lowell Inn, Stillwater, Minnesota

Ingredients

Directions (Makes one 9-inch pie)

1 quart blueberries ·················· Line greased pie tin with pastry. Combine berries, sugar and butter and pour into pastry shell. (Do not add thickening agents.) Top with crust. Bake in 450° oven for 10 minutes. Reduce heat to 350° and bake for about 30 minutes longer or until crust is golden brown. Serve runny in a fairly deep dish.

1 1/4 cups sugar

4 tablespoons melted butter

Blueberry Pie

Ingredients

Directions (Makes one 8-inch pie)

1 (No. 2) can blueberries–syrup pack ·················· Drain juice from blueberries and add water, if necessary, to make 1 cup of liquid.

3 tablespoons sugar ·················· Mix dry ingredients and combine with liquid. Cook over low heat until thickened and clear, stirring constantly. Remove from heat.

1/4 teaspoon salt

2 tablespoons cornstarch

1 tablespoon lemon juice ·················· Add juice and butter to the above mixture and fold in the berries. Fill pie shell with the blueberry mixture.

1 tablespoon butter

1 baked 8-inch pie shell

3 egg whites–beaten stiff

6 tablespoons sugar ·················· Beat sugar gradually into the beaten egg whites. Beat until peaks are formed. Spread over the blueberry filling. Bake 15 to 20 minutes in a 325° oven or until meringue is lightly browned.

The Duncan Hines Dessert Book

Raspberry Pie

John Ebersole's Restaurant, White Plains, New York

Ingredients

Directions (Makes one 9-inch pie)

2 cups frozen raspberries ············· Defrost and drain raspberries; reserve juice.

1/4 cup cold water ························ Combine berry juice with cold water and other ingredients and place over low
2 tablespoons butter   heat.
1/2 cup sugar
1 teaspoon lemon juice
Pinch of salt

3 tablespoons cornstarch ············· Dissolve cornstarch with cold water and add to above. Cook until thick, stirring
1/4 cup cold water   constantly. Remove from fire; add berries; let cool. Pour into 9-inch baked pie
1 baked 9-inch pie shell   shell. Serve with whipped cream.

Riverside Lodge Fresh Raspberry Pie

(Makes one 9-inch pie) Use recipe for Riverside Lodge Fresh Strawberry Pie except substitute 1 quart fresh raspberries, which have been washed and stemmed, for the strawberries.

Cherry Pie

Stagecoach Inn, Manitou Springs, Colorado

Ingredients

Directions (Makes one 9-inch pie)

CRUST

2 1/2 cups sifted flour ·················· Mix flour and salt. Cut shortening into it until pieces are size of bean. Mix well
1 teaspoon salt   with water until dough comes together and can be shaped into a ball. Divide into
3/4 cup shortening   two parts. Roll out into two 9- inch pie crusts. Line a 9-inch pie plate with pastry.
1/4 cup water
2 cups fresh or frozen sour
  pitted cherries   **FILLING**
1 tablespoon flour ······················ Mix flour and sugar; then stir in with the flavor and cherries. Pour into pastry
1 1/2 cups sugar   shell; dot with butter. Cover with pastry top. Bake slowly for 45 minutes in a 350°
1 tablespoon butter   oven.
1/4 teaspoon almond extract

Apricot Pie

Mrs. John R. Shields, Bogota, New Jersey

Ingredients

1 lb. apricots–canned or fresh
1 cup apricot juice
1/2 cup sugar
1 tablespoon cornstarch
Drop of yellow coloring
1 baked 9-inch pie shell
1 pt. whipping
  cream–whipped

Directions (Makes one 9-inch pie)

Drain juice from canned apricots. Combine juice, sugar, and cornstarch. Mix. Cook until thick and clear; add a drop of yellow coloring. Chill until partially set. In a good rich 9-inch baked pie shell fill as follows: First ½ pint whipped cream. Second canned or fresh apricots. Third ½ pint whipped cream. Cover with chilled apricot cooked juice.

Serve hot fruit pies with cream.

Peach Praline Pie

Ingredients

4 cups sliced fresh peaches
3/4 cup sugar
1 1/2 teaspoons cornstarch
1 1/2 teaspoons lemon juice
1/4 cup flour
1/3 cup firmly packed brown
  sugar
1/2 cup chopped pecans
3 tablespoons butter
1 unbaked 9-inch pie shell

Directions (Makes one 9-inch pie)

Combine opposite ingredients in large bowl and mix well.

Combine opposite ingredients in small bowl.

Mix butter into the above mixture until it is crumbly. Sprinkle one third of this mixture in the bottom of the pie shell. Cover with the peach mixture. Then sprinkle the remaining pecan mixture over the top. Bake in hot oven 425° for about 45 minutes.

Fresh Peach Crumb Pie

Ingredients

Directions (Makes one 9-inch pie)

1/2 cup soft butter ·······················
1/2 cup sugar
1 1/2 cups sifted flour
Pinch of salt

Crumb together the opposite ingredients with pastry blender, fork, or fingers until well mixed. Set aside ¾ cup of the crumbs. Press remaining crumbs into the bottom of a 9-inch spring form pan and about ¾ inch up the sides.

4 cups sliced fresh peaches ···········
2 tablespoons cornstarch
1/2 cup sugar
1 tablespoon lemon juice

Combine in a bowl the opposite ingredients and mix well. Then arrange peach mixture in crumb shell. Bake in hot oven 425° for 20 minutes. Remove from oven and sprinkle top with reserved crumbs. Return to the oven and continue to bake 20 to 30 minutes longer or until the shell is browned.

Riverside Lodge Fresh Peach Pie

(Makes one 9-inch pie) Use recipe for Riverside Lodge Fresh Strawberry Pie except substitute 1 quart fresh peaches, which have been peeled and sliced, for the strawberries.

Peach Plum Pie

Ingredients

Directions (Makes one 9-inch pie)

1 recipe pastry ·····························
6 medium peaches–pitted, ···········
  pared, and sliced
4 red plums–pitted and sliced
1 cup sugar
3 tablespoons cornstarch
Pinch of salt
1/2 teaspoon grated orange
  rind
1 1/2 tablespoons butter

Line a 9-inch pie pan with one-half the pastry.
Fill pie shell with fruit. Combine sugar, cornstarch, and salt and pour over the fruit. Add rind and dot with butter. Cover with lattice top. Bake in hot oven 425° for 50 to 60 minutes.

Deep Dish Plum Pie

Ingredients

1 uncooked pastry shell
1 pastry top
2 lbs. blue prune plums
1/3 cup cold water
1 cup sugar
1/2 teaspoon salt
2 tablespoons plus
  1 teaspoon cornstarch
3 tablespoons cold water
1/2 cup chopped walnuts
6 tablespoons orange
  marmalade

Directions (Makes one 9-inch deep pie)

Line a deep 9-inch pie pan with pastry and chill. Have ready a pastry top.

Wash and pit plums. If they are large, quarter; if small, halve. Put plums in saucepan, add sugar and water and bring to a boil. Lower heat at once and simmer for 4 minutes.

Dissolve cornstarch in water and add to plums. Cook slowly, stirring constantly from the bottom of the pan until the mixture is thick and clear. Remove from fire and let get cold.

When mixture is cold stir in walnuts. Spread bottom of pie pastry with marmalade and cover with plum filling. Put on top crust and slit to allow steam to escape. Bake in 450° oven for 25 to 30 minutes or until crust is done and lightly browned.

Apricot Cream Pie

Mills Restaurants of Ohio (Cincinnati, Columbus and Cleveland)

Ingredients

3/4 cup sugar
3 1/2 cups milk
4 tablespoons cornstarch
1/2 cup cold milk
2 egg yolks–beaten slightly
1/2 teaspoon salt
1 teaspoon vanilla
1 1/2 tablespoons butter
1 cup cooked apricots
1 baked 9-inch pie shell

Directions (Makes one 9-inch pie)

Put sugar and milk in double boiler and bring to scalding point.

Soak cornstarch in milk and add to above. Cook until mixture thickens.

Add a small amount of the above hot mixture to the eggs, mix and pour back into the double boiler. Cook until thick.

Add opposite ingredients to above and blend well.

Cut in pieces and add to above. Stir well. Cool. Put in baked pie shell and cover with meringue.

Apricot Meringue

Ingredients	Directions
6 egg whites	Whip egg whites until stiff and dry; add sugar gradually.
3/4 cup sugar	
3/4 cup cooked apricots	Drain well and add to above. Spread on pie and serve. DO NOT BROWN IN OVEN.

Rhubarb Pie

Sunset Farm, Whittier, North Carolina

Ingredients

Directions (Makes one 9-inch pie)

CRUST

1 cup flour	Sift dry ingredients together. Work in shortening quickly with fingers until of crumb consistency. Add just enough cold water to make stiff dough. Roll out and line 9-inch pie pan.
1 teaspoon baking powder	
1/4 teaspoon salt	
1/3 cup shortening	
2 tablespoons cold water (about)	

FILLING

4 cups rhubarb	Cut in ½-inch cubes. Place in uncooked pastry shell.
1 1/2 cups sugar	Mix together and sprinkle over rhubarb.
1/2 cup flour	
2 eggs	Beat whole eggs well and put by spoonfuls over rhubarb.
2 tablespoons butter	Break in small pieces and sprinkle over pie. Strip pie with thin strips of pastry. Bake in oven 350° until done.

Egg whites, several days old, will beat up better than those which are strictly fresh.
A watery egg white gives better volume than a thick white.

Baked Cream Pie

Ingredients

1 pint coffee cream ·····················
1 tablespoon cornstarch
1 box (1 lb.) powdered sugar
2 egg whites ·····························
1 uncooked pie crust

Directions (Makes one 9-inch pie)

At breakfast time combine cornstarch and sugar. Pour cream over sugar; mix well and let stand until an hour before lunch.

Beat egg whites stiff and stir into cream and sugar mixture. Place in uncooked pie crust and bake in 450° oven for 15 minutes. Reduce heat to 300° and bake until done.

Coconut Cream Pie

El Encanto Tea Shop, Los Angeles, California

Ingredients

1 cup milk ·······························
1 1/3 cups sugar
Pinch of salt
2 egg yolks–beaten ·····················
2 tablespoons cornstarch
1 tablespoon milk
2 1/2 teaspoons unflavored ··········
  gelatin
1 tablespoon milk
1/2 cup coconut ·························
1 cup whipped cream
1 teaspoon vanilla
2 egg whites–beaten ····················
1 baked 10-inch pastry shell

Directions (Makes one 10-inch pie)

Combine opposite ingredients in saucepan. Bring to a boil.

Blend cornstarch and milk and mix with eggs. Add to hot milk above and cook slightly.

Dissolve gelatin in milk and pour hot mixture over it. Let set until firm. Put in electric beater and beat well.

Add opposite ingredients to above mixture and put in refrigerator for 10 minutes.

Fold in stiff egg whites; pour in baked pastry shell; cover with whipped cream and sprinkle with coconut.

French Cream Coconut Pie

Ingredients

1 pint milk ·······················

1 cup sugar

4 1/2 tablespoons cornstarch ········

5 egg yolks

2/3 cup milk

4 2/3 tablespoons butter ············

1 pinch salt

1 tablespoon vanilla ················

1/2 can coconut or 1/2 fresh ········
  coconut–grated

1/2 pint whipping ·················
  cream–whipped ·················

Directions (Serves 6 to 8)

Scald.

Mix together and add slowly to above, stirring constantly until mixture thickens. Remove from fire.

Add to above mixture and stir until butter is dissolved.

Stir into mixture, and pour immediately into baked pie shell.

Put on top of filling.

Put on top of coconut.

To vary this pie, stir into finished cream filling 3 ½ squares unsweetened melted chocolate, or top with fresh fruit such as red raspberries, before topping with whipped cream. Place in refrigerator before serving.

Custard Pie

Stone's Restaurant, Marshalltown, Iowa

Ingredients

3 eggs–beaten lightly ···············

2 1/2 cups milk

1 cup sugar

Pinch of salt

2 tablespoons melted butter

Directions (Makes one 9-inch pie)

Mix together all ingredients and put in uncooked pie shell. Sprinkle top with grapenuts or graham cracker crumbs. Do not stir. Bake in 400° oven for 12 to 15 minutes. Then reduce heat to 300° and cook until custard is set in the center of the pie.

Continental Cream Pie

Ingredients

Directions (Makes one 9-inch pie)

CRUST

14 ginger cookies or graham crackers ·········· Roll fine.

5 tablespoons butter–melted ········· Mix well with above. Pat evenly in a 9-inch spring form pan. Bake in 300° oven for 10 minutes or until lightly brown.

FILLING

4 egg yolks–beaten ····················· Slowly add milk to eggs.

2 cups milk–scalded

1 1/2 tablespoons cornstarch ········· Combine sugar and cornstarch and stir into the above. Cook over simmering water for 20 minutes, or until custard generously coats spoon. Remove from the fire.

1/2 cup sugar

1 envelope (1 tablespoon) ············· Soak gelatin in cold water for about 5 minutes. Add to the custard while it is still unflavored gelatin hot. Let cool.

4 tablespoons cold water

4 egg whites–beaten ····················· Beat egg whites very stiff; gradually beat in sugar and add to custard while it is still soft and smooth. Fill the pie crust and set it in the refrigerator. Sprinkle with candied fruit.

1/2 cup sugar

Candied fruit

Special Continental Cream Pie

(Makes one 9-inch pie) Use recipe for Continental Cream Pie adding 2 tablespoons brandy when the egg white meringue is folded into the cooled custard.

Our favorite American man's dessert is good apple pie with a flaky crust and coffee to go with it. There are three ways to improve that apple pie. One is to add a scoop of rich, creamy ice cream. Another is to serve a piece of good, strong cheese with it–the kind that bites back at you. And the third–and least known–is to place a thin slice of ham on top of it.

Chocolate Cream Pie

Ingredients

2 squares unsweetened ⋯⋯⋯
  chocolate
2 1/2 cups milk

6 tablespoons flour ⋯⋯⋯⋯
1/4 teaspoon salt

1 cup sugar ⋯⋯⋯⋯⋯⋯
2 egg yolks–slightly beaten

2 tablespoons butter ⋯⋯⋯⋯
1 1/2 teaspoons vanilla
1 baked 9-inch pie shell

1/2 cup whipping ⋯⋯⋯⋯⋯
  cream–whipped

Directions (Makes one 9-inch pie)

Combine chocolate and milk in top of double boiler. Cook and stir over boiling water until the chocolate is melted. Beat with rotary egg beater until the mixture is blended.

Combine opposite ingredients and add gradually to the chocolate mixture. Cook until the mixture is thickened (about 10 minutes longer), stirring occasionally.

Pour a small amount of the chocolate mixture over the egg yolks, stirring vigorously. Return to the double boiler and cook 5 minutes longer.

Add butter and vanilla to the chocolate mixture. Turn into baked pie shell. Cool.

Garnish with whipped cream.

Sour Cream Pie

Mrs. A. W. Boswell, Monmouth, Illinois

Ingredients

3 egg yolks ⋯⋯⋯⋯⋯⋯
3/4 cup sugar
1 teaspoon cinnamon
1 cup sour cream
1 cup seedless raisins
1/2 cup chopped pecans
1 unbaked 9-inch pie shell

3 egg whites ⋯⋯⋯⋯⋯⋯
6 tablespoons sugar

Directions (Makes one 9-inch pie)

Beat the yolks of 3 eggs; add ¾ cup sugar, cinnamon, sour cream, raisins, and nuts. Mix well and pour into unbaked crust. Bake in 400° oven for 10 to 15 minutes. Reduce heat to 325° and bake ½ hour or until well set.

Cover with meringue by whipping the egg whites stiff, and adding 6 tablespoons sugar gradually. Brown slowly in low oven.

Pumpkin Pie

Ingredients

3 cups pumpkin ·························
1 1/2 cups granulated sugar
4 eggs–beaten
1 teaspoon salt
2 teaspoons cinnamon
1 teaspoon ginger
1 cup cream
2 cups milk
2 unbaked 8-inch pie shells

Directions (Makes two 8-inch pies)

Beat all together thoroughly and pour into 8-inch unbaked pie shells. Bake at 350° for 45 minutes or until set.

Pumpkin Pie

Ingredients

1 cup pumpkin ·······················
1 cup sugar
1 1/2 tablespoons flour
1 teaspoon cinnamon
1/2 teaspoon nutmeg
1/2 teaspoon salt
1 1/2 cups hot milk
1 egg ······························
1 unbaked 9-inch pie shell

Directions (Makes one 9-inch pie)

Mix pumpkin with dry ingredients.

Separate egg. Beat yolk and add with milk to dry ingredients. Beat egg white and fold carefully into mixture.
Pour into pie shell. Bake for 10 minutes at 450°. Reduce heat and bake for 35 minutes at 350° until firm. May be topped with whipped cream and chopped Brazil nuts when served.

To vary pumpkin pie add cider, good brandy, or sherry to the custard.

Orange Pumpkin Pie

Ingredients

1 1/2 cups milk ·············
2 eggs–beaten
2 tablespoons orange juice
1 teaspoon orange rind

1 1/4 cups pumpkin ···········
3/4 cup brown sugar
1 teaspoon cinnamon
1/2 teaspoon ginger
1/2 teaspoon nutmeg
1/2 teaspoon salt
1 unbaked 9-inch pie shell

1/2 cup walnuts ·············
1/2 teaspoon orange rind
1 cup whipped cream

Directions (Makes one 9-inch pie)

Combine milk, beaten eggs, orange juice and rind.

Mix opposite ingredients well and add to above mixture. Pour into unbaked 9-inch pie shell. Bake in 420° oven for 10 minutes. Reduce temperature to 350° and bake for 40 minutes.

When cool cover with whipped cream and sprinkle with nut meats and orange rind.

Lemon Chiffon Pie

Stone's Restaurant, Marshalltown, Iowa

Ingredients

4 egg yolks–beaten ···········
1/2 cup sugar
1/2 cup lemon juice
1 lemon rind–grated
Pinch of salt

1 envelope (1 tablespoon) ··········
  unflavored gelatin
1/4 cup cold water

4 egg whites–beaten ···········
1/2 cup sugar

Directions

Cook opposite ingredients in double boiler, stirring constantly until consistency of custard.

Soak gelatin in cold water for about 5 minutes. Then add to hot custard.

Beat sugar into egg whites. Fold hot custard into egg whites carefully. Put in baked pie shell and chill 3 hours.

Lime Chiffon Pie

Brook Farm Restaurant, Chevy Chase, Maryland

Ingredients

4 egg yolks–slightly beaten ·········
3/4 cup sugar
1/4 teaspoon salt

1 envelope (1 tablespoon) ·········
 unflavored gelatin
1/4 cup cold water

1/2 cup lime juice ·········
2 tablespoons grated lime rind
2 drops green vegetable
 coloring

4 egg whites ·········
1/4 cup sugar
1 baked 10-inch pie shell

Directions (Makes one 10-inch pie)

Combine opposite ingredients in top of double boiler and stir constantly.

Soak the gelatin in the cold water about five minutes then add this to the above hot custard, stirring until dissolved.

Add this to the above mixture and remove from heat.

While custard is cooling, beat egg whites dry and stiff; fold sugar into egg whites. Fold the beaten egg whites and cooled custard together. Pour into baked pie shell and place in refrigerator. Spread with whipped cream before serving.

Florida Lime Chiffon Pie

Johnston's Coffee Shop, Daytona Beach, Florida

Ingredients

1 can sweetened condensed ·········
 milk
Grated rind of 1 lime
1/2 cup lime juice
3 egg yolks

3 egg whites ·········
1 baked 9-inch pie shell

Directions (Makes one 9-inch pie)

Beat these ingredients together with an egg beater until thick.

Whip the whites of the eggs stiff, and fold into this mixture. (If you wish, you may use the whipped egg whites as a meringue adding 3 tablespoons of sugar. Brown in oven.) Pour filling into baked pie shell and cool.

Butterscotch Chiffon Pie

Ingredients

3/4 cup brown sugar ·················
4 egg yolks ·····························
1/2 teaspoon salt
1/2 cup milk
1 envelope (1 tablespoon)
  unflavored gelatin
1/4 cup cold water
4 egg whites–beaten stiff
1/4 cup sugar ··························

Directions (Makes one 9-inch pie)

Cook opposite ingredients in double boiler until thick.
Soak gelatin in cold water and add to the above mixture. Let cool.

Add sugar to beaten egg whites and beat well. Fold into the above mixture. Place in 9-inch pie shell and cover with whipped cream.

Pumpkin Chiffon Pie

Ingredients

1 cup brown sugar ·················
3 egg yolks
1 1/4 cups pumpkin
2 teaspoons cinnamon
1/2 teaspoon ginger
1/4 teaspoon allspice
1/2 teaspoon salt
1 envelope (1 tablespoon) ···········
  unflavored gelatin
1/4 cup cold water
3 egg whites–beaten ··············
2 tablespoons sugar
1 baked 10-inch pie shell

Directions (Makes one 10-inch pie)

Put opposite ingredients in double boiler and cook until it begins to thicken.

Soak gelatin in water for 5 minutes. Add to hot mixture and stir until thoroughly dissolved. Cool.

Beat sugar into whites and fold into mixture. Pour into baked pie shell and chill. Serve garnished with whipped cream.

Pecan Chiffon Pie

Ingredients

Directions (Makes one 9-inch pie)

1 cup milk ·············· Combine opposite ingredients in saucepan and bring just to a boil.
1/4 cup water
1/2 cup sugar
Pinch of salt

1/4 cup cornstarch ·············· Dissolve cornstarch in milk. Add to the above mixture. Cook and stir until thick.
1/4 cup milk Remove from fire.

1 teaspoon vanilla ·············· Add vanilla and butter to the above.
1 teaspoon butter

4 egg whites ·············· Beat egg whites stiff; add sugar gradually, beating until stiff peaks are formed.
1/4 cup sugar

1/4 cup chopped, toasted ·············· Fold in chopped pecans. Fold this meringue easily into the hot cooked mixture.
  pecans Place in baked pie shell and chill thoroughly. Garnish with whipped cream and
1 baked 9-inch pie shell sprinkle with chopped nuts. (A few drops of brown coloring gives mixture the
 color of pecans.)

Lemon Fluff Pie

Stoddard's Atop Butler Hall, New York City

Ingredients

Directions (Makes one 8-inch pie)

4 egg yolks–beaten ·············· Cook opposite ingredients in double boiler for about 12 minutes, stirring
Juice of 2 lemons constantly. If it gets lumpy beat with egg beater after removing from fire. It is
Rind of 1 lemon–grated better not to let it get lumpy.

3/4 cup sugar ·············· Beat sugar into egg whites and fold into mixture. Pour into baked pie shell.

2 egg whites–beaten ·············· Beat egg whites until foamy and then add sugar gradually. Beat until stiff peaks
1 teaspoon sugar are formed. Spread over filling and brown in moderate oven 350° for about
1 baked 8-inch pie shell 15 minutes.
2 egg whites–beaten
1/4 cup sugar

Spread whipped cream over the top of chiffon and cream pies providing you're not counting calories.

The Duncan Hines Dessert Book

Sherry Chiffon Pie

The Derings, Green Lake, Wisconsin

Ingredients

1 cup milk
1/2 cup sugar
3 egg yolks
1/4 teaspoon nutmeg
1/4 teaspoon salt
1/2 cup sherry wine
1 envelope (1 tablespoon)
  unflavored gelatin
4 tablespoons cold milk

3 egg whites
1 cup heavy cream–whipped
1 baked 9-inch pie shell
Grated bitter chocolate

Directions (Makes one 9-inch pie)

Combine the milk and sugar in the top of a double boiler and heat. Add the well beaten egg yolks, nutmeg and salt, and stir constantly until thickened. Add the wine slowly and the gelatin which has been softened in the cold milk. Cool.

Fold in the stiffly beaten egg whites and finally the stiffly whipped cream. Pour into a baked pie shell; top with a layer of sweetened whipped cream; chill. Add grated bitter chocolate just before serving.

Sunny Silver Pie

High Hampton, Cashiers, North Carolina

Ingredients

4 egg yolks
2 or 3 tablespoons lemon juice
Rind of 1 lemon–grated
1/8 teaspoon salt
1/2 cup sugar

1 1/2 teaspoons unflavored
  gelatin
1/3 cup cold water

4 egg whites–beaten
1/2 cup sugar

1 baked 9-inch pie shell

1 cup whipping cream

Directions (Makes one 9-inch pie)

Combine opposite ingredients and cook in double boiler until thick, stirring constantly. Remove from fire.

Soak gelatin in cold water and add to the above.

Beat together well. Fold into the above mixture.

Place in baked pie shell and set in refrigerator for 2 or 3 hours.

Whip and spread on top of pie.

New Year Eggnog Pie

Ingredients

2 teaspoons unflavored gelatin
1/4 cup cold water
3 egg yolks
1 cup milk
1/2 cup sugar
1/4 teaspoon salt
3 tablespoons rum
3 egg whites–beaten stiff
1 baked 9-inch pie shell
1 cup heavy cream

Directions (Makes one 9-inch pie)

Soften gelatin in cold water about 5 minutes.

Make a custard of egg yolks, milk, sugar and salt and stir in the gelatin while custard is hot.

When mixture is cool, add rum. When it begins to thicken, fold in egg whites.

Pour into either a baked pie crust or a graham cracker crust.

Whip cream, do not sweeten. Spread over pie and sprinkle with nutmeg. Chill until ready to serve.

Eggnog Pie

The Carr House, Wolfeboro, New Hampshire

Ingredients

1 envelope (1 tablespoon) unflavored gelatin
1/4 cup cold water
4 egg yolks–beaten
1/2 cup sugar
1/2 teaspoon salt
1/2 cup hot water
4 egg whites–beaten
1/4 cup sugar
3 teaspoons rum
1 baked 9-inch pie shell

Directions (Makes one 9-inch pie)

Soak gelatin in cold water for five minutes.

Put opposite ingredients in double boiler and cook until custard consistency. Add gelatin and cool.

Add sugar gradually to beaten egg whites, beating until smooth and glossy. Fold in egg white meringue and rum and fill baked pie shell. Place in refrigerator to set. Serve with thin layer of whipped cream over top and grated nutmeg.

Eggnog Pie

Santa Maria Inn, Santa Maria, California

Ingredients

3 envelopes (3 tablespoons) ·········· unflavored gelatin
2 tablespoons cold water
2 cups boiling water
8 egg whites–beaten stiff ···········
2 1/2 cups sugar
4 oz. rum
1 pint whipped cream ················
2 baked 9-inch pie shells

Directions (Makes two 9-inch pies)

Soak gelatin in cold water; then add boiling water. Allow to cool and begin to set before proceeding with the following.

Add sugar gradually to beaten egg whites, beating until smooth and glossy. Add rum and then fold into gelatin.

Fold whipped cream into above mixture and pour into previously baked pie shells. Place in a cool place and allow to set. Top with additional whipped cream.

Lime Pie

Brown's, Fort Lauderdale, Florida

Ingredients

2 tablespoons sugar ···················
3 egg yolks
1 can condensed milk ·················
1/2 cup lime juice ·····················
1 baked 9-inch pie shell ············
3 egg whites ·····························
3 tablespoons sugar

Directions (Makes one 9-inch pie)

Beat together.

Beat condensed milk into the egg mixture.
Add and stir thoroughly. DO NOT COOK.
Pour mixture into pie shell.
Whip up egg whites, adding the sugar gradually. Spread over the pie and put in 350° oven a few minutes to brown the top.

The secret for that mile-high effect in lemon chiffon pie: first let the egg whites warm to room temperature before beating–this gives more volume. Second, fold the egg meringue into the custard mixture–not the custard into the meringue. Finally, use the correct pie pan.

Frozen Lime Pie

Ingredients

1/2 cup lime juice ························
24 marshmallows

2 whole eggs ·····························
1/4 cup sugar
Pinch of salt
Grated rind of 2 limes
2 or 3 drops green vegetable
   color

2 cups graham cracker crumbs ·······
1/3 cup melted butter

1 cup heavy cream–whipped ·········

Directions (Makes one 9-inch pie)

Melt marshmallows in double boiler with lime juice.

Beat eggs until light in color. Gradually add sugar and salt beating until thick. Pour into this the above mixture, beating during the addition. Add lime rind and green color and mix thoroughly. Let get cold.

Combine crumbs and butter and mix well. Line a 9-inch pie tin with ¾ of the mixture. Set in refrigerator to chill.

When filling is cold and crust is chilled, add whipped cream to filling and mix well. Pour into pie shell; top with remaining crumbs and cover with aluminum foil. Set in freezing compartment for at least 6 hours.

Frosted Lime Pie

Vera Kirkpatrick, San Mateo, California

Ingredients

1 1/2 cups hot water ·····················
1 1/4 cups sugar

7 tablespoons cornstarch ············
7 tablespoons cold water (or
   1/2 scant cup)

2 large egg yolks (or 3 small ········
   ones)

Directions (Makes 6 individual pies or one 10-inch pie)

Put sugar and water in top of double boiler and bring to a boil over direct heat.

Mix opposite ingredients to a thin paste and add to the above and cook over hot water until thick and smooth, stirring frequently.

Beat yolks slightly and add to above. Cook a few minutes longer. Remove from fire.

1/3 to 1/2 cup fresh lime juice ······· Mix opposite ingredients and add to the above. Chill slightly and pour in baked
   depending on strength and   pie shells, top with meringue.
   taste
1 teaspoon grated lime rind
1 tablespoon butter
A few drops of green coloring

MERINGUE

1/4 lb. marshmallows ···················· Melt marshmallows in double boiler. Beat egg whites stiff and combine with
2 large egg whites (or 3 small   sugar, lime juice and marshmallows. Pile gently on top of the pie filling. Pies may
   ones)   be browned slightly under the broiler, but are nicest chilled and garnished with
1/4 cup sugar   springs of fresh mint leaves dipped in egg white and bar sugar.
1 tablespoon lime juice

Nell Palmer's Pecan Pie

Lowell Inn, Stillwater, Minnesota

Ingredients   **Directions** (Makes one 9-inch pie)

3 eggs ································· Beat until light.
3/4 cup sugar ····················· Slowly beat opposite ingredients into the eggs.
1/4 lb. butter–melted
1 cup dark corn syrup
1 uncooked 9-inch pie shell ··········· Pour above into uncooked pie shell and bake slowly in 300° oven for 40 minutes.
      Completely cover the pie with whole pecan halves and return to a 350° oven and
1 cup pecan halves   bake for another 10 to 15 minutes. May be served with whipped cream.

Pick tart, juicy apples such as Winesaps, Jonathans and Wealthies for pie making.

Mrs. Murphy's Pecan Pie

Mrs. Thomas J. Murphy, Wyoming, Cincinnati, Ohio

Ingredients

Directions (Makes one 8 ½-inch pie)

1/2 cup sugar ···························· Cream together opposite ingredients.

2 eggs–beaten

2 tablespoons flour

2 tablespoons butter

1 teaspoon vanilla

1 cup white corn syrup ············ Stir syrup into the above and add pecans. Put into unbaked pie shell and bake at

1 cup pecan halves   325° for 40 minutes or until brown on top.

1 unbaked 8 1/2-inch pie shell

Pecan Pie

The Derings, Green Lake, Wisconsin

Ingredients

Directions (Makes one 9-inch pie)

3 eggs ································· Beat eggs slightly; add sugar, syrup, nuts, salt, and vanilla. Pour into unbaked pie

1 cup granulated sugar   shell and bake in slow oven 325° for 40 minutes or until done.

1 cup maple syrup

1 cup pecans–chopped

1/2 teaspoon salt

1 teaspoon vanilla

1 unbaked 9-inch pie shell

Use heat resistant glass or enamelware pans for browned undercrusts.

Pie a la mode is all right if it is good pie and the ice cream is top-grade vanilla–
but heaven forbid using chocolate.

Pecan Pie

Pine Tree Inn, Lynnhaven, Virginia

Ingredients

3 eggs–slightly beaten ⋯⋯⋯⋯⋯
1 cup dark corn syrup
1/8 teaspoon salt
1 cup granulated sugar
1 teaspoon vanilla extract
1 unbaked 9-inch pie shell
2/3 cup pecan meats

Directions (Makes one 9-inch pie)

Mix together all ingredients except nuts. Pour into unbaked pie shell. Place nut meats carefully over top of mixture in attractive patterns. Bake in hot oven at 450° for 10 minutes. Then reduce heat to 350° and bake for about 30 minutes or until a clean knife blade inserted into center of pie comes out clean.

Pecan Pie

New Perry Hotel, Perry, Georgia

Ingredients

3 eggs ⋯⋯⋯⋯⋯⋯⋯⋯⋯⋯⋯⋯
1 cup sugar ⋯⋯⋯⋯⋯⋯⋯⋯
1 cup white corn syrup
1/4 lb. melted butter
1 teaspoon vanilla
1 cup chopped pecans
1 uncooked 9-inch pie shell

Directions (Makes one 9-inch pie)

Beat well.

Add ingredients, in order given, to eggs. Pour in uncooked pie shell and cook in preheated oven, 350°, for 30-45 minutes.

Spiced Nut Pie

Ingredients

Directions (Makes one 9-inch pie)

3 eggs-separated ················ Cream together egg yolks, butter and sugar.

1/2 cup sugar

1/4 lb. butter

1 cup mixed nuts—················ Mix opposite ingredients and add all to above.

    pecans and walnuts

1 cup steamed seedless raisins

1/2 teaspoon cinnamon

1/2 teaspoon cloves

1 teaspoon nutmeg

1/4 teaspoon salt

2 tablespoons cider vinegar

3 egg whites ···················· Beat egg whites stiff and slowly beat sugar into whites. Fold into above.

1/2 cup sugar

1 uncooked 9-inch pie shell ··········· Bake in moderate oven 350° in uncooked pastry shell about 40 minutes.

Date Nut Pie

Villula Tea Garden, Seale, Alabama

Ingredients

Directions (Makes one 8-inch pie)

12 dates-chopped fine ················ Mix all ingredients except egg whites and extract. Fold in egg whites and extract. Put in 8-inch pie pan which has been greased. Bake 30 minutes at 350°, or until light brown. Let cool before cutting.

1 cup pecans-chopped fine

1 cup sugar

12 premium crackers-rolled
    fine

1/2 teaspoon baking powder

1 teaspoon almond extract

3 egg whites-stiffly beaten

The Duncan Hines Dessert Book

Hazelnut Pie

Plentywood Farm, Bensenville, Illinois

Ingredients

3 eggs

1/2 cup sugar

1/4 teaspoon salt

1 cup dark corn syrup

1/2 teaspoon vanilla

1 cup toasted chopped hazelnuts

Directions (Makes one 9-inch pie)

Beat eggs slightly and add other ingredients in order. Mix well. Line pie tin with plain pastry; pour in filling and bake 45 minutes in 300° oven. Serve with whipped cream.

1 cup golden table syrup instead of dark corn syrup makes a maple flavored pie.

Treasure Chest Pie

Ingredients

1 pie shell–unbaked

1/2 cup butter

1 cup sugar

3 egg yolks–beaten

1 egg white–beaten

1/2 cup cooked raisins

1/2 cup mincemeat

1/2 cup walnuts–broken

1/2 cup pecans–broken

2 tablespoons orange juice

1 teaspoon vanilla

1/2 teaspoon salt

2 tablespoons Apple Jack brandy

Directions

Make a rich flaky crust but do not bake it first.

Cream butter and sugar together.

Stir yolks and white into mixture until it foams.

Add remaining ingredients to mixture and pour into pie shell, uncooked. Put a criss-cross crust on top and bake in 400° oven for 12 to 15 minutes or until the filling sets and then cover the pie with an inverted pie pan; lower the temperature to 350° and bake until the top crust becomes brown and the filling is well set. May be served with whipped cream, but that is not necessary.

Black Walnut Pie

Ingredients

1/4 lb. butter
1 cup sugar
1 cup dark corn syrup
3 eggs
1 teaspoon cinnamon
1/4 cup black walnut meats
2 tablespoons boiling water
1 uncooked 9-inch pie shell

Directions (Makes one 9-inch pie)

Melt butter; add sugar and corn syrup and stir to dissolve. Beat eggs and add to mixture. Put walnut meats in cloth and beat to pulp. Add to mixture with cinnamon and stir in water. Bake in uncooked pie shell in 350° oven for 50 minutes.

Sour Cream Raisin Pie

Ingredients

1 10-inch baked pastry shell

Directions (Makes one 10-inch pie)

Prepare.

FILLING

1/2 cup seedless raisins
1/2 cup nut meats

Chop raisins and nuts and mix together.

1 cup sugar
2 1/2 tablespoons flour
1 teaspoon cinnamon
1/4 teaspoon ground cloves

Mix together dry ingredients and add to raisins and nuts.

1 1/2 cups sour cream

Pour over above mixture and stir all together thoroughly. Place in double boiler and bring to a boil.

3 egg yolks

Beat egg yolks together and add gradually to above mixture, stirring constantly to prevent lumping. Cook all together until thick. Let cool and pour into pastry shell.

3 egg whites
6 tablespoons sugar

Beat the egg whites together and add the sugar gradually. Top the pie with the meringue and brown in a slow oven.

Brownie Pie

Ingredients

2 squares unsweetened ·············· chocolate

2 tablespoons butter

3 eggs–well beaten ·····················

1/2 cup sugar

3/4 cup dark corn syrup

2/3 cup pecan halves

1 unbaked 9-inch pie shell

Directions (Makes one 9-inch pie)

Melt chocolate and butter together over hot water.

Add chocolate, sugar, and corn syrup to the beaten eggs and beat thoroughly. Stir in pecan halves. Pour mixture into unbaked pie shell. Bake in moderate oven 375° for 40 to 50 minutes.

English Toffee Pie

Pendarvis House, Mineral Point, Wisconsin

Ingredients

2 cups heavy sour cream ···············

2 1/4 cups sugar

1 teaspoon ground cloves

3 eggs

2 egg yolks

3 cups seedless raisins ··················

1/2 cup chopped walnuts

1/2 cup quartered blanched almonds

1/2 cup chopped hazelnuts

1 teaspoon vanilla

1/4 cup sherry

2 unbaked 9-inch pie shells

Directions (Makes two 9-inch pies)

Combine sugar, cream and cloves. Blend well. Beat together whole eggs and egg yolks and stir into the sugar mixture.

Stir into above mixture the remaining ingredients and blend well. Pour into the unbaked pie shells and bake in 400° oven for 15 minutes. Reduce heat to 350° and bake 35 to 40 minutes or until a silver knife inserted in center comes out clean. Serve with vanilla ice cream if you like. Note: If 2 pies are not wanted, one might be wrapped in aluminum foil and put in the freezer for a short time. When wanted, let defrost and warm in the oven at about 350° just long enough to get warm through.

Grandma Obrecht's Lemon Pie

Lowell Inn, Stillwater, Minnesota

Ingredients

1 1/2 cups sugar
5 tablespoons cornstarch
1/2 teaspoon salt

1 1/2 cups boiling water

2 teaspoons butter
4 egg yolks–slightly beaten

1/2 cup lemon juice
Grated rind of 1 lemon

Directions (Makes one 9-inch pie)

Mix opposite ingredients together.

Add water to above; cook over direct heat, stirring constantly until mixture boils. Then place in double boiler; cover and cook until thick.

Remove from fire; add butter and egg yolks; return to fire and cook two minutes.

Add lemon juice and rind to above. Cook until thick. Pour into baked pie shell.

MERINGUE

4 egg whites
8 tablespoons granulated
  sugar
1/4 teaspoon cream of tartar

Beat egg whites very stiff, add sugar and cream of tartar gradually and beat until blended. Spread over pie; sprinkle with a little sugar before baking. Bake in preheated 350° oven until brown.

Chess Pie

Mrs. Earle Forbes, Greenville, North Carolina

Ingredients

3 eggs
1 cup sugar
1/4 teaspoon salt
1/4 teaspoon nutmeg
1/2 cup butter
1/4 tablespoon tart jelly

Directions (Makes one 8-inch pie)

Beat lightly.
Mix dry ingredients together and add slowly to eggs, beating all the while.

Melt and add to above.
Stir into above, mixing well. Pour into unbaked pie crust and place in 350° oven for 10 minutes and then reduce heat to 300° for 20 minutes or until it sets.

The Duncan Hines Dessert Book

Chess Pie

Mrs. R. G. Price, Bowling Green, Kentucky

Ingredients

Directions (Makes one 9-inch pie)

1/4 lb. butter .... Melt butter; stir and add sugar slowly; remove from fire.

1 1/2 cups sugar

1 1/2 teaspoons mild white .... If vinegar is strong, reduce amount of vinegar a bit and dilute with water. Add to
  vinegar   above with corn meal. Cool slightly.

1 1/2 teaspoons cornmeal

3 eggs .... Beat eggs slightly and add to above. Pour into uncooked pastry shell and bake for

1 uncooked 9-inch pie shell   10 minutes at 425°. Lower heat to 300° or 275° is better, for almost an hour. Take
from oven when pie still shakes slightly.

Lemon Pie

Ingredients

Directions (Makes one 8-inch pie)

2 tablespoons flour–scant .... Add flour to sugar; mix well.

1 cup sugar

1/4 cup lemon juice .... Mix thoroughly the opposite ingredients and add to the above. Cook over boiling

Rind of 1 lemon–grated   water until thick.

4 egg yolks

2 egg whites

1 cup water

1 pinch salt

1 tablespoon butter .... Add butter to the above mixture. Cool. Pour into baked pie shell.

1 baked 8-inch pie shell

2 egg whites .... Beat egg whites until foamy and then add sugar gradually. Beat until stiff peaks

1/4 cup sugar   are formed. Spread over filling and brown in moderate oven 350° for about
15 minutes.

An 8-inch pie cuts into 5 or 6 servings and a 9-inch pie cuts into 7 or 8 pieces.
It all depends upon how big one's appetite is.

Jelly Pie

Ingredients

1/2 cup butter

2 cups sugar

4 eggs

1/2 cup tart jelly

1 cup light cream

Pinch of salt

1 unbaked 8-inch pie shell

Directions (Makes one 8-inch pie)

Cream butter until soft; add sugar gradually and cream together until light and fluffy. Add eggs, one at a time, and beat well. Add jelly and continue to beat until smooth. Turn into unbaked pie shell. Bake in hot oven 450° for 10 minutes; reduce temperature to 325° and continue to bake for 50 minutes longer. Cool and garnish with whipped cream, if desired.

French Chocolate Mint Pie

Lamkin Lake Shore Lodge, Good Hart, Michigan

Ingredients

1 1/2 cups powdered sugar

1/4 lb. butter (half margarine and half butter may be used although butter is better)

2 eggs

2 squares melted unsweetened chocolate

6 drops oil of peppermint

1 baked vanilla wafer pie shell or plain pastry shell

Directions (Makes one 9-inch pie)

Cream butter and sugar together.

Beat eggs well. Add melted chocolate. Mix thoroughly.

Add peppermint to mixture and beat until light and fluffy. Put into vanilla wafer pie shell or thin pastry shell and let stand in refrigerator overnight. Note: The secret of the success in this dessert is in the beating; beat thoroughly and the mixture will be light and fluffy and delicate.

Custard pies should be stored in a cool place as soon as they have cooled naturally.

Pineapple-Mint Parfait Pie

Ingredients

1 package lime-flavored gelatin
1 1/4 cups hot pineapple juice (if not enough juice, add water to make 1 1/4 cups)
Few drops mint extract
1 pint vanilla ice cream
1 cup drained canned, crushed pineapple
1 baked 9-inch pie shell
1 cup whipping cream—whipped

Directions (Makes one 9-inch pie)

Dissolve gelatin in hot liquid in a 2-quart saucepan. Add mint extract. Add ice cream by spoonfuls, stirring until melted. Chill mixture until thickened but not set (25 to 35 minutes).

Fold drained pineapple into the above mixture. Turn into pie shell. Chill until firm, about 15 to 25 minutes.

Garnish with whipped cream.

Frozen Chocolate Peppermint Pie

Hotel Anderson, Wabasha, Minnesota

Ingredients

4 egg whites
1/2 teaspoon cream of tartar
1 cup sugar

2 3/4 cups whipping cream
2 cups fudge sauce
1/2 teaspoon oil of peppermint

1 qt. vanilla ice cream

Directions (Makes one 12-inch pie)

Beat egg whites until frothy. Add cream of tartar. Beat until whites are stiff. Add sugar slowly a tablespoon at a time beating until mixture is thick and glossy. Line a deep 12-inch pie pan with meringue and bake in pre-heated 300° oven for 50 to 60 minutes. Cool.

Whip cream until stiff. Slowly add fudge sauce and oil of peppermint.

Soften a bit in electric beater. Spoon into cooled meringue shell. Do not let ice cream get too soft–just enough to manage. Pour over this the chocolate whipped cream mixture. Freeze until firm. Note: If you do not have a 12-inch pan, use two 9-inch pie pans.

Fudge Pie with Peppermint Ice Cream

Mrs. Ashby, Bowling Green, Kentucky

Ingredients

2 squares semi-sweet ·················· baking chocolate

3 eggs

1 cup sugar

1/4 cup flour

1/2 cup melted butter ··················

1/2 cup pecans

1 teaspoon vanilla

1/4 teaspoon salt

1/2 pint vanilla ice cream ············

1/4 cup crushed peppermint candy

Couple of drops of red coloring

Directions (Makes one 9-inch pie)

Melt chocolate in double boiler. Beat eggs; add sugar and flour to the beaten eggs and mix well. Add this mixture to the melted chocolate.

Add the opposite ingredients to the above. Grease a 9-inch pie pan with shortening; pour in mixture and bake in slow oven 275° for about 30 minutes or until set. Cool.

Whip vanilla ice cream and blend in crushed peppermint candy. Add a little coloring to the ice cream to make it pink enough. (Do not put too much candy into the ice cream as it will make it syrupy.) Refreeze the ice cream and serve on top of the Fudge Pie.

Strawberry Parfait Pie

Ingredients

1 package strawberry-flavored ···· gelatin

1 1/4 cups boiling berry juice (add water to make 1 1/4 cups)

1 pint vanilla ice cream

Directions (Makes one 9-inch pie)

Dissolve gelatin in boiling liquid in a 2-quart saucepan. Add ice cream by spoonfuls, stirring until melted. Chill mixture until thickened but not set (15 to 20 minutes).

The Duncan Hines Dessert Book

| 1 box (12 oz.) frozen strawber- | ······· Fold drained strawberries into the above mixture. Turn into pie shell. Chill until |

1 box (12 oz.) frozen strawber- ······· Fold drained strawberries into the above mixture. Turn into pie shell. Chill until
   ries–defrosted and drained   firm, about 20 to 30 minutes.
1 baked 9-inch pie shell
1 cup whipping ···················· Garnish with whipped cream.
   cream–whipped

Holiday Pie

Ye Old College Inn, Houston, Texas

Ingredients

Directions (Makes two 9-inch pies)

PUMPKIN CUSTARD

2 cups sugar ··························· Cream together.
4 eggs
4 cups custard ······················ Add in order given to the sugar and egg mixture.
   pumpkin–canned
1 teaspoon salt
2 teaspoons cinnamon
2 teaspoons allspice
3 cups milk

MINCEMEAT BASE FILLING

3/4 lb. prepared mincemeat ·········· Line two 9-inch pie pans with your favorite crust. Build up sides as high as
8 oz. chopped tart apples   possible–crimp around edges. Spread one half of the mincemeat filling in each
Pastry for two 9-inch pie shells   pie shell. Then pour pumpkin custard on top. Bake in 350° oven for approxi-
                                     mately 45 minutes. This results in a two layer pie of unusual taste.

Prick pastry with a fork to prevent puffing during baking.
If the pastry still puffs, reach quickly in the oven and prick again.

White Christmas Pie

Ingredients

Directions (Makes one 9-inch pie)

1 package (1 tablespoon) ············· Combine opposite ingredients in saucepan.
  unflavored gelatin

1/2 cup sugar

1/4 cup flour

1/4 teaspoon salt

1 3/4 cups milk ····························· Stir milk into the above mixture. Cook over low heat, stirring constantly, until the mixture comes to a boil. Remove from heat and cool. When slightly thickened, beat with rotary egg beater until smooth.

3/4 teaspoon vanilla ····················· Fold extracts and whipped cream into the above mixture.

1/4 teaspoon almond extract

1/2 cup whipping
  cream–whipped

3 egg whites ································ Beat egg whites until foamy. Add sugar gradually, beating until mixture stands in stiff peaks. Fold the meringue and coconut into the gelatin mixture. Pour into baked pie shell. Chill until set.

1/2 cup sugar

1 cup shredded coconut–cut

1 baked 9-inch pie shell

Christmas Pie

Brevard Hotel, Cocoa, Florida

Ingredients

Directions (Makes one 9-inch pie)

CRUST

1 1/2 cups ground Brazil nuts ········ Mix nuts and sugar thoroughly. Line bottom and sides of pie tin and bake in 400° oven for 8 minutes or until lightly browned. Watch carefully for it scorches easily.

3 tablespoons sugar

FILLING

1 envelope (1 tablespoon) ············· Soak gelatin in cold water about 5 minutes.
  unflavored gelatin

The Duncan Hines Dessert Book

1/4 cup cold water

3 egg yolks ·········· Beat egg yolks slightly with a fork, add salt. Add sugar gradually. Then stir in

1/4 cup sugar gradually and carefully the hot milk. Place in double boiler and cook over boiling

1/8 teaspoon salt water until it coats a metal spoon. Remove at once and stir in gelatin. Cook; then

1 1/2 cups scalded milk chill custard until it mounds when dropped from a spoon. Beat with an egg

beater until smooth.

1/2 cup glacéed cherries ·············· Stir in cherries which have been sliced thin. Beat in carefully the rum. Beat egg

2 tablespoons light rum whites until stiff. Add gradually the sugar and beat until stiff and dry. Fold into

3 egg whites the custard. Pour into cooled baked Brazil nut crust. Place in the refrigerator

1/4 cup sugar until the following day or for at least 4 hours, until firm.

1/2 pint cream ··········· Whip at least a half pint of cream and spread over the pie. Top with sliced Brazil

Sliced Brazil nuts nuts.

Chocolate Angel Pie

Ingredients

Directions (Makes one 9-inch pie)

1/2 cup sugar ······························· Sift sugar and cream of tartar. Beat egg whites stiff, not dry. Add sifted sugar

1/8 teaspoon cream of tartar gradually while beating until smooth and glossy. Line well buttered 9-inch pie

2 egg whites pan with mixture. Keep center hollowed out to ¼-inch thickness. Do not spread

1/2 cup nuts on rim of pan. Sprinkle with nuts. Bake in slow oven 275° for one hour or until

delicate brown. Cool thoroughly.

3/4 cup semisweet chocolate ········· Melt chocolate in double boiler. Stir in water. Cook until thick. Cool slightly. Add

3 tablespoons hot water vanilla. Fold in whipped cream. Fill shell and chill in refrigerator for 3 or 4 hours.

1 teaspoon vanilla

1 cup heavy cream—whipped

Heavenly Pie

Ingredients	Directions
3 egg whites–beaten	Beat egg whites stiff and dry. Add sugar gradually.
1/2 cup sugar	
1/3 cup confectioners' sugar	Fold into mixture. Bake in ungreased glass pie plate in 275° to 325° oven for 1 hour. About 2 hours before serving, crush the top slightly.
1 cup whipping cream	Whip and spread over the pie. Place in the refrigerator until ready to serve. Shred bitter chocolate over the top.

Butterscotch Pie

Ingredients

Directions (Makes one 9-inch pie)

Ingredients	Directions
1 1/4 cups firmly packed brown sugar	Combine opposite ingredients in top of double boiler and cook over direct heat for 5 minutes, stirring constantly.
1/4 teaspoon salt	
2 tablespoons water	
2 cups milk	Blend a small amount of the milk with the cornstarch. Add this with the remaining milk to the above mixture. Cook over boiling water for about 20 minutes or until thick and smooth, stirring constantly.
4 1/2 tablespoons cornstarch	
3 egg yolks–slightly beaten	Stir a small amount of the hot mixture over the beaten eggs and mix well; return to the double boiler and cook 5 minutes longer. Add butter and vanilla. Pour into baked pie shell and chill.
2 tablespoons butter	
1/2 teaspoon vanilla	
1 baked 9-inch pie shell	
1/2 cup pecans–chopped	Just before serving, sprinkle top with nuts and garnish with whipped cream.
1 cup whipping cream–whipped	

Lemon Angel Pie

Vera Kirkpatrick, San Mateo, California

Ingredients

4 egg whites ·····················
1 teaspoon cream of tartar
1 cup sugar

4 egg yolks ·····················
1/2 cup sugar
1 1/2 lemons–juice and rind

1 cup heavy cream ·····················
2/3 teaspoon vanilla

Directions (Makes one 9- or 10-inch pie)

Beat egg whites stiff, add cream of tartar and sugar and beat until smooth and glossy. Put in buttered pit tin and bake for 60 minutes, 200°. Cool when done.

Beat egg yolks with sugar, add juice of the lemons and grated rind of the lemons. Cook in top of double boiler over boiling water until thick. Let cool.

Whip cream, sweeten to taste and add vanilla. Spread half of whipped cream on cold meringue, put custard filling on cream, then remainder of cream on top. Chill 3 hours before serving. Garnish with mint leaves and fresh strawberries.

Angel Pie

Quaker House, Orchard Park, New York

Ingredients

3 egg whites ·····················
1/2 teaspoon vinegar
1/2 cup sugar ·····················

3 egg yolks ·····················
1/2 cup sugar
1 lemon–juice and grated rind

1 1/2 cups whipping cream ··········
1/4 cup sugar
1 teaspoon vanilla

Directions (Serves 6 to 8)

Beat whites with vinegar until stiff but not dry.

Add gradually. Spread this meringue in a buttered 9-inch pie plate in the shape of a pie shell. Bake at 300° for one hour. Cool.

Beat yolks until light and thick. Add sugar gradually. Add juice and cook this mixture in top of double boiler until thick. Add lemon rind. Cool and spread on baked meringue shell.

Whip cream until thick. Add sugar and vanilla to whipped cream. Spread on top of lemon mixture in meringue. Chill in refrigerator 6 to 24 hours.

Maid of the Mist Pie

Ingredients	Directions
CRUST	
14 graham crackers ····················	Crush graham crackers with rolling pin. Blend butter with crumbs and pat into pie pan.
1/4 cup butter–melted	
FILLING	
3 egg yolks ·······························	Beat sugar and eggs well together; add lemon juice; place in double boiler and cook to custard consistency.
1 cup sugar	
Juice of two large lemons	
3 egg whites ·····························	Beat egg whites very stiff; fold into custard; blend thoroughly; put into crust and bake in very moderate oven, about 325° until set.
1/2 pt. whipping cream ·············	Whip until stiff; cover pie when cool, just before serving.

Banana Butterscotch Pie

Dorothy Brehmer Klassen, Fond du Lac, Wisconsin

Ingredients	**Directions** (Makes one 8-inch pie)
1 cup brown sugar ····················	Mix brown sugar and flour and put in top of double boiler.
4 tablespoons flour	
1 cup milk ·······························	Add slowly to the above. Cook, stirring constantly until it thickens.
2 egg yolks–beaten ···················	Add to mixture and cook 3 minutes longer. Remove from fire.
4 tablespoons butter ·················	Add to mixture. Cool.
1/2 teaspoon vanilla ··················	Add to mixture.
1 baked 8-inch pie shell ············	Line pie shell with banana slices, and pour over the mixture.
2 large bananas–sliced	
2 egg whites–beaten 2 table- ······· spoons sugar	Make a meringue and cover pie, and brown in oven, or
1 cup whipped cream	Cover pie with whipped cream.

Graham Cracker Pie

Ingredients

Directions (Makes two 8-inch pies)

30 graham crackers–crushed ·········· Mix opposite ingredients and press in pie pan.
2 tablespoons flour
2 tablespoons cinnamon
1/2 cup sugar
1 cup melted butter
1/2 cup lard–melted

FILLING

1 quart milk ································· Heat.
8 egg yolks–beaten ····················· Mix this filling, add the heated milk and cook until thick. Then fill the pie shells.
4 tablespoons cornstarch
2 teaspoons vanilla
Pinch of salt
2 tablespoons melted butter
1/2 cup sugar
8 egg whites–beaten ···················· Make a meringue of these ingredients and cover pies. Brown in 350° oven.
1/2 cup sugar
1 pinch of salt
1 teaspoon vanilla

Boiled Cider Pie

Ingredients

Directions (Makes one 8-inch pie)

1 cup sugar ·····························

2 tablespoons cornstarch

1/2 cup boiled cider

2 eggs yolks–slightly beaten

3/4 cup boiling water

1 tablespoon butter

1 baked 8-inch pie shell

Combine sugar and cornstarch in saucepan. Add boiled cider gradually, mixing well. Stir in the egg yolks and then add boiling water. Cook over low heat until clear and thick, stirring constantly. Add butter and remove from heat. Cool slightly and pour into baked pie shell.

2 egg whites ·····························

1/4 cup sugar

Beat egg whites until very soft peaks are formed. Add sugar, a tablespoon at a time, beating after each addition. Beat until meringue will stand in stiff peaks. Spread over filling and bake in 350° oven for about 10 minutes or until lightly browned.

Barbara Fritchie Sugar House Pie

Water Gate Inn, Washington, D. C.

Ingredients

Directions (Makes one 9-inch pie)

1 pie shell–unbaked ·····················

Make your favorite pie crust and line pie tin. Put into refrigerator to chill while you make the filling.

2 tablespoons flour ·····················

1/4 cup evaporated milk

1/2 cup brown sugar

1/2 cup light corn syrup

2 egg yolks

1 tablespoon melted butter

Mix flour with a portion of the milk to make a smooth paste. Add sugar, syrup, beaten egg yolks, remainder of milk and butter. Mix well. Cook in upper part of double boiler over hot water, stirring constantly until thick and smooth. Remove from fire.

The Duncan Hines Dessert Book

| 1/2 teaspoon flavoring– | Add flavoring and salt to above mixture. Beat egg whites stiff and fold into mixture. Pour into uncooked pie shell and sprinkle with nutmeg. Bake in 425° oven for 10 minutes. Reduce heat to 300° and bake about 45 minutes longer or until a knife blade inserted in center comes out clean. Serve cold. If you like you may garnish each piece as it is served with tablespoon of rum-flavored whipped cream. |

1/2 teaspoon flavoring–
  vanilla, lemon, or rum
1/2 teaspoon salt
2 egg whites
Nutmeg

Add flavoring and salt to above mixture. Beat egg whites stiff and fold into mixture. Pour into uncooked pie shell and sprinkle with nutmeg. Bake in 425° oven for 10 minutes. Reduce heat to 300° and bake about 45 minutes longer or until a knife blade inserted in center comes out clean. Serve cold. If you like you may garnish each piece as it is served with tablespoon of rum-flavored whipped cream.

Cavalier Pie Supreme

Beach Plaza Hotel, Virginia Beach, Virginia

Ingredients

2 envelopes (2 tablespoons)
  unflavored gelatin
1 pt. warm water
1 qt. whipping cream
6 egg yolks–beaten
1 cup powdered sugar
Pinch of salt
1 teaspoon vanilla
2 baked 8-inch pie shells
1 pt. whipping cream
1/3 cup powdered sugar
1/2 teaspoon vanilla
4 oz. bitter-sweet chocolate

Directions (Makes two 8-inch pies)

Dissolve gelatin in warm water and let cool.

Whip until stiff.

Add opposite ingredients to cream and whip again for 1 minute. Add gelatin and whip well again. Pour into baked pie shells, and put into refrigerator to congeal.

Whip until stiff.

Add sugar and vanilla to whipped cream, and spread over pies above.

Grate chocolate and spread over pies and return to refrigerator until ready to serve.

Black Bottom Pie

Dolores Restaurant, Oklahoma City, Oklahoma

Ingredients

Directions (Makes one 9-inch pie)

CRUST

14 crisp ginger snaps .... Roll snaps out fine. Add butter to cookie crumbs and pat evenly into a 9-inch
5 tablespoons melted butter   pan. Bake 10 minutes in 300° oven. Allow to cool.

FILLING

2 cups milk–scalded .... Add eggs slowly to hot milk.

4 egg yolks–beaten

1/2 cup sugar .... Combine sugar and cornstarch and stir into above. Cook in double boiler for
1 1/4 tablespoons cornstarch   20 minutes, stirring occasionally until it generously coats a spoon. Remove from
                                 flame and take out 1 cup.

1 1/2 squares chocolate .... Add to the cup of custard and beat well.

1 teaspoon vanilla .... As custard cools, add vanilla; pour into pie crust and chill.

1 envelope (1 tablespoon)   Soak gelatin in cold water and add to remaining hot custard. Let cool, but not
   unflavored gelatin   thick.

4 tablespoons cold water

MERINGUE

4 egg whites .... Beat egg whites, sugar, and cream of tartar into a meringue and fold into custard.

1/2 cup sugar

1/4 teaspoon cream of tartar

2 tablespoons rum .... Add rum. As soon as chocolate custard has set, add this. Chill again until it sets.

1 cup whipped cream .... Spread on top of pie.

1/2 square chocolate .... Shave and sprinkle over pie and serve.

216   The Duncan Hines Dessert Book

Shoofly Pie

Mrs. Edwin Bowen, Shillington, Pennsylvania

Ingredients

Directions (Makes two 7-inch pies)

2 unbaked pie shells ·················· Prepare.

1 1/2 cups flour ···················· Blend opposite ingredients together to make crumbs.

1/2 cup light brown sugar

1/2 cup dark brown sugar

1/4 cup butter

3/4 teaspoon baking soda ·········· Mix soda with hot water; add syrup and salt and blend thoroughly. In pie shells,

3/4 cup hot water place layer of crumbs, layer of liquid, layer of crumbs, layer of liquid and top with

3/4 cup dark corn syrup layer of crumbs. Bake at 475° for 10 minutes, then reduce heat to 375° and bake

1/4 teaspoon salt for 30 minutes.

Jefferson Davis Pie

Mrs. McKenzie Moss, Bowling Green, Kentucky

Ingredients

Directions (Makes two 9-inch pies)

3 cups sugar ······················· Cream butter and sugar together.

1 cup butter

4 eggs–beaten lightly ············· Add eggs to the above.

1 cup milk ························· Stir milk into mixture.

1 tablespoon flour ················ Blend remaining ingredients into mixture. Then beat all the above like the devil.

1/4 teaspoon salt Line 2 pie pans, that have first been well buttered, with pie crust. Pour in the

1 teaspoon vanilla filling and bake in 450° oven for 10 minutes, then reduce heat to 350° for another

30 to 35 minutes.

Soufflés, Fondues, Sponges, and Whips

TO MAKE PERFECT SOUFFLÉS THERE ARE CERTAIN RULES THAT YOU SHOULD FOLLOW. THE EGG YOLKS should be beaten until thick and lemon-colored. The egg whites should be beaten only to the point where the peaks are slightly rounded. A quick, deft hand is necessary in mixing a soufflé in order to get the greatest volume and yet not break down the air cells. Last of all, butter only the bottom of the baking dish and not the sides as this method allows the soufflé to rise more. If these few rules are followed, success will be yours and you will never again fret for fear of a flat, soggy failure.

Soufflés should be served at once because they fall very quickly.

Chocolate Soufflé

Mrs. W. B. Taylor, Bowling Green, Kentucky

Ingredients	Directions
2 tablespoons butter	Blend together.
2 tablespoons flour	
3/4 cup milk	Gradually add to the above. Cook until it reaches the boiling point.
1 1/2 squares chocolate–melted	Mix together and add to the above mixture and stir until smooth.
1/3 cup sugar	
2 tablespoons hot water	Add to above mixture. Let cool.
3 egg yolks–beaten	Fold into mixture. Turn into baking dish and bake in 350° oven for 25 minutes, or until done. Serve hot with hard sauce.
3 egg whites–beaten	
1/2 teaspoon vanilla	

Lemon Soufflé

L. S. Ayres & Co., Tea Room, Indianapolis, Indiana

Ingredients

Directions (Serves 8)

Ingredients	Directions
1 1/4 cups sugar	Mix sugar, salt, and flour. Add butter, lemon juice, rind and beaten egg yolks, blended with the milk. Beat well. Fold in stiffly beaten egg whites. Pour into a buttered casserole; place in a pan of boiling water and bake for 30 minutes in an oven at 350°. Be accurate as to baking time as bottom remains a thick liquid, which serves as a sauce.
1/8 teaspoon salt	
2 1/2 tablespoons flour	
2 1/2 tablespoons butter	
2 1/2 lemons and rind–grated	
3 eggs–separated plus one extra white	
1 1/4 cups milk	

"Of all books produced," said Joseph Conrad, "since the most remote ages by human talents and industry, those only that treat of cooking are, from a moral point of view, above suspicion."

Date Soufflé

Ingredients

Directions (Serves 8)

2 tablespoons butter ···················· Cream together.
3 tablespoons sugar

3 egg yolks ······························· Add to above.
2 tablespoons flour····················· Add to the above, alternately with milk.
3/4 cup milk

3 egg whites–beaten ················· Beat together and fold into mixture.
1 teaspoon salt

1 package dates–chopped ············· Fold into mixture. Pour into greased 1 ½ or 2-quart casserole dish. Set in pan of
  (14 oz.)   hot water and bake in 350° oven for 35 minutes. Serve with Orange Sauce

ORANGE SAUCE

1 cup sugar ····························· Mix together and cook in a double boiler until it coats a spoon.
1 cup orange juice
1 orange rind–grated
1 lemon–juice
1 teaspoon cornstarch
1 tablespoon butter
1 egg yolk

Do not open the oven when baking a soufflé.

For a soufflé with a "top hat," cut a circle around the top of the mixture
with a sharp knife about 2 inches from the edge before putting in the oven.

Orange Soufflé

Ingredients

Directions (Serves 6)

6 egg whites ·· Beat egg whites stiff and beat in sugar gradually.

6 tablespoons sugar

4 tablespoons orange ················· Mix into the above. Put in a double boiler that holds 3 quarts. Cook slowly for
  marmalade 1 hour. Turn out on a round platter. (It should stand up like a man's silk hat.)

1 teaspoon orange extract Pour sauce around it and serve.

SAUCE

6 egg yolks–beaten ················· Beat together until smooth.

1 cup sugar

Pinch of salt

1 pint whipped cream ················· Add to the sauce just before serving.

2 tablespoons curacao

Candied kumquats–sliced ············· Decorate each portion with kumquats.

Rum Soufflé

Ingredients

Directions (Serves 4)

4 egg yolks ·· Combine yolks and sugar and beat until thick and lemon-colored.

1/4 cup sugar

1/2 teaspoon vanilla ······················ Add to the above mixture.

Pinch of salt

4 egg whites–stiffly beaten ············· Fold into egg yolk mixture. Pour into flat baking dish. (Mixture should be about
  1-inch high.) Bake in slow oven 325° for 25 minutes or until firm.

1/4 cup Jamaica rum ····················· Pour over soufflé. Ignite and serve immediately.

Vanilla Soufflé

Ingredients

1/4 cup butter ···························
1/4 cup flour ·····························
1/4 teaspoon salt
3/4 cup milk
3 egg yolks ······························
1/2 cup sugar
1 teaspoon vanilla ···················
3 egg whites ····························
1/4 teaspoon cream of tartar

Directions (Serves 8)

Melt in saucepan.
Add opposite ingredients to the above mixture and blend together. Cook over low heat, stirring constantly, until thick and smooth. Remove from heat.

Beat egg yolks until thick and lemon-colored. Add sugar gradually and continue beating.

Add vanilla to milk mixture and blend into egg yolk mixture.
Combine and beat until stiff. Gently fold in egg yolk mixture. Pour into greased 2-quart baking dish. Place baking dish in pan of hot water. Bake in moderate oven 350° about 45 minutes or until golden brown. Serve immediately with whipped cream and sliced toasted almonds.

Party Soufflé

Ingredients

9 egg whites ·····························
3/4 teaspoon cream of tartar
1/8 teaspoon salt
9 tablespoons sugar ················
3 teaspoons vanilla ·················
1 quart crushed, sweetened
  strawberries

Directions (Serves 12)

Combine opposite ingredients and beat until stiff peaks are formed.

Beat in very gradually.
Add and mix thoroughly. Pour into greased 10-inch tube pan. Place tube pan in pan of hot water (1-inch deep). Bake in slow oven 275° about 1 ½ hours. Carefully invert onto hot serving dish. Spread with Eggnog Sauce. Pour over the top and around souffle. Serve immediately.

EGGNOG SAUCE

2 egg yolks ·····························
1/2 cup sifted confectioners'
  sugar
1/2 cup heavy cream–whipped ·······
2 tablespoons Jamaica rum

Beat egg yolks until thick and lemon-colored. Add sugar gradually and continue to beat until thick.

Fold into above.

Chocolate Sponge Pudding

Ingredients

4 oz. sweet chocolate ······················
3 egg yolks ································
2 tablespoons sugar
3 egg whites ·······························
Pinch of salt
2 tablespoons sugar
1 teaspoon vanilla

Directions (Serves 5)

Melt chocolate in top of double boiler.

Beat yolks until thick and lemon-colored. Add sugar and continue beating until very thick. Set aside.

Beat egg whites with salt until mixture will stand in soft moist peaks. Add sugar gradually, then vanilla, and beat until stiff but not dry. Add hot melted chocolate slowly to egg yolk mixture, mixing well. Fold into egg whites. Pile lightly into sherbet glasses with ladyfingers, macaroons, or vanilla wafers, cut in quarters, or strips of sponge cake. Fill glasses with chocolate mixture. Top with whipped cream and serve.

Chocolate Fondue

Ingredients

2 squares unsweetened ···············
  chocolate
1 cup milk
1/2 cup fine bread crumbs ···········
1 tablespoon butter–melted
1/2 cup sugar
1/4 teaspoon salt
3 egg yolks ································
1 teaspoon vanilla
3 egg whites–stiffly beaten ···········

Directions (Serves 5 to 6)

Heat together in saucepan, stirring constantly, until chocolate is melted and mixture blended.

Add opposite ingredients and mix well.

Beat yolks slightly in bowl. Gradually add chocolate mixture stirring constantly. Add and blend.

Fold above mixture into egg whites. Pour into greased 1 ½-quart casserole. Place casserole in pan of hot water. Bake in moderate oven 350° about 40 minutes or until silver knife inserted comes out clean. Serve with cream, whipped cream, Foamy Sauce, or Plain Custard Sauce. (See Dessert Sauces Section for sauces.)

Chocolate Custard Sponge Pudding

Ingredients

Directions (Serves 6 to 8)

2 squares unsweetened ················· Combine in top of double boiler. Cook and stir over hot water until chocolate is
  chocolate   melted. Beat with rotary egg beater until smooth and blended.

2 cups milk

1/4 cup flour ································· Combine opposite ingredients together in bowl.

1/2 cup sugar

1/4 teaspoon salt

2 tablespoons butter–melted ········· Add butter and yolks to above mixture. Then gradually add hot chocolate

3 egg yolks–slightly beaten   mixture, blending well.

3 egg whites ·································· Beat to soft peaks. Fold gently into chocolate mixture. Pour into greased 8-inch
                       round baking dish. Place baking dish in pan of hot water. Bake in moderate oven
                       350° for 45 to 50 minutes. Serve warm or cold, with whipped cream.

Date-Applesauce Whip

Ingredients

Directions (Serves 6)

2 egg whites ·································· Beat egg whites with salt until foamy throughout. Add sugar, 2 tablespoons at a

1/4 teaspoon salt   time, beating after each addition. Continue beating until stiff peaks are formed.

1/4 cup sugar

1 1/4 cups thick sweetened ············ Combine opposite ingredients. Fold gently into beaten egg whites. Blend well.
  applesauce

1 tablespoon lemon juice

3/4 cup chopped dates

2/3 cup chopped walnuts

Ladyfingers or vanilla wafers ········· Arrange along the inside of sherbet glasses. Place mixture into sherbet glasses.

Prune Whip

Ingredients

Directions (Serves 4)

2 egg whites ···························· Beat egg whites with salt until foamy throughout. Add sugar, 2 tablespoons at a
1/8 teaspoon salt   time, beating after each addition. Continue beating until stiff peaks are formed.
1/4 cup sugar

1 1/2 cups prune pulp ··········· Combine and fold into beaten egg whites. Blend well. Place mixture into sherbet
2 tablespoons lemon juice   glasses and chill. Serve plain or with Plain Custard Sauce. (See Dessert Sauces
Section.)

Prune Whip

Ingredients

Directions (Serves 4 to 6)

5 egg whites ··························· Combine and beat until foamy throughout.
1/8 teaspoon salt

1/4 teaspoon cream of tartar ······· Add and continue beating until stiff.

1 cup sweetened prune pulp ······· Fold in. Pour into greased 9-inch baking dish. Place baking dish in pan of hot
water. Bake in slow oven 300° about 1 hour. Serve hot with Plain Custard Sauce.
(See Dessert Sauces Section.)

Quick Strawberry Fluff

Ingredients

Directions (Serves 5)

1 cup fresh ····························· Combine in bowl and beat at high speed of electric mixer until light and fluffy.
  strawberries–capped
1 egg white
1 cup sugar
2 teaspoons lemon juice

1/2 cup heavy cream–whipped ····· Fold into fruit mixture. Pour into sherbet glasses and chill.

Strawberry Marshmallow Cream

Ingredients

1 egg white ································
Pinch of salt

1 cup heavy cream–whipped ···········
1 cup marshmallows-cut in
  small pieces

1 cup fresh strawberries or ···········
  1 box frozen strawberries–
  defrosted and drained

Directions (Serves 6)

Beat egg white with salt until stiff.

Fold whipped cream and marshmallows into beaten egg white and chill.

Crush berries and fold in just before serving.

Baked and Steamed Puddings

PUDDINGS ARE A SUBTLE BLEND OF FLAVORS. THEY MAY BE FRAGRANT AND SPICY OR MILD AND DELICATE. WHEN served with the right sauce they become luxurious desserts.

For generations steamed puddings have been associated with the three winter holidays, Thanksgiving, Christmas, and New Year's. Plum Pudding is as traditional as turkey and cranberry sauce at holiday time. The first Plum Pudding was very different from our present pudding. It consisted of a mixture of mashed plums mixed with butter, rice and barley. Whole grains of rice and barley were included as it was believed that these would guarantee an abundant harvest for the coming year. Later Plum Pudding was made of a mixture of meat broth, spices, and dried raisins. By the early 19th century the familiar English Plum Pudding of flour, spices, raisins, currants, ground suet, sugar, eggs and brandy had evolved. The only major difference between the puddings of the early days and those of today is that formerly the pudding was wrapped in a cloth and placed in boiling water to cook, while today our Plum Pudding is steamed. ▶

The colonial settlers, forced to be thrifty and resourceful, made a new variation of Plum Pudding. Their adaption, called Suet Pudding, was made of flour, spices, fruit and molasses and although not as rich as the original English Pudding it filled the need for such a dessert. Since the time of the Suet Pudding many steamed fruit variations have been developed.

From the early settlers we also derive another steamed pudding–the Indian Pudding. As the name implies, this recipe was taught to the Puritans by the Indians. It consists of a mixture of cornmeal, molasses, milk, and spices. Indian Pudding has a very unusual flavor and texture, and the secret of its preparation is long slow baking or steaming.

In the South, especially in Virginia, Colonial women competed with one another in serving elegant puddings. To this day, we still have desserts which were developed as a result of this competition. The Duke of Gloucester Pudding and the Queen Charlotte are examples of the fine puddings which came from this era.

Puddings as a group really fall in no special social class. They can be highfalutin or plain Jane. They can be used to bolster a simple meal or can keep company with the most lavish dinner. They can be heavy and hearty or light and tasty. I have enjoyed them in frontier camps as well as in the most elegant metropolitan cafes. Universal though it may be there is still one thing a pudding must avoid: it must not weep.

When serving you may want to hold out a little portion for a late snack or tomorrow's light lunch. Keep this little nugget in the refrigerator and try it smothered with cold milk. You will find it tasty and filling.

Chocolate Steam Pudding

Ingredients

Directions (Serves 6)

3 tablespoons butter ·················· Cream and blend together opposite ingredients.
2/3 cup sugar
1 egg–beaten
2 1/4 cups flour ·················· Sift together dry ingredients and mix into the above.
4 1/2 teaspoons baking
  powder
1/2 teaspoon salt ·················· Add milk to mixture.
1 cup milk
2 1/2 squares unsweetened ·········· Melt and add to mixture. Turn into molds, filling no more than half-full. Steam
  chocolate   2 hours and serve with sauce.

SAUCE

1/4 cup butter ·················· Work until very soft.
1 cup powdered sugar ·················· Gradually add to the butter.
1/2 teaspoon vanilla ·················· Add vanilla and salt to mixture.
Pinch of salt
1/4 cup whipping cream ············· Whip and fold into the sauce.

Suet Pudding

Mrs. Roy B. Morningstar, Bowling Green, Kentucky

Ingredients

1/2 teaspoon salt
1 3/4 cups flour
1/2 cup chopped suet
1/2 cup sorghum molasses
1/2 cup buttermilk
1/2 teaspoon soda
1 cup raisins

Directions (Serves 6 to 8)

Mix salt, flour, and suet together.

Mix molasses, milk, and soda. Add to this enough of the flour mixture to make a stiff batter (not dough).

Flour raisins lightly and add to the above mixture. Fill cans half-full and steam for three hours. (Use three 12 oz. baking powder cans or any similar containers.) If pressure cooker is used for steaming, go by chart for steaming puddings. Serve with Wine Sauce or Clear Brown Sugar Sauce and top with whipped cream. Note: Be sure to use suet that can be easily broken into pieces and is free from fine fibers; ask the butcher for kidney fat.

Steamed Blackberry Pudding

Ingredients

2 cups sifted flour
4 teaspoons baking powder
1 teaspoon salt
4 tablespoons butter
1 3/4 cups milk
1 cup blackberries

Directions (Serves 6 to 8)

Sift together dry ingredients into bowl.

Cut butter into flour mixture with pastry blender until coarse crumbs are formed.

Add milk to the above mixture and stir until blended.

Add berries to the above mixture and stir until mixed. Pour batter into greased mold and steam for about 1 ½ hours. Serve with cream or Brandy Sauce. (See Dessert Sauces Section.)

Cranberry Steamed Pudding

Ingredients

1 cup boiling water ·····················
1 cup chopped cranberries
2 tablespoons butter
1 egg–well beaten
1/2 cup sugar ·····················
1/2 cup molasses
1 1/2 cups sifted flour ·····················
1 teaspoon salt
1 teaspoon soda

Directions (Serves 8)

Pour water over cranberries and butter.

Add sugar and molasses to beaten egg. Add above mixture and stir until well blended.

Sift together dry ingredients and stir into the above mixture. Pour into well greased 1-qt. mold. Steam for 2 hours. Serve with Foamy Sauce. (See Dessert Sauces Section.)

Steamed Vanilla Pudding

Ingredients

1 1/2 cups sifted flour ·····················
1/2 teaspoon salt
3 teaspoons baking powder
1/4 cup butter ·····················
1/2 cup sugar
1 egg–well beaten
1 teaspoon vanilla
2/3 cup milk ·····················

Directions (Serves 6)

Sift together dry ingredients.

Cream butter and sugar together until light and fluffy. Add egg and beat well. Stir in vanilla.

Add dry ingredients alternately with the milk to the above mixture. Pour into greased and sugared 1-quart mold. Cover. Steam for 1 ½ hours. Serve with Fruit Sauce. (See Dessert Sauces Section.)

Raisin Pudding

(Serves 6) Use recipe for Steamed Vanilla Pudding adding 1 cup raisins with the creamed mixture. Serve with Lemon Sauce.

Plum Pudding

Mrs. Charles Normand, Belton, Texas

Ingredients

Directions (Serves 8 to 10)

1/2 lb. citron ···································· Chop fruit.

1/4 lb. candied lemon peel

1/4 lb. candied orange peel

1 lb. raisins

1 lb. currants

1 lb. suet ······································· Put suet through food chopper. Mix all these ingredients together.

1/4 teaspoon cloves

1/3 teaspoon cinnamon

1/4 teaspoon allspice

6 eggs–beaten ··························· Mix sugar and eggs together and stir into above mixture.

2 cups sugar

1 cup sherry wine

2 cups flour

2 teaspoons baking powder ·········· Thicken the wine with flour and baking powder and pour over fruit mixture. Dip a cloth in hot water and line with flour. Pour in the pudding and tie. Have the water boiling and keep boiling for 6 hours. Keep the pudding covered with water during this process.

English Plum Pudding

Anchorage-by-the-Sea, Mattapoisett, Massachusetts

Ingredients

Directions (Serves 10 to 12)

1 cup flour ································· Sift flour over fruit and mix well. Set aside.

1 lb. seedless raisins

4 oz. candied citron–cut fine

4 oz. candied lemon peel–
  cut fine

4 oz. candied orange peel–cut
  fine

1/2 cup chopped almonds ··········	Mix opposite ingredients.
1/2 lb. bread crumbs	
1/2 cup sugar	
1 teaspoon baking powder	
1 teaspoon ground cinnamon	
1/2 teaspoon ground allspice	
1/2 teaspoon ground cloves	
1 teaspoon salt	
1 cup suet–chopped fine ··········	Work suet, evenly, into the above mixture.
3 eggs–beaten ····················	Add remaining ingredients with the floured fruit to the above mixture. Pour mixture into buttered molds filling two-thirds full. Cover; place in steamer of boiling water; steam slowly and steadily for 4 to 8 hours, according to the size of the molds. When ready to serve, reheat by steaming one-half hour or more. Serve with Hard Sauce or Wine Sauce.
1 cup molasses	
1 cup pickled peach syrup or other fruit juice	

Chocolate Bread Pudding

Robert G. Brehmer, Jr., Fond du Lac, Wisconsin

Ingredients	Directions (Serves 8)
2 tablespoons butter ················	Melt butter and chocolate in double boiler.
4 squares unsweetened chocolate	
1/2 cup sugar ·····················	Add sugar and salt to the above.
1/4 teaspoon salt	
4 egg yolks–beaten ················	Add yolks and milk to mixture and cook until slightly thickened.
1/2 cup milk	
2 cups fresh bread crumbs ··········	Add opposite ingredients to the above and mix thoroughly.
1 teaspoon vanilla	
1/2 cup nut meats	
4 egg whites–beaten ················	Fold egg whites into mixture. Turn into molds filling about one-half full. Steam for 25 minutes. Serve with Butter Sauce or whipped cream, either hot or cold.

Raisin Puffs

Ingredients

1/2 cup butter ·····························
1 cup sugar
2 eggs–beaten ·····························
2 cups flour ·····························
2 teaspoons baking powder
1 cup milk
1 cup raisins–cut up ·····················

Directions (serves 8 to 10)

Cream together butter and sugar.

Add eggs to above mixture.

Sift together dry ingredients and add to mixture, alternately with milk.

Flour raisins and add to mixture. Steam in cups ¾ of hour. Serve with whipped cream.

Persimmon Pudding

Mammoth Cave Hotel, Mammoth Cave, Kentucky

Ingredients

1 cup persimmon pulp ·················
1 tablespoon butter
1 cup sugar
2 teaspoons soda
1/2 cup milk
1 cup flour
1 teaspoon vanilla
1 1/2 teaspoons baking
  powder
Pinch of salt

Directions (Serves 6 to 8)

Mix together opposite ingredients and turn into molds, filling two-thirds full. Steam for 3 hours. Serve with sauce.

SAUCE

2 egg yolks–beaten ·····················
1 cup sugar
1/2 cup sherry wine ····················
1/2 pint whipping ·······················
  cream–whipped

Beat together yolks and sugar.

Add wine to eggs.

Add cream to mixture just before serving.

Pudding Saxon

Ingredients

2 cups sugar ·································
4 eggs–beaten
3 oz. citron peel–chopped
6 oz. raisins
1 pint milk
8 slices bread–diced
Rind of 1 orange–grated
3 oz. melted butter

Directions (Serves 8)

Mix all ingredients and blend. Pour into a greased mold and set in hot water. Bake in 375° oven for 30 minutes. Serve hot. This is a man's dessert.

Raisin Pudding

Mrs. K's Toll House Tavern, Silver Spring, Maryland

Ingredients

1 cup sugar ·································
1 cup flour
2 teaspoons baking powder
1/2 cup sweet milk
1 cup raisins
1 1/3 cups brown sugar ·············
2 cups hot water
1 tablespoon butter

Directions (Serves 6 to 8)

Mix together in order given and pour into greased baking dish.

Dissolve sugar in hot water and add butter. Stir until melted. Pour over above and bake in 350° oven for 45 minutes.

Queen of Pudding

Ingredients

2 slices bread
1 pint fresh milk
2 egg yolks
Rind of 1/2 lemon–grated
1 tablespoon butter
1/2 cup powdered sugar
2 egg whites
4 tablespoons granulated
  sugar
2 tablespoons coconut
1/4 teaspoon vanilla

Directions (Serves 6)

Cube the bread; heat milk to scalding point. Pour milk over bread cubes. Mash through strainer.

Add to the above mixture the egg yolks, lightly beaten, grated rind of lemon, butter, and sifted powdered sugar. Place mixture in lightly greased baking pan and bake in 350° oven for one hour or until done.

Beat egg whites until fluffy. Add granulated sugar gradually beating until stiff peaks are formed. Fold in coconut and vanilla. Spread evenly over pudding. Toast meringue under broiler or in hot oven and serve hot or cold.

Chocolate "Brot"

Ingredients

3 squares unsweetened
  chocolate–melted
4 oz. almonds–chopped
6 egg whites
1/8 teaspoon salt
1 cup powdered sugar
1 teaspoon vanilla

Directions (Serves 6 to 8)

Combine chocolate and chopped almonds.

Beat egg whites and salt until stiff. Add sugar, 2 tablespoons at a time, and continue beating until blended. Add vanilla. Fold in chocolate-almond mixture. Pour into greased square pan and bake in slow oven 300° for 45 to 50 minutes.

Butterscotch Graham Cracker Pudding

Baron Steuben Hotel, Corning, New York

Ingredients

1 quart milk

3 tablespoons butter

3/4 cup brown sugar

2 cups graham crackers–ground

2 eggs

1/2 teaspoon salt

1 teaspoon vanilla extract

1/4 teaspoon nutmeg

Directions (Serves 6)

Scald milk in top of double boiler.

Melt butter; add ½ cup of sugar; stir and cook until brown. Add to scalded milk in top of double boiler and stir as it cooks.

Add to above mixture.

Beat eggs and remainder of sugar together. Stir into the milk.

Add remaining ingredients to mixture. Pour into greased pan. Place pan in a water bath and bake at 350° for 75 minutes. Serve warm or cold with whipped cream, Hard Sauce, or Vanilla Sauce. (See Dessert Sauces Section.)

Grated Sweet Potato Pudding

Mayfair Hotel, Searcy, Arkansas

Ingredients

1/2 cup sugar

1/2 cup butter

1/2 cup chopped nuts

3 eggs

4 cups grated sweet potato (raw)

1 cup corn syrup (light or dark)

2 cups sweet milk

1 teaspoon salt

1 teaspoon nutmeg

1 teaspoon cinnamon

1 teaspoon cloves

Directions (Serves 12)

Cream butter, sugar, and nuts.

Add eggs, one at a time, and beat well.

Add grated potato, syrup, milk and spices and bake 2 hours in moderate oven in well buttered iron skillet. When brown crust forms on top, stir down and let brown again. (If pudding gets too dry while baking, add another cup milk, stir lightly and let brown again.) Serve plain or with whipped cream, either hot or cold. This pudding makes a delicious cold weather dessert and is handed down from the old days of Dutch oven baking.

Brown's Rice Pudding

Brown's Restaurant, Ft. Lauderdale, Florida

Ingredients

1/4 cup raw rice
1 qu. whole milk
1/4 cup sugar
1/2 teaspoon vanilla
Pinch of salt
Pinch of cinnamon
1/2 cup raisins

Directions (Serves 4)

Wash rice thoroughly and place in earthen-ware casserole. Add milk, sugar, salt, cinnamon and vanilla. Cook in 250° oven for 3 ½ hours stirring frequently.

Then add raisins, more if you like, and cook half an hour longer. Raisins will curdle milk if added before pudding is almost done.

Baked Indian Pudding

The Toll House, Whitman, Massachusetts

Ingredients

3 cups milk
3 tablespoons Indian meal
1/3 cup molasses
1/2 cup sugar
1 egg–beaten
1 tablespoon butter
1/2 teaspoon ginger
1/2 teaspoon cinnamon
1/4 teaspoon salt
1 cup milk

Directions (Serves 8)

Scald the milk.

Mix together and stir into hot milk and cook until it thickens. Stir constantly to prevent scorching. Remove from fire.

Add opposite ingredients to mixture and mix thoroughly. Pour into a buttered baking dish and put in 300° oven.

In ½ hour pour the milk over it and continue baking for 2 hours.

Riz a l'Imperatriee

Grand Hotel Victoria-Jungfrau, Interlaken, Switzerland

Ingredients

1/3 cup citron–chopped ················

1/3 cup candied lemon
  peel–chopped

1/3 cup candied orange
  peel–chopped

3 oz. Kirschwasser

2 cups milk ·····························

1 tablespoon vanilla or one
  1-inch stick vanilla

1/2 cup water ·····················

1/2 cup sugar

3/4 cup rice

2 tablespoons (2 envelopes) ·········
  unflavored gelatin

1/2 cup cold water

1 pint heavy cream ····················

SAUCE

1 box frozen strawberries ··············
  or raspberries

1/2 cup sugar

Directions (Serves 10 to 12)

Combine fruits and marinate in Kirschwasser while making the pudding. Stir occasionally.

Add vanilla to milk and heat in top of double boiler.

Combine water and sugar in saucepan and let come to a boil. Wash and drain rice and drop into boiling syrup. Cook five minutes, stirring constantly. Drop the rice mixture by spoonfuls into above hot milk and let cook until almost all of the liquid is absorbed. Stir occasionally. (About 1 hour.)

Soak gelatin in water about 5 minutes and add to above mixture, stir to dissolve. Let set until cool.

Whip cream until almost stiff and add to fruits and Kirschwasser. Add whipped cream and fruits to rice mixture and pack into a 2-quart oiled mold. Let stand overnight or until well set. Unmold and serve with sauce.

Combine opposite ingredients in saucepan and simmer until well blended. Chill and serve over Riz a l'Imperatriee.

Old Fashioned Indian Pudding

Ingredients

Directions (serves 8)

4 cups milk .... Scald in double boiler.

5 tablespoons Indian meal .... Gradually add meal to the above and cook 15 minutes, stirring constantly.

2 tablespoons butter .... Add these ingredients to the mixture.

1 teaspoon salt

1/2 teaspoon ginger

1/2 teaspoon cinnamon

1 cup molasses

2 eggs–well beaten

1 cup sweet apples–sliced .... Stir into mixture and turn into buttered baking dish.
  very thin

1 cup cold milk .... Pour over all and bake in 325° oven for 1 hour. Serve with vanilla ice cream.

The Duncan Hines Dessert Book

Frozen Desserts

BELIEVE IT OR NOT, ICE CREAM HAS BEEN KNOWN FOR CENTURIES, BUT FOR MANY YEARS IT WAS served only to royalty.

There is some disagreement as to who discovered ice cream but Emperor Nero is usually credited with being the first to serve this dish to his guests. As the story goes, his slaves ran down from the mountain tops carrying fresh snow, which was then flavored with juices and fruits by his kitchen staff.

Many years later Marco Polo returned to Venice from Japan with a recipe for frozen milk ice. This was probably the first of our prepared frozen desserts. Eventually cream was substituted for the milk and this was called "cream ice." This new dessert spread quickly through Europe, and the recipe was no longer the property of royalty alone. When Charles I of England heard about this dessert, which was so popular on the continent, he immediately hired a French chef to make it for him. The popularity of ice cream grew steadily in England, and when the colonists came to America, they brought the recipe with them. Years later when Dolly Madison served this dessert, she reversed the name on the White House Menu, and we have the first recorded reference to ice cream.

In the United States we eat more ice cream than all the rest of the world combined. This is not surprising because we have a flavor for every taste. For example, in California it is possible to buy avocado ice cream, in the South, buttermilk ice cream, and in upstate New York, green corn ice cream. There is even a baked bean and ketchup ice cream! However, no matter how many different flavors we have available, the three most popular continue to be chocolate, vanilla and strawberry.

Ice cream is not the only frozen dessert. This group can be classified into four definite types:

Ice creams made of cream sweetened or flavored with or without a custard base or other thickening.

Ices made of fruit juices sweetened and combined with water.

Sherbets which are a water ice to which milk, beaten egg whites, or gelatin have been added to change the flavor and texture.

Mousses and parfaits which are a whipped cream dessert, frozen without stirring. A mousse may or may not have a foundation thickened with gelatin or another material. A parfait has a foundation of syrup cooked with beaten egg whites or yolks.

All these mixtures can be frozen by packing in a freezing unit of a refrigerator or, if available, a home freezer.

There are many party desserts made of an ice cream or sherbet base. They are simple and easy to make, but they add that extra gourmet's touch to your meals. Ice cream tarts, pies, and that very special treat, Baked Alaska, all are worthy additions to the frozen dessert section.

I am passing on to you many recipes for frozen desserts, and suggest that you vary the old favorites with different fruits or sauces.

How to Make Ice Cream in the Crank Freezer

1. Chill the freezer can and the mixture first.

2. Put the can in the freezer tub. Set dasher in place. Fill can with ice cream mixture 2/3 full to allow for expansion. Put on cover and adjust crank.

3. Pack freezer tub 1/3 full of crushed ice. Add remaining crushed ice alternately with layers of coarse rock salt until the tub is full. (Use 3 to 6 parts ice to 1 part salt depending upon how fast you want the ice cream to freeze. More salt will bring quicker results, but the ice cream is not as smooth.)

4. Turn crank slowly at first. Then turn rapidly until the crank turns with difficulty.

5. Draw off water. Wipe off lid and remove it. Take out dasher; plug opening in lid; scrape dasher; and pack down ice cream.

How to Make Ice Cream in Automatic Refrigerators

1. Use a thickening ingredient such as gelatin, eggs, flour or cornstarch to get a smooth ice cream.

2. Set control at highest point. Pour mixture into freezing tray.

3. Beat or stir mixture several times while freezing to make a smooth creamy mixture.

4. Freeze until firm. Turn down control so it will not be too hard.

Vanilla Ice Cream

Ingredients

Directions (Makes 3 quarts)

3 pts. cream ·········· Scald cream in double boiler.

1 1/4 cups sugar ·········· Add sugar to hot cream and stir to dissolve sugar.

8 egg yolks ·········· Beat egg yolks until thick and creamy. Add sugar and cream mixture gradually, beating well to make custard.

1/4 teaspoon salt ·········· Stir opposite ingredients into above. Let cool. Freeze, using 2 parts cracked ice to 1 part rock salt.

1 teaspoon vanilla

1/8 teaspoon almond extract

French Vanilla Ice Cream

Ingredients

Directions (Makes 2 quarts)

3/4 cup sugar ·········· Mix together sugar, flour, and salt. Then stir in milk. Cook over boiling water, stirring constantly, until slightly thickened. Put on cover and continue to cook 10 minutes longer.

1 tablespoon flour

1/8 teaspoon salt

2 cups milk

*6 egg yolks–slightly beaten ·········· Stir a little of the hot milk mixture into the eggs. Then add it to the above mixture. Cook over hot water (about 5 minutes), stirring constantly, or until mixture coats the spoon. Remove top section of double boiler from hot water. Chill.

2 teaspoons vanilla ·········· Add opposite ingredients to the chilled mixture. Freeze according to directions given for ice cream in a crank freezer.

2 cups light cream

*For an ice cream which is less rich, use 2 whole eggs.

Banana Ice Cream

Ingredients

Directions (Makes 2 quarts)

2 cups mashed, ripe bananas ········· Mix together opposite ingredients.
  (5 or 6 bananas)
1 1/2 tablespoons lemon juice
1/2 cup sugar
1/2 teaspoon salt ·························· Add salt, eggs, milk and vanilla to banana mixture.
2 eggs–well beaten
1 cup milk
2 teaspoons vanilla
2 cups whipping cream ················· Stir whipping cream into above mixture. Freeze in hand or electric freezer until firm.

Butter-Crunch Ice Cream

Use recipe for French Vanilla Ice Cream, adding ⅔ lb. finely crushed butter-crunch just before serving.

Graham Cracker Ice Cream

Ingredients

Directions (Serves 6 to 8)

1 cup graham ···························· Combine graham crackers, sugar, and cream.
  crackers–crushed
1/3 cup granulated sugar
1 pint coffee cream
1 teaspoon vanilla ······················ Add vanilla and pour into refrigerator tray and freeze. Stir once in tray during freezing otherwise the crumbs are likely to come to the top of the mixture.

Chocolate Ice Cream

Ingredients

Directions (Serves 20)

2 eggs–beaten ·································· Cream together opposite ingredients.
1 cup sugar
1 tablespoon flour
1 quart milk ·································· Scald milk and mix a little with the chocolate, making a smooth paste. Add the balance of the milk, and pour over the egg mixture. Cook in double boiler, stirring until a custard.
3 squares unsweetened chocolate–melted
1 1/2 cups sugar ·································· Add sugar to custard and cool.
1 teaspoon vanilla ·································· Add remaining ingredients to mixture. Put in freezer and freeze.
Pinch of salt
1 quart cream

Macaroon Ice Cream

Ingredients

Directions (Makes 3 pints)

24 stale macaroons ·································· Roll macaroons to a crumb.
1 quart whipping cream ·································· Scald cream and whip.
1/2 pint sherry wine ·································· Dissolve the sugar in wine. Combine the two liquids.
1 cup sugar
1 cup shredded almonds ·································· Add almonds to combined liquids. Fold in crumbs and put in freezer. Freeze and pack for at least 4 hours.

Coffee Ice Cream

Use recipe for French Vanilla Ice Cream. Add ⅓ cup ground coffee to 2 cups milk. Cook over medium heat until milk reaches the scalding point. Strain through a piece of fine cheesecloth and then proceed as directed for French Vanilla Ice Cream, using the coffee-milk mixture for the 2 cups of milk.

Lemon Ice Cream

Ingredients

24 marshmallows ·······················
1/2 cup lemon juice

1 pint sweet milk ·······················

2 egg yolks ·······························
1/2 cup sugar

Grated rind of 2 lemons ···············

1 pint whipping cream ···················

Directions (Makes 2 quarts)

Put marshmallows in top of double boiler with lemon juice and let melt.

Scald milk.

Beat egg yolks until thick; add sugar gradually and beat until light colored. Gently pour in scalded milk and mix well. Add marshmallow mixture and lemon rind.

Mix well and let cool.

Whip cream and fold into lemon mixture. Pour into ice cream tray and freeze.

Peppermint-Stick Ice Cream

Use recipe for French Vanilla Ice Cream. Omit sugar and vanilla; when ready to freeze add 2 cups (½ pound) finely crushed peppermint-stick candy.

Persimmon Ice Cream

Ingredients

2 ripe Japanese ·······························
  persimmons–sieved

1 tablespoon sugar

1/4 cup lemon juice

1 cup heavy cream–whipped ········

Directions (Serves 4)

Combine together opposite ingredients.

Fold whipped cream into the above mixture. Pour into refrigerator tray and freeze until firm.

Pistachio Ice Cream

Use recipe for French Vanilla Ice Cream reducing vanilla to 1 ½ teaspoons and adding ¾ teaspoon almond extract. Add 1 cup finely chopped blanched pistachio nuts and green coloring just before freezing.

Raspberry Ice Cream

Use recipe for French Vanilla Ice Cream. Just before freezing add 2 cups crushed raspberries, sweetened, with ½ cup sugar.

Sherry Almond Ice Cream

Ingredients	Directions (Serves 8)
1 envelope (1 tablespoon) unflavored gelatin	Soak gelatin in cold water for about 5 minutes.
1/4 cup cold water	
1 cup boiling water	Add boiling water and sugar to gelatin and stir well until dissolved. Cool. When it begins to set, beat with an egg beater until frothy.
1 1/4 cups sugar	
6 egg whites–beaten	Fold into mixture.
1/3 cup sherry	Add opposite ingredients to mixture.
1/2 teaspoon almond extract	
1 cup almonds–chopped	Fill ring mold with alternate layers of mixture and nuts. Put in deep freeze and let set for 2 hours.
SAUCE	
6 egg yolks–beaten	Cook yolks and milk in double boiler until mixture coats a spoon.
1 pint milk	
1/4 cup sugar	Add opposite ingredients to mixture and let cool.
1/8 teaspoon salt	
1/2 teaspoon vanilla	
3 tablespoons sherry	Add sherry to cooled mixture.
1/2 pint whipping cream–whipped	Just before serving, fold whipped cream into mixture, and fill the center of the mold.

Lime Sherbet

Ingredients

1 1/4 teaspoons unflavored gelatin
1/4 cup cold water
3/4 cup water
2/3 cup sugar
1/2 cup lime juice
2 drops green coloring (about)
2 egg whites–stiffly beaten
Pinch of salt

Directions (Serves 4)

Soak gelatin in cold water about 5 minutes.

Combine sugar and water in saucepan and boil for 10 minutes. Dissolve soaked gelatin in hot syrup. Cool.

Add juice and coloring to the above mixture.

Fold beaten egg whites and salt into the mixture. Pour into refrigerator tray and freeze until firm. Stir or beat once or twice to give a smoother sherbet.

Lemon Sherbet

Ingredients

2 teaspoons unflavored gelatin
1/4 cup cold water
2 1/4 cups water
3/4 cup sugar
1 teaspoon grated lemon rind
3/4 cup lemon juice
2 egg whites–stiffly beaten
Pinch of salt

Directions (serves 4 to 6)

Soak gelatin in cold water about 5 minutes.

Combine sugar and water in saucepan and boil for 10 minutes. Dissolve soaked gelatin in hot syrup. Cool.

Add rind and juice to the above mixture.

Fold beaten egg whites and salt into the above mixture. Pour into refrigerator tray and freeze until firm. Stir or beat once or twice to give a smoother sherbet.

Lemon Sherbet

Mrs. Ralph Prince, Gladewater, Texas

Ingredients

3 cups sugar ···························

1 cup lemon juice

Grated rind of 4 lemons

2 quarts whole milk ··················

1/4 teaspoon salt

Directions (Makes about 3 quarts)

Combine opposite ingredients and let set 1 hour.

Combine milk and salt with the above mixture. Put in electric or hand freezer and freeze. (Do not get upset if it appears to curdle; it's all right.)

Orange Sherbet

Ingredients

2 teaspoons unflavored gelatin ·····

1/4 cup cold water

1 cup water ·····························

2/3 cup sugar

1 teaspoon grated orange rind ······

1 teaspoon grated lemon rind

1 1/2 cups orange juice

1/3 cup lemon juice

2 egg whites–stiffly beaten ···········

Pinch of salt

Directions (Serves 4 to 6)

Soak gelatin in cold water about 5 minutes.

Combine water and sugar in saucepan and boil for 10 minutes. Dissolve soaked gelatin in hot syrup. Cool.

Add opposite ingredients to the above mixture.

Fold beaten egg whites and salt into the above mixture. Pour into refrigerator tray and freeze until firm. Stir or beat once or twice to give a smoother sherbet.

A la mode your desserts: chocolate brownies, fruit tarts, Indian pudding, dessert dumplings, hot gingerbread or chocolate cake, baked fruit, hot doughnuts, pies and warm fruitcake slices.

"Five Threes" Sherbet

Mrs. E. E. Forbes, Greenville, North Carolina

Ingredients

3 cups sugar
3 cups water
3 lemons–juice
3 oranges–juice
3 bananas–mashed through a
  sieve
1 small can pineapple
1/2 pint cream (optional)

Directions (Makes 2 quarts)

Combine opposite ingredients and boil about two minutes. Not until it strings but just enough to dissolve thoroughly.

Add opposite ingredients to syrup and freeze.

Three Fruit Ice

Mrs. Wallace J. Rigby, Larchmont, New York

Ingredients

2 cups sugar
3 cups water
3 bananas
1 cup lemon juice
1 cup orange juice

Directions (Makes 2 quarts)

Heat water and dissolve sugar in water. Let cool.

Slice bananas thin and make puree by passing through sieve. Add to above with juices. Freeze in refrigerator. If an old-fashioned freezer is used, it is not necessary to puree the bananas but chop fine.

Black Raspberry Ice

Virginia McDonald's Tea Room, Gallatin, Missouri

Ingredients

2 quarts black raspberries
5 cups sugar
3 cups hot water
Juice of 6 lemons

Directions (Makes about 2 ½ quarts)

Run raspberries through colander; then squeeze through coarsely woven cloth, extracting every possible bit of pulp but no seeds. Mix sugar and hot water; stir and bring to boil. Boil for 15 minutes. Combine lemon juice, raspberries, and syrup. Cool and freeze.

Coffee Parfait

Ingredients

Directions (Serves 6 to 8)

1/3 cup sugar ·
1/2 cup strong coffee

Combine sugar and coffee in saucepan. Cook over medium heat, stirring constantly, until sugar is dissolved. Then boil without stirring until the syrup spins a thread (238° F.).

2 egg whites–stiffly beaten · · · · · · · · · · ·

Gradually add the hot syrup, in a fine stream, to the beaten egg whites, beating constantly until the mixture is cool. Chill.

1 pint whipping ·
    cream–whipped

Fold into above mixture. Pour into individual molds or freezing tray and freeze until firm.

Maple Parfait

Ingredients

Directions (Makes 1 ½ quarts)

6 egg yolks–slightly beaten · · · · · · · · · ·
3/4 cup maple syrup
Pinch of salt

Combine opposite ingredients in top of double boiler. Cook and stir over boiling water until mixture is thick and coats a metal spoon. Remove top section of double boiler from boiling water. Pour into a bowl and beat with egg beater or wire whisk until it is cold.

1 pint whipping ·
    cream–whipped

Fold whipped cream into the above mixture. Pour into refrigerator trays or mold and freeze until firm.

Parfait comes from the French meaning "perfect." It is less cold and more creamy than ice cream. "Mousse" is French for foam.

Serve ices in meringue shells topped with whipped cream for a delicious summer dessert.

Maple Walnut Parfait

Use recipe for Maple Parfait, folding in ½ cup finely chopped walnuts with the whipped cream.

Apple Mousse

The Derings, Green Lake, Wisconsin

Ingredients

1 cup thick, strained, ...
  sweetened applesauce
1 tablespoon lemon juice
1 cup whipping cream
1/2 cup sugar

Directions (Serves 4)

Combine the applesauce and the lemon juice. Whip the cream and add to it the sugar. Fold the two mixtures together and turn into freezing trays or a mold to freeze.

Gooseberry Mousse

Ingredients

1 quart gooseberries ....
1/2 lb. sugar
1/2 pint water
1 tablespoon brandy ....
A little green coloring
1 pint whipping ....
  cream—whipped

Directions (Serves 6)

Combine and cook opposite ingredients slowly until tender enough to put through a sieve.

Add brandy and coloring. Let cool.

Fold whipped cream into mixture. Put in refrigerator trays and freeze. Any fresh fruit, minus the coloring, may also be used.

Raspberry Mousse

Use recipe for Strawberry Mousse substituting 1 pint fresh raspberries for the strawberries.

Strawberry Mousse

Ingredients

1 pint strawberries–washed
  and stemmed
1 cup sugar
2 egg whites–stiffly beaten
1 pint whipping
  cream–whipped
Pinch of salt
1 tablespoon lemon juice
  (optional)

Directions (Serves 8)

Crush berries. Add sugar to berries and heat until sugar is dissolved. Chill.

Fold opposite ingredients into the above mixture. Pour into freezing tray and freeze.

Baked Alaska

Ingredients

3 egg whites
6 tablespoons sugar

Pound cake
1 pint very firm brick ice
  cream–any flavor

Directions (Serves 4)

Beat egg whites until foamy throughout. Add sugar, 2 tablespoons at a time, beating after each addition until blended. Continue beating until stiff peaks are formed.

Slice cake ½ inch thick. Place on board or baking sheet, covered with heavy paper. Cut ice cream into 4 slices, slightly smaller than cake; place on cake. Spread with meringue, covering completely. Bake in hot oven 450° for 5 minutes or until lightly browned. Serve at once.

Butterscotch-Almond Ice Cream Cake

(Serves 4) Line bottom of freezing tray with strips of pound cake. Spread with 1 pint softened coffee or vanilla ice cream. Pack ice cream down smoothly. Freeze. Serve slices with Butterscotch Sauce (See Dessert Sauces Section) and toasted slivered almonds.

Ice Cream Royale

Ingredients

Directions (Serves 4)

1 pint chocolate ice cream ·········· Layer the ice cream in parfait glasses with the chocolate on the bottom, then
1 pint vanilla ice cream   vanilla and strawberry.
1 pint strawberry ice cream
1/2 pint heavy cream–whipped ····· Top with whipped cream and chopped walnuts.
Walnuts–chopped

Biscuit Tortoni

Ingredients

Directions (Serves 4 to 6)

1 pint heavy cream–whipped ········ Combine opposite ingredients.
1/3 cup powdered sugar
1 teaspoon vanilla
3 tablespoons sherry wine
Pinch of salt
2 egg whites–stiffly beaten ·········· Fold beaten egg whites and macaroon crumbs into the above mixture. Pour into
1 cup macaroon crumbs   individual paper cups or freezing tray. Sprinkle with finely chopped, blanched
                                       toasted almonds, if desired. Freeze until firm.

Ice Cream Pie

Ingredients

Directions (Serves 6)

2 squares unsweetened ··············· Melt chocolate and butter over hot water, stirring until blended.
  chocolate
2 tablespoons butter
2 tablespoons hot milk ·············· Combine milk and confectioners' sugar. Add to chocolate mixture, stirring well.
2/3 cup sifted confectioners'
  sugar
1 1/2 cups coconut–toasted ·········· Add coconut to above mixture and mix well. Spread on bottom and sides of
1 quart vanilla ice cream   greased 9-inch pie pan. Chill until firm. Fill with ice cream just before serving.
                                         Serve with Chocolate Sauce, if desired. (See Dessert Sauces Section.)

Marshmallow Ice Cream Pie

Ingredients	Directions (Serves 8)
1 egg white 2 tablespoons sugar	Beat egg white until foamy throughout. Add sugar and beat until mixture will stand in soft peaks.
1 tablespoon light corn syrup 1 teaspoon vanilla	Add corn syrup and vanilla to the egg white mixture.
2 cups coconut–finely cut	Fold cut coconut into the above mixture. Press firmly into the bottom and sides of a well buttered 9-inch pie pan, using the back of a fork to press the mixture into the pie pan. Bake in moderate oven 350° for 15 minutes or until lightly browned. Cool.
1 1/2 pints firm vanilla ice cream	Spoon ice cream into cooled shell.
1 cup crushed, sweetened strawberries–drained	Spread crushed strawberries over ice cream. Reserve juice for meringue. Cover with marshmallow meringue. Seal the edges carefully. Bake in hot oven 450°for 5 minutes or until golden brown. Chill at least 2 hours before serving.

MARSHMALLOW MERINGUE

16 marshmallows 2 tablespoons strawberry juice	Combine opposite ingredients in top of double boiler. Cook over boiling water until marshmallows melt. Cool slightly.
2 egg whites Pinch of salt 1/4 cup sugar	Beat egg whites and salt until foamy throughout. Add sugar gradually and continue beating until mixture will stand in stiff peaks. Carefully fold in marsh-mallow mixture.

Refrigerator-Tray Pie

Ingredients	Directions (Serves 6)
1 1/2 cups chocolate wafer crumbs 1/4 cup butter 1/4 cup sugar 1 1/2 pints vanilla or coffee ice cream–softened	Cream butter and add crumbs and sugar. Blend together. Pack half the crumb mixture into a refrigerator tray. Chill. Spoon ice cream over crumb mixture and pack down well. Press remaining crumbs on top of the ice cream. Spread with whipped cream, if desired. Return to refrigerator to freeze.

Frozen Praline Pie

Ingredients	Directions
4 egg whites 1/2 teaspoon cream of tartar	Beat egg whites until frothy and add cream of tartar. Beat whites stiff and dry.
1 cup sugar	Add sugar slowly and beat until mixture is glossy. Line a 9-inch spring form pan with meringue. Bake in 300° oven for 50 to 60 minutes. Cool. While the meringue is baking make the Butterscotch Sauce.

Butterscotch Sauce

1 3/4 cups light corn syrup 2 cups sugar 1 cup butter 1 cup cream	Combine opposite ingredients in a saucepan and cook until it reaches the soft ball stage.
1 cup cream	Add cream to the above and let cook until the candy thermometer says 218° F.
1 teaspoon vanilla	Add vanilla. When the Butterscotch Sauce is done and cool, complete as follows:
2 quarts vanilla ice cream 1 cup whole pecan halves 1 cup ground pecans	Soften 1 quart ice cream in mixer until sufficiently soft to spoon into meringue shell. Pour over it a thick layer of Butterscotch Sauce and cover with pecan halves. Put in freezer and let get firm, about an hour and a half. Soften the other quart of ice cream and put on top of frozen filling. Top with Butterscotch Sauce, reserving some of the sauce for serving with the wedges. Cover entirely with ground pecans. Wrap tightly with aluminum foil and freeze. Unwrap and serve in wedges with a spoonful of sauce on top.

Ice Cream Tarts

Fill baked tart shells with fresh, sliced, sweetened peaches or strawberries. Top with a scoop of vanilla ice cream. Serve with additional fruit, if desired

Chocolate Meringues

Fill cooled Meringue Shells (see Pie Section) with scoops of chocolate ice cream. Top with Chocolate Sauce. (See Dessert Sauces Section.)

Frozen Eggnog

Ingredients

5 egg yolks–beaten ················
1 3/4 cups sugar
3/4 cup Bourbon ···················
Nutmeg to taste
5 egg whites–beaten ···············
1 pint whipping ···················
  cream–whipped

Directions (Makes 2 quarts)

Beat yolks and sugar together until light and creamy.

Add Bourbon and nutmeg to mixture.

Fold beaten egg whites into mixture.

Add whipped cream to mixture. Put in freezer and freeze. Pack until ready to serve. This can also be made in refrigerator trays.

Strawberry Meringues

Fill cooled Meringue Shells (see Pie Section) with scoops of vanilla ice cream. Top with crushed, sweetened strawberries.

Chocolate Charlotte

Ingredients

Ladyfingers–split ·················
3 tablespoons sherry wine ··········
1 pint chocolate ice ···············
  cream–softened
Whipped cream ····················

Directions (Serves 6)

Line bottom and sides of freezing tray with ladyfingers.

Sprinkle sherry wine over ladyfingers.

Spread ice cream over the ladyfingers. Freeze.

Just before serving spread with whipped cream.

Cookies

COOKIES CAN BE DIVIDED INTO FIVE GENERAL CLASSES; DROPPED, SPREAD, ROLLED, REFRIGERATOR, and pressed. Rolled, pressed, and refrigerator cookies are made with a stiffer dough than the dropped and spread cookies. Dropped, rolled, refrigerator, and pressed cookies should be baked on a lightly greased baking sheet. This allows for even heat conduction and makes removal of the baked cookies easier. They should be baked on the top shelf of the oven to eliminate the chance of burning on the bottom. When the cookies are done remove them immediately from the baking sheet, using a flat knife or spatula. Place the cookies on a wire rack to cool. Spread cookies, on the other hand, are baked in a greased sheet pan. They are usually cooled in the pan before removing, as this prevents them from drying out. Store the cooled cookies immediately, storing crisp and soft cookies separately in tightly covered boxes, cans, or jars. To keep soft cookies from drying out add a piece of bread or a slice of apple. ▶

Cookie may be decorated by sprinkling with chopped nuts, candied or dried fruit, coconut, colored candies, or grated chocolate before baking. Rolled cookies may be cut into unusual shapes with a cookie cutter, and especially at holiday time, attractive and appropriate designs can be prepared.

Betty Cass' Brown Sugar Cookies

Mrs. R. T. Cooksey, Madison, Wisconsin

Ingredients

Directions (Makes about 5 ½ dozen)

2 cups brown sugar ····················· Mix ingredients in the order given and drop from a teaspoon onto a buttered
1/2 cup shortening   baking sheet. Press a pecan half into each one. Bake in 350° oven for 15 minutes.
1/2 cup butter
2 eggs
2 cups flour
1 teaspoon baking powder
2 teaspoons vanilla
1 cup chopped pecans

Quick Brown Sugar Drop Cookies

Ingredients

Directions (Makes about 7 dozen)

1 lb. butter ································· Mix all together.
2 cups brown sugar
2 egg yolks
3 1/2 cups flour
2 teaspoons vanilla
1 cup chopped nuts ···················· Drop mixture from the end of a teaspoon into the nuts. Place on baking sheet
and bake in 400° to 450° oven about 10 minutes or until done.

Soft Molasses Cookies

Ingredients

Directions (Makes about 4 dozen)

2 cups sifted flour ······················· Sift together opposite ingredients. Set aside.

1/2 teaspoon salt

1 teaspoon soda

1 teaspoon ginger

1 teaspoon cinnamon

1/2 cup soft vegetable ················· Combine shortening, sugar, egg, and molasses and beat well.
  shortening

1/3 cup sugar

1 egg

1/2 cup molasses

3/4 cup sour milk ······················· Add flour mixture to the above, alternately with liquid, mixing well after each addition. Drop from teaspoon onto lightly greased baking sheet. Bake in moderate oven 375° for 8 to 10 minutes.

French Cookies (Tulles)

Villa LaFayette, Mountain View, California

Ingredients

Directions (Makes 40)

4 egg whites–beaten ················· Beat together opposite ingredients.

1 cup sugar

1 teaspoon vanilla

1 cup almonds ························· Blanch and grind almonds fine. Add to the above.

1/4 lb. butter–melted ··············· Add butter to mixture.

1 cup flour ······························· Stir flour in slowly. Drop from a teaspoon onto a buttered pan. Bake in 350° oven for 15 minutes. Let cool on rack before putting them away.

Rocks

Ingredients

1 cup butter
1 cup granulated sugar
4 egg yolks
2 1/4 cups flour
1 teaspoon cinnamon
1 teaspoon cloves
1 cup black walnut meats
1 1/2 cups raisins
1 teaspoon soda
1 1/2 tablespoons boiling water
4 egg whites

Directions (Makes 4 dozen)

Cream butter and add sugar, beating until smooth.

Beat in the egg yolks.

Sift flour, cinnamon, and cloves together. Add walnuts and raisins to the flour. Stir this mixture into the above, mixing well.

Dissolve soda in boiling water and add to batter.

Beat whites until stiff and fold into batter. Drop from teaspoon onto baking sheet and bake in 350° oven for 15 to 20 minutes or until done.

Cherry Nut Cookies

Richards Treat Cafeteria, Minneapolis, Minnesota

Ingredients

1 1/3 cups butter
2 cups brown sugar
4 cups flour
1 teaspoon soda
1 teaspoon salt
3 eggs

1 1/3 cups nuts
   (peanuts or walnuts)
1 1/3 cups candied cherries
1 1/3 cups dates

Directions (Makes 60 cookies)

Cream together butter and sugar.

Sift these ingredients together and add a portion to the above.

Add the eggs to the creamed mixture and continue mixing. (If an electric mixer is used, the bowl and beater should be scraped down thoroughly.) Add nearly all the remaining flour.

Chop and dredge opposite ingredients with the remaining flour and add to the mixture. Drop cookies on a greased and floured sheet pan and bake about 15 minutes in 375° to 400° oven until brown. This dough can be kept in refrigerator and baked as needed.

Cornucopias

Ingredients

1 egg ·····················
1/3 cup sugar
2 tablespoons water ··············
1/2 cup sifted cake flour ··············

Directions (Makes 1 dozen)

Beat egg slightly in small deep bowl. Add sugar, and continue beating until very thick.

Add water gradually to the above mixture, beating constantly until very thick and light.

Add flour all at once, and fold in until just blended. Grease baking sheet and dust lightly with flour, tapping sheet to remove any excess flour. Drop dough from tablespoon onto sheet, spreading each cookie with a spoon into a very thin 5-inch circle.) Best to bake only 3 at a time so they may be rolled quickly when baked.) Bake in moderate oven 350° for 10 minutes, or until golden brown. Immediately remove from baking sheet with a spatula and roll at once into a cone. (If necessary, place baking sheet over low heat or return to oven for a minute or two in order to remove cookies easily.) Set aside to cool. When cold, fill with Strawberry Whipped Cream, Cocoa Whipped Cream, or Lemon Whipped Cream. Serve at once.

Salted Peanut Cookies

The Ruttger's Lodge, Deerwood, Minnesota

Ingredients

1 cup butter–melted ·····················
2 cups brown sugar
2 eggs ·····················
2 cups flour ·····················
1 teaspoon baking powder
1 teaspoon soda
1 teaspoon salt
2 cups oatmeal ·····················
1 cup cornflakes
1 cup whole salted peanuts

Directions (Makes about 5 dozen)

Blend together butter and sugar.

Beat eggs well and add to above.

Sift together opposite ingredients and add to mixture.

Stir remaining ingredients into mixture and drop from teaspoon onto a greased cookie sheet. Bake in 350° oven for 15 to 20 minutes.

Chocolate Drop Cookies with Icing

Grace Peterson Adams, Chicago, Illinois

Ingredients

Directions (Makes 36 cookies)

1/2 cup butter ·················· Cream together butter and sugar.

1 cup brown sugar

1 egg–beaten ·················· Add egg to the above.

2 cups sifted flour ·················· Sift dry ingredients and alternately add to the mixture with the milk.

1/2 teaspoon salt

1/2 teaspoon soda

3/4 cup milk

2 squares unsweetened ·················· Blend together opposite ingredients and add to the mixture. Drop from teaspoon
  chocolate–melted   onto greased baking sheets and bake in 400° oven for 15 minutes.

1/2 cup nuts–chopped

1 teaspoon vanilla

Icing

2 tablespoons butter ·················· Melt together chocolate and butter in double boiler.

2 squares unsweetened
  chocolate

4 tablespoons cream ·················· Blend all these ingredients and add chocolate and butter mixture. Beat until

2 cups powdered sugar   smooth.

Pinch of salt

1 egg-beaten ·················· Fold into mixture and spread on cookies.

When recipe calls for sour milk or cream and you have none of your own, you may
add 1 tablespoon vinegar or lemon juice to each cup of sweet milk, and sour your own.

     The Duncan Hines Dessert Book

Lebkuchen

Ingredients

2 1/2 cups sifted flour ⋯⋯⋯⋯
1/2 teaspoon cinnamon
1/2 teaspoon cloves
1/4 teaspoon soda
1/4 teaspoon allspice
2 eggs ⋯⋯⋯⋯⋯⋯⋯⋯⋯
1 cup sugar
1/3 cup honey ⋯⋯⋯⋯⋯⋯
3/4 cup unblanched, slivered
  almonds
1/3 cup chopped candied ⋯⋯⋯
  orange peel
2 tablespoons chopped
  candied lemon peel

Directions (Makes about 3 dozen)

Sift together opposite ingredients. Set aside.

Beat eggs and sugar together until light and fluffy.

Add honey and almonds to the above and mix well. Add dry ingredients and blend.

Add fruit to the batter and mix well. Chill. Roll ½-inch thick on lightly floured board. Cut with cookie cutter. Place on lightly greased baking sheet. Bake in moderate oven 350° for about 20 minutes.

Shortbread

Mrs. David Donald, Pittsfield, Massachusetts

Ingredients

1 lb. butter–soft, but not ⋯⋯⋯
  melted
6 cups flour ⋯⋯⋯⋯⋯⋯⋯
1 1/2 cups sugar
1 egg

Directions (Makes about 4 dozen)

Cut butter into flour until like coarse sand, as for a pie crust.

Mix all ingredients together and roll or knead into larger cakes about ½-inch thick and cut with a cookie cutter. Prick each piece several times with a fork. Place on baking sheet and bake in 300° oven for 20 to 30 minutes.

Orange Cookies

Villa LaFayette, Mountain View, California

Ingredients

1/2 cup butter ·······················
1 cup sugar
Rind of 1 orange–grated
1 egg–beaten
1/2 cup orange juice
3 cups flour
4 teaspoons baking powder

Directions (Makes 36)

Mix in the order given. More flour may be required. Roll into a sheet; cut in rounds. Place on lightly greased baking sheet. Dredge with sugar and bake in 350° oven for about 20 minutes, or until brown. This recipe makes soft cookies; if crisp ones are desired, use ¼ cup of orange juice.

Butter Cookies

Mr. Francis E. Fowler, Jr., Los Angeles, California

Ingredients

1 lb. butter ······················
1 cup sugar
6 cups flour ·······················
Pinch of salt

Directions (Makes about 5 ½ dozen)

Cream together butter and sugar.

Sift flour and salt and add to mixture. Roll out thin; cut. Place on lightly greased baking sheet and bake in a 375° oven for 10 to 12 minutes.

Sugar Cookies

Ingredients

2 cups sifted flour ·····················
2 teaspoons baking powder
1/2 teaspoon salt
1/2 cup soft butter ·····················
1 cup sugar
2 eggs ·····················
1 tablespoon milk
1/2 teaspoon vanilla

Directions (Makes about 3 dozen)

Sift together dry ingredients. Set aside.

Cream butter and sugar together until light and fluffy.

Add remaining ingredients to the above mixture and beat well. Chill several hours. Roll out thin on lightly floured board. Cut with cookie cutter. Place on lightly greased baking sheet. Bake in hot oven 400° for 10 to 15 minutes.

Filled Cookies

(Makes about 1 ½ dozen) Prepare recipe for Sugar Cookies. Roll out the dough thin on a lightly floured board. Cut into rounds with cookie cutter. (The upper round may be cut with a doughnut cutter to permit the filling to show through.) Place jam or filling (for filling see below) between 2 rounds or place the filling on half a round and fold over the other half. Seal the edges of the cookies with a floured fork. Bake as directed for Sugar Cookies.

FILLING

Ingredients	Directions
1 cup chopped raisins, figs, or dates	Combine all ingredients in saucepan and cook and stir over medium heat until thick.
1/3 cup sugar	
1/3 cup boiling water	
1/2 teaspoon grated lemon rind	
1 tablespoon butter	
Pinch of salt	

Soft Ginger Cookies

Ingredients	**Directions** (Makes 2 to 3 dozen)
1/2 cup sugar	Cream sugar and butter. Stir in molasses.
1/2 cup butter	
1/2 cup molasses	
3 cups flour	Sift together flour, soda, spices, and salt. Add flour mixture, alternately with the sour milk, to the above mixture. Roll out on lightly floured board about ¼-inch thick. Cut. (Can be sprinkled with sugar.) Place on lightly greased baking sheet and bake at 400° for about 10 to 15 minutes or until lightly browned.
2 teaspoons soda	
1 teaspoon ginger	
1 teaspoon cinnamon	
1/4 teaspoon cloves	
Pinch of nutmeg	
1/2 teaspoon salt	
1/2 cup sour milk	

Ginger Snaps

Ingredients

1/2 cup butter ·······················
1 cup sugar
1/2 cup lard

2 eggs–beaten ··························

1/2 cup molasses ····················

4 1/2 cups flour ·······················
3 teaspoons ginger
1 teaspoon salt
1 teaspoon soda

Directions (Makes about 30)

Cream together opposite ingredients.

Stir eggs into the above.

Add molasses to above and mix well.

Sift together remaining ingredients and stir into the above. Let stand in refrigerator overnight. Roll out thin on lightly floured board and cut with round cookie cutter. Bake in 400° oven for 15 to 20 minutes.

Dream Cookies

Ingredients

1 cup butter ·····························
3/4 cup sugar ··························
2 cups sifted flour ·····················
1 teaspoon baking powder
2 teaspoons vanilla
40 blanched almond halves ···········
  (about)

Directions (Makes about 40)

Melt and brown butter slightly in saucepan. Cool.

Add sugar to butter and beat until fluffy.

Sift together dry ingredients. Stir into above mixture. Add vanilla and stir until blended and smooth.

Shape dough into balls about the size of a walnut. Place on lightly greased baking sheet. Press almond into each cookie. Bake in slow oven 250° for 30 minutes or until golden brown.

Swedish Oatmeal Cookies

Ingredients

3 cups finely ground quick-
  cooking oats
3/4 cup soft butter
1/2 cup sugar
1 teaspoon vanilla
36 pecan halves (about)

Directions (Makes about 3 dozen)

Mix together oats, butter, sugar and vanilla thoroughly with hands. Shape into small balls and place on lightly greased baking sheet.

Place a pecan half on top of each. Bake in a slow oven 325° 15 to 20 minutes or until lightly browned.

Peanut Butter Cookies

Ingredients

1 cup butter
1 cup granulated sugar
1 cup brown sugar
2 eggs
1 cup peanut butter
3 cups flour
2 teaspoons soda
Pinch of salt
1 teaspoon vanilla

Directions

Cream butter; add both cups sugar gradually and beat until smooth.

Drop in eggs and beat until blended. Add peanut butter and stir until well blended.

Sift flour; measure and sift again with soda and salt. Stir into above mixture and stir until smooth. Add vanilla. Flatten small balls between palms and crisscross with fork tines. Place on greased cookie sheets and bake in 350° oven for 12 to 15 minutes or until done.

Pecan Puffs

Mrs. Louis M. Weathers, Elkton, Kentucky

Ingredients

Directions (Makes about 2 dozen)

1/2 cup butter · · · · · · · · · · · · · · · · · · Beat butter until soft.

2 tablespoons sugar · · · · · · · · · · · · Add sugar and vanilla and beat until creamy.

1 teaspoon vanilla

1 cup pecans–put through a · · · · · · · Mix these together and stir into the butter mixture. Roll into small balls and place
   meat grinder on greased baking sheet. Bake in 300° oven for 45 minutes. While hot, roll in

1 cup cake flour–sifted powdered sugar and when cooled, roll again in powdered sugar.

Powdered sugar

Pecan Cookie Balls

Mrs. Alfred North, Philadelphia, Pennsylvania

Ingredients

Directions (Makes 10 to 12 dozen)

1 cup shortening · · · · · · · · · · · · · · · Blend shortening with salt and vanilla; add the sugar gradually. Cream well.

1 teaspoon salt

2 teaspoons vanilla

1/2 cup confectioners' sugar

2 cups sifted flour · · · · · · · · · · · · · · Sift flour; add flour and chopped nuts to the above mixture. Beat well. Shape the

2 cups finely chopped pecans stiff dough into little balls, slightly larger than a marble. Place on greased cookie

Powdered sugar sheet and bake about 15 minutes in moderate oven 350°. Remove from pan and
quickly, but carefully, roll the hot cookies in sifted powdered sugar. This forms a
frosting-like coating over the cookies. Cool, then roll again in powdered sugar.
Store in an air tight container.

Recrisp "once crisp" cookies in a slow oven for about 5 minutes before serving them.

Refrigerator Cookies

Ingredients

Directions (Makes about 6 dozen)

4 cups sifted flour ·························· Sift together opposite ingredients. Set aside.

1 teaspoon baking powder

1/4 teaspoon soda

1 teaspoon salt

1 1/3 cups soft butter ···················· Cream together butter, sugar, and eggs until light and fluffy.

1 cup firmly packed brown
  sugar

2/3 cup sugar

2 eggs

1 1/2 teaspoons vanilla ················ Add vanilla with flour to the creamed mixture; blend thoroughly. Shape into rolls 3 inches in diameter. Wrap in waxed paper and chill thoroughly. Cut into thin slices with a sharp knife. Place on an ungreased baking sheet. Bake in hot oven 400° for 5 to 8 minutes or until lightly browned.

Chocolate Refrigerator Cookies

(Makes about 6 dozen) Use recipe for Refrigerator Cookies adding 4 squares unsweetened chocolate, melted and cooled, to the creamed mixture.

Coconut Refrigerator Cookies

(Makes about 6 dozen) Use recipe for Refrigerator Cookies adding 1 ¾ cups finely cut coconut to the creamed mixture.

Date-Nut Refrigerator Cookies

(Makes about 6 dozen) Use recipe for Refrigerator Cookies adding 1 cup finely chopped walnuts and 1 cup finely chopped, pitted dates to the creamed mixture.

Nut Refrigerator Cookies

(Makes about 6 dozen) Use recipe for Refrigerator Cookies adding 1 cup finely chopped black walnuts or pecans to the creamed mixture.

Refrigerator Nut Cookies

The Maine Maid, Jericho, Long Island, New York

Ingredients

2 cups brown sugar
1 cup butter
2 eggs
1 teaspoon soda
1 teaspoon water
3 3/4 cups all-purpose flour
1 teaspoon salt
1 teaspoon vanilla
1 cup chopped nuts

Directions (Makes about 6 dozen)

Cream butter; add sugar and beat until creamy. Beat eggs and add.

Dissolve soda in water and add to sugar mixture.

Sift salt with flour twice and add to above mixture; mix well.

Add vanilla and nuts. Line loaf pan with waxed paper; pack in cookie mixture. Chill overnight in refrigerator. Next day slice thin. Place on lightly greased baking sheet and bake in 325° oven for 10 to 15 minutes. This will keep several days in the refrigerator.

Pinwheel Refrigerator Cookies

(Makes about 6 dozen) Prepare Refrigerator Cookies. Divide the dough into two parts. To one part add 2 squares unsweetened chocolate, melted and cooled. Leave the other part plain. Roll each part as thin as possible in a lightly floured board. Place one on top of the other and roll jelly-roll fashion. Chill; slice and bake as directed.

Boiling water poured over seedless raisins makes them plump.

Ginger Crisps

Miss Katharine L. Little, Chicago, Illinois

Ingredients

1 cup shortening
1 cup granulated sugar
2 eggs–beaten
1/2 cup molasses
4 1/2 cups flour
3 teaspoons ginger
1 teaspoon soda
1 teaspoon salt

Directions (Makes 36 cookies)

Cream shortening until soft and waxy.
Add sugar gradually to above and cream until fluffy.
Stir in eggs.
Add molasses and beat until well blended.
Sift together opposite ingredients and add to the mixture. Mold into roll and place in refrigerator until thoroughly set. Slice as thin as desired. Place on lightly greased baking sheet. Bake in 325° oven until the cookies are brown.

Easy Mix Cookies

Duncan Hines Division, Nebraska Consolidated Mills Company, Omaha, Nebraska

(Using White or Spice Cake Mix)

Ingredients

2 eggs
1/4 teaspoon soda
1/4 lb. soft or barely melted
  butter or margarine
1 package (19 oz.) White or
  Spice Cake Mix
3/4 cup sifted all-purpose flour

Directions

Beat eggs with soda.

Add shortening to above mixture and beat well.

Stir cake mix package contents into butter-egg mixture until all moistened.

Add flour to the above and mix well. Drop by heaping teaspoonfuls, 2 inches apart, on ungreased cookie sheet. Bake at 350°, on rack above center, 12 to 15 minutes. Remove from pan at once. Note: For crisp cookies use 1 egg and 2 tablespoons water instead of 2 eggs.

Oatmeal Cookies

Use recipe for Easy Mix Cookies (using either White or Spice Cake Mix) and substitute ¼ cup flour and 1 cup rolled oats for the ¾ cup sifted flour. (Add fruit variations desired.) Bake as directed for Easy Mix Cookies.

Lemon Coconut Drops

Use recipe for Easy Mix Cookies (using either White or Spice Cake Mix) and add ⅔ cup cut coconut and ¼ teaspoon lemon extract. Stir these ingredients in with the flour. Bake as directed for Easy Mix Cookies.

Fruit Cookies

Use recipe for Easy Mix Cookies (using either White or Spice Cake Mix) and add ⅔ cup finely cut raisins or dates and ½ teaspoon vanilla. Stir these ingredients in with the flour. Bake as directed for Easy Mix Cookies.

Refrigerator Cookies

Use recipe for Easy Mix Cookies (using either White or Spice Cake Mix) and increase flour to 1 cup. Use fruit variation desired. Shape in long rolls. Wrap in waxed paper. Store in refrigerator until used. Slice thin. Place on ungreased cookie sheet. Bake about 10 minutes at 350°.

Easy Mix Cookies
Duncan Hines Division, Nebraska Consolidated Mills Company, Omaha, Nebraska

(Using either Yellow or Devil's Food Cake Mix)

Ingredients	Directions
2 eggs	Beat eggs with soda.
1/4 teaspoon soda	
1/4 lb. soft or barely melted butter or margarine	Add shortening to above mixture and beat well.
1 package (19 oz.) Yellow or Devil's Food Cake Mix	Stir cake mix package contents into butter-egg mixture until all moistened.
1/2 cup sifted all-purpose flour	Add flour to the above and mix well. Drop by heaping teaspoonfuls, 2 inches apart, on ungreased cookie sheet. Bake at 350°, on rack above center, 12 to 15 minutes. Remove from pan at once. Note: For crisp cookies use 1 egg and 2 tablespoons water instead of 2 eggs.

Fruit Cookies

Use recipe for Easy Mix Cookies (using either Yellow or Devil's Food Cake Mix), adding ⅔ cup finely cut raisins or dates and ½ teaspoon vanilla. Stir these ingredients in with the flour. Bake as directed for Easy Mix Cookies.

Oatmeal Cookies

Use recipe for Easy Mix Cookies (using either Yellow or Devil's Food Cake Mix) and substitute 1 cup rolled oats for the ½ cup sifted flour. (Add fruit variations desired.) Bake as directed for Easy Mix Cookies.

Chocolate Chip Cookies

Use recipe for Easy Mix Cookies (using either Yellow or Devil's Food Cake Mix) and adding ⅔ cup semi-sweet chocolate bits. Stir in with the flour. Bake as directed for Easy Mix Cookies.

Refrigerator Cookies

Use recipe for Easy Mix Cookies (using either Yellow or Devil's Food Cake Mix) and increasing flour to ¾ cup. Use fruit variation desired. Shape in long rolls. Wrap in waxed paper. Store in refrigerator until used. Slice thin. Place on ungreased cookie sheet. Bake about 10 minutes at 350°.

Brownies

Ingredients

2 squares unsweetened chocolate
1/2 cup butter
1 cup sugar
2 eggs
1 teaspoon vanilla
1 cup nuts–broken
3/4 cup flour
1/2 teaspoon baking powder
1/2 teaspoon salt

Directions (Makes about 2 ½ dozen)

Melt together chocolate and butter over hot water.

Add sugar and eggs to above and beat thoroughly.

Add vanilla and nuts to mixture.

Sift together opposite ingredients and add to mixture. Stir in thoroughly. Pour into a greased and floured 12x12x2-inch baking pan and bake in 350° oven for 25 to 30 minutes. When cool, cut into squares. These may be iced before serving.

Date Squares

Ingredients

1 1/2 cups rolled oats ················
1 1/2 cups flour
1 cup brown sugar
1/2 teaspoon soda
3/4 cup shortening—half butter
  and half vegetable
  shortening
1/2 teaspoon salt

Directions (Makes 10 to 12)

Mix opposite ingredients together like pie crust. Divide and spread half the mixture on the bottom of a greased 9x9x2-inch square pan, patting down mixture with hands.

Filling

3/4 pound dates—cut up ··········
1/2 cup sugar
1/2 cup water
Juice of 1/2 lemon

Cook opposite ingredients until transparent (about 5 minutes). Cool and spread over first layer. Cover with remaining mixture. Bake 25 minutes in 350° oven. When cold, cut in squares and serve with whipped cream as dessert. Or may be cut in smaller squares like brownies and served with tea.

Fudge Squares

Ingredients

1/2 cup butter ·······················
2 squares unsweetened
  chocolate or 1/3 cup cocoa
  plus 1 tablespoon butter
1/2 cup cake flour ················
1 1/4 cups sugar
1/8 teaspoon salt
3 eggs—beaten ·····················
1 teaspoon vanilla
3/4 cup chopped nuts (walnuts
  or pecans)

Directions (Makes about 16)

Melt butter and chocolate

Sift dry ingredients twice and add to above.

Mix opposite ingredients into mixture. Pour into a greased 9x9x2-inch square pan. Bake in 350° oven for 25 minutes.

The Duncan Hines Dessert Book

Penuche Coconut Bars

Ingredients

1/2 cup soft butter ·······················
1/2 cup firmly packed
  brown sugar
1 cup sifted flour ·······················
1/2 teaspoon salt
1 tablespoon milk ·······················

2 eggs–well beaten
1 cup firmly packed ·······················
  brown sugar
1 teaspoon vanilla
2 tablespoons flour ·······················
1/2 teaspoon baking powder
1/4 teaspoon salt
1 1/2 cups coconut–finely cut
1 cup chopped pecans

Directions (Makes about 3 dozen)

Cream together butter and sugar until light and fluffy.

Sift together dry ingredients and add to sugar mixture. Blend well.

Stir milk into above mixture and mix well. Spread mixture in a lightly greased 9x9x2-inch pan and bake in slow oven 325° for 20 minutes or until lightly browned.

Add sugar and vanilla to beaten eggs and continue beating until thick and lemon-colored.

Stir remaining ingredients into the above mixture and mix well. Spread over baked mixture and return to oven and bake 25 minutes longer or until golden brown. Cool and cut into small bars.

You will not have burned cookies if you use a small timer clock or the clock on the range.

Jackson Cookies

Mrs. Mathew Jackson, Chicago, Illinois

Ingredients

Directions

1 cup butter ·································· Cream together butter and sugar.

1 1/2 cups sugar

3 eggs–beaten ······························ Add eggs to above.

1/4 cup milk ································ Stir opposite ingredients into mixture.

1/2 teaspoon soda

Pinch of salt

2 cups flour ······························ Sift together and add to mixture.

1 teaspoon nutmeg

1 teaspoon cinnamon

1 1/2 cups raisins ···················· Mix raisins and pecans well and stir into mixture. Spread on shallow well-greased

1/2 cup chopped pecans or   pans and bake in 375° oven for 10 to 12 minutes. Remove from oven and cut into
   walnuts   squares.

Carmens

Ingredients

Directions (Makes 1 cookie sheet)

1 cup butter ································ Cream together butter and sugar until light.

2 cups brown sugar–sifted

4 egg yolks–beaten ····················· Add eggs to the above.

2 egg whites–beaten

1 cup milk ······························ Mix these together.

1 teaspoon vinegar

1 teaspoon soda

2 1/4 cups pastry flour ················ Sift together dry ingredients. Alternately add a little of the milk mixture, then the

1 teaspoon cinnamon   flour mixture to the butter and eggs. Mix well.

1/2 teaspoon cloves

1 teaspoon allspice

The Duncan Hines Dessert Book

1 teaspoon vanilla	Fold vanilla into the mixture and spread on cookie sheet about ⅜-inch thick.
3 egg whites–beaten stiff	Make a meringue and spread over the dough. Bake about 40 minutes in 350° oven. Cut in small pieces. These are very delicate and should be carefully handled.
1 cup brown sugar	
1/2 cup chopped nuts	

Berliner Krautzen

Mrs. Howard Gilbert, Sioux Falls, South Dakota

Ingredients

Directions (Makes about 5 dozen)

1 lb. butter	Cream butter and sugar together.
1 cup sugar	
4 egg yolks–hard cooked and mashed	Add hard cooked egg yolks and then add raw egg yolks, one at a time. Beat well.
3 egg yolks–raw	
3 1/2 to 4 cups flour	Add enough flour to roll out the dough. Roll with palm of hand to the size of a pencil. Shape into a figure 8. (Cookie press may be used.)
1 egg white–slightly beaten	Dip in egg white and then in sugar. Place on lightly greased baking sheet and bake in moderate oven 350° about 10 minutes or until light brown.
Loaf sugar–crushed	

Spritz

Ingredients

Directions (Makes about 6 dozen)

1 cup soft butter	Mix opposite ingredients together thoroughly with hands.
2/3 cup sugar	
3 egg yolks	
1 teaspoon vanilla	
2 1/2 cups sifted flour	Add flour and salt to the above mixture and work with hands until well mixed. Force the dough through a cookie press onto an ungreased baking sheet, using any desired design. Bake in moderate oven 400° for 8 to 10 minutes. (Cookies do not brown on top.)
Pinch of Salt	

Cocoa Kisses

Ingredients

1 cup sifted powdered sugar ·········
2 egg whites
1 cup chopped walnuts
1 cup chopped dates
1/4 cup sliced glaced cherries
1 large tablespoon cocoa
1 teaspoon vanilla
Pinch of salt

Directions (Makes about 2 dozen)

Beat egg whites stiff. Add sugar slowly. Stir in gently all ingredients. Drop from a teaspoon onto a greased cookie sheet. Bake in 325° oven for 15 minutes, or until done, but not dry. These should be gummy when cool. Must be removed from tin quickly.

Nut Macaroons

McDonald Tea Room, Gallatin, Missouri

Ingredients

2 cups powdered sugar–sifted ········
1/2 cup flour–sifted
1 teaspoon baking powder
5 egg whites ·····································
1 lb. chopped nuts

Directions (Makes 6 or 7 dozen)

Blend these ingredients.

Do not beat. Stir into the dry ingredients.
Add the nuts. Drop from a teaspoon onto a greased cookie sheet. Bake in 300° oven 15 minutes or until set. Do not bake too hard or they won't be good.

Dessert Sauces

A SAUCE SHOULD ENHANCE A DESSERT BY ADDING COLOR, TEXTURE, FLAVOR AND MOISTNESS. IT should never mask the true flavor of the dessert. Too few people realize the importance of a sauce on the right dessert.

There are two kinds of dessert sauces, cooked and uncooked. Cooked sauces are usually thickened with whole eggs, egg yolks, flour, cornstarch or tapioca. When you want a fruit sauce to have a bright clear color thicken with cornstarch or tapioca. An appetizing color will greatly add to your sauce's eye appeal. Liquor, fruit juice (when used as a flavoring) and all other flavoring ingredients should be added only when the sauce is cool. If they are added when the sauce is still hot, some of the flavor will evaporate.

Some desserts which are improved by the use of a sauce are: ice creams, sherbets, steamed puddings, simple puddings, dumplings, plum pudding and sponge, angelfood and pound cake squares. ▶

Rum, sherry, brandy and Madeira all add a good flavor and piquance to a dessert sauce. However, be sure to serve the right sauce with the right pudding, as not all flavors blend well together. There are a few simple rules which should be followed when choosing a sauce for your pudding. A sauce should complement the pudding. If a pudding is citrous, serve a bland sauce with it; if the pudding is bland then serve a rich sauce. If you have a rich dessert, shun whipped cream and try a fruit sauce. The success of the pudding and the sauce will depend on your own discrimination.

A "hard sauce" with a butter foundation is a traditional supplement for many desserts which are served warm, such as baked and steamed puddings, dumplings and some fruit pies. A chilled hard sauce served over such a dessert has a delicate flavor that mingles well with the hardier flavor of the pudding.

A sauce does not need to be complicated to be good. The most important point is to learn the correct combination of flavors. A simple sauce, such as a custard or lemon sauce, can be transformed into a sauce of fluffy consistency by adding beaten egg whites or whipped cream. An easy uncooked fruit sauce can be made from left over fruit, fresh or stewed, with the flavor enhanced by the addition of a little wine or cordial.

Most cooked sauces require low heat or the use of a double boiler. In making a cooked sauce it is a good idea to use a saucepan large enough to allow for cooking without danger of overflowing, but not so large that the mixture forms only a thin layer at the bottom of the pan. Your sauce will have a better consistency if it is deep enough in the pan to enable easy stirring.

Most chefs classify a sauce as a "pick up," which is their term for a finishing touch that will add a dash of glamour and distinction to a dessert. Especially in ice cream, sauces are used to create color contrast. Popular crushed strawberries or raspberries over vanilla ice cream are good examples of this touch. This combination makes a good taste contrast too.

Any restaurant owner will tell you that one of the most popular desserts on the menu is ice cream served as a sundae. No matter how full you may be there is always just a little room left for this dish with a special sauce. In this section I discuss several sauces that are well suited for ice cream desserts. I know you will enjoy the caramel fudge, butterscotch, pecan and brandy sauces when you try them.

Chocolate Sauce for Ice Cream

Ingredients

1/2 lb. marshmallows ·················
2 squares unsweetened ················
  chocolate
2 squares sweet chocolate
1/2 cup cream

Directions (Makes about 1 ½ cups)

Cut marshmallows into small pieces.
Shave the chocolate. Place all ingredients in a double boiler and let stand over boiling water until dissolved. Stir often. Serve on ice cream. Will keep well in covered jar in refrigerator.

Regal Chocolate Sauce

Ingredients

1/2 cup light corn syrup ··············
1 cup sugar
1 cup water
Pinch of salt
3 squares unsweetened ················
  chocolate
1 teaspoon vanilla
1 cup evaporated milk

Directions (Makes about 2 ½ cups)

Combine opposite ingredients in saucepan. Cook to the soft-ball stage or to a temperature of 236° F. Remove from heat.

Add chocolate to the above mixture and stir until chocolate melts. Add vanilla. Slowly add evaporated milk and mix thoroughly. Serve on ice cream.

Don't forget the whipped cream! Spoonfuls of whipped cream around the edge of a pie will give it that professional touch, and although it may add calories–it's worth it! A dab of whipped cream also goes well on gelatin desserts, puddings, and baked desserts.

Always remember that cold desserts should be served cold and hot desserts should be served hot.

Chocolate Sherry Sauce

Old Southern Tea Room, Vicksburg, Mississippi

Ingredients

Directions (Makes about 3 cups)

4 squares unsweetened .... chocolate

Melt chocolate in top of double boiler. Add sugar, cream, and butter. Stir well and cook for 7 minutes. Let cool.

2 cups confectioners' sugar

3/4 cups cream

1 tablespoon butter

1/4 cup sherry ....

When sauce is cool, add sherry. Serve over vanilla ice cream in parfait glasses. Also may be served on a square of angelfood cake with white icing on top, a scoop of vanilla ice cream, chocolate sauce, and then a red cherry. Dessert is called "Angelfood Sherry Delight."

Caramel Sauce

Ingredients

Directions (Makes 1 ½ cups)

3 cups sugar ....

Heat sugar in heavy skillet over low heat, stirring constantly until sugar has melted and changed to a golden brown syrup. Remove from heat and slowly stir in hot water. Return to heat and boil slowly until mixture thickens. Remove from heat.

2 cups hot water

2 tablespoons butter ....

Add opposite ingredients to above mixture.

1/4 teaspoon salt

1 teaspoon vanilla

Caramel Fudge Sauce

Ingredients

Directions (Makes 1 cup)

1 1/2 cups sugar ....

Melt sugar in heavy frying pan over low heat, stirring constantly. When golden brown in color, remove from heat and stir in water. Add butter and return to heat. Boil until very soft ball stage has been reached or to a temperature of 230° F.

1 cup boiling water

1 tablespoon butter

3/4 teaspoon vanilla ....

Remove from heat and add vanilla. Stir. Serve hot or cold on ice cream.

Butterscotch Sauce

Ingredients

3/4 cup firmly packed brown ········· Boil sugar, syrup, and butter for 5 minutes, stirring until the sugar is dissolved.
    sugar

1 cup light corn syrup

1/3 cup butter

1 cup light cream ····················· Add cream and bring to a boil. Serve hot or cold on ice cream.

Directions (Makes 3 cups)

Foamy Sauce

Ingredients

1/2 cup butter ······················· Cream butter until soft. Add sugar gradually and cream together until light and fluffy. Add egg yolk and vanilla and beat until blended. Place the sauce over hot water and beat and cook until slightly thickened. Remove from heat.

1 cup powdered sugar–sifted

1 egg yolk

1 teaspoon vanilla

1 egg white–stiffly beaten ·········· Fold into the above mixture. Serve hot or cold.

Pinch of salt

Directions (Makes about 2 cups)

Eggnog Sauce

Ingredients

2 1/2 tablespoons sugar ············· Combine opposite dry ingredients in top of double boiler. Add egg yolk and beat well. Gradually add milk, stirring constantly. Cook over rapidly boiling water 5 minutes, stirring occasionally. Remove from heat. Cool.

1 tablespoon flour

Pinch of salt

1 egg yolk

1 1/4 cups milk

Pinch of nutmeg ····················· Add nutmeg and rum to the above.

1 tablespoon rum

1 egg white ·························· Beat egg white until frothy. Add sugar gradually, beating until mixture will stand in soft peaks. Fold in cooled custard mixture.

1 tablespoon sugar

Directions (Makes about 2 cups)

Fruit Sauce

Ingredients

1 cup unsweetened fruit juice
2/3 cup sugar
1 tablespoon cornstarch
2 teaspoons lemon juice
3 tablespoons butter
1 cup crushed fruit–fresh or
stewed

Directions (Makes 1 ½ cups)

Combine opposite ingredients in saucepan. Stir and cook until mixture comes to a boil. Remove from heat.

Add lemon juice and butter to the above mixture. Cool.

Add fruit to sauce mixture. Return to heat and cook and stir until thick. Serve over cake, puddings, or ice cream.

Gold Sauce

Ingredients

4 egg yolks
1/4 cup sugar
1/8 teaspoon salt
1/2 teaspoon vanilla

Directions (Makes about 2 cups)

Beat egg yolks in top of double boiler until very thick and lemon-colored.
Beat sugar and salt into the above mixture. Beat until the sugar is dissolved. Place top section of double boiler over hot water. (Never let water boil.) Cook sauce, beating constantly for about 5 minutes or until mixture is the consistency of whipped cream. Remove from heat and add vanilla. Serve hot or cold over puddings and cakes.

Brandy Gold Sauce

(Makes 2 cups) Use recipe for Gold Sauce, adding 3 tablespoons of brandy just before removing sauce from heat. Beat into mixture thoroughly.

Orange Gold Sauce

(Makes 2 cups) Use recipe for Gold Sauce, adding ⅛ cup orange juice and 1 ½ teaspoons grated orange rind before cooking the sauce. Omit vanilla.

The Duncan Hines Dessert Book

Lemon Sauce

Purefoy Hotel, Talladega, Alabama

Ingredients

1/2 cup sugar
1 tablespoon cornstarch
1/8 teaspoon salt
1 cup boiling water

1 egg yolk–beaten
3 tablespoons butter
2 tablespoons lemon juice

Directions (Makes about 1 ½ cups)

Mix sugar, cornstarch, and salt. Add boiling water slowly, stirring constantly. Boil for 5 minutes. Remove from fire.

Pour above mixture over beaten egg yolk, and add butter and lemon juice. This is good with pineapple or apricot upside down cake.

Orange Sauce

Ingredients

1 1/2 tablespoons cornstarch
1/3 cup sugar
1 1/2 tablespoons grated
  orange rind
1 cup orange juice
1/2 cup water
1 tablespoon lemon juice

Directions (Makes about 1 ½ cups)

Combine cornstarch, sugar, and rind in saucepan. Stir in orange juice and water. Bring to a boil, stirring constantly. Boil until clear. Add lemon juice. Serve hot or cold on steamed puddings.

Pecan Sauce

Ingredients

1 cup light brown sugar
Pinch of salt
2 tablespoons cornstarch
1 cup cold water
3 tablespoons butter
2/3 cup chopped pecans

Directions (Makes about 1 ½ cups)

Mix sugar, salt and cornstarch in saucepan. Stir in cold water. Cook, stirring constantly, over low heat. Boil until clear. Remove from heat.

Add butter and pecans.

Pineapple Sauce

Ingredients

1 1/2 tablespoons cornstarch ········

1/2 cup sugar

1 cup canned, crushed
  pineapple

3/4 cup water

1 1/2 tablespoons lemon juice ·······

Directions (Makes about 1 ½ cups)

Combine cornstarch and sugar in saucepan. Stir in crushed pineapple and water. Bring to a boil, stirring constantly. Boil until clear. Chill

Add lemon juice. Serve on puddings or ice cream.

Clear Sauce

Ingredients

1 cup sugar ····························

2 tablespoons cornstarch

2 cups boiling water ····················

2 tablespoons butter ····················

1/2 teaspoon nutmeg

1/4 cup whiskey

Directions (Makes about 2 cups)

Mix sugar and cornstarch together in a saucepan.

Stir boiling water in gradually. Bring to a boil and boil for 1 minute or until clear, stirring constantly. Remove from heat.

Add remaining ingredients. Serve hot over Bread Pudding.

Plain Custard Sauce

Ingredients

2 cups milk ···························

2 eggs–slightly beaten ···············

1/4 cup sugar

1/8 teaspoon salt

1 teaspoon vanilla ····················

Directions (Makes about 2 cups)

Scald milk in the top of a double boiler. Combine eggs, sugar, and salt in bowl.

Add scalded milk gradually to the egg mixture, stirring constantly. Return mixture to top of double boiler. Cook custard over hot water, stirring constantly until thickened and will coat a metal spoon without running off. (Takes 15 to 20 minutes.) Remove from heat and pour into a bowl or jar to cool. (Cover with waxed paper to prevent a scum from forming.)

Add vanilla when cool.

Russian Sauce

Ingredients

4 egg yolks ....
1 cup sugar
1 tablespoon flour
Juice and pulp of 2 oranges
Grated rind of 1 orange
2 tablespoons coconut ....
1/2 pint whipped cream

Directions (Makes about 2 ½ cups)

Mix opposite ingredients in double boiler and cook until mixture thickens.

Add coconut while still hot. Let cool and add whipped cream. Serve over slices of angelfood cake.

Brandy Sauce

Dolores Restaurant, Oklahoma City, Oklahoma

Ingredients

1 cup sugar ....
1 tablespoon cornstarch
1/4 teaspoon salt
1 tablespoon butter
1 cup boiling water
1/4 cup or more brandy ....

Directions (Serves 8)

Mix together dry ingredients. Add butter and boiling water. Mix well and cook 6 minutes or until clear.

Add brandy after you remove saucepan from the fire. Serve quite warm over any little plain cake or pudding.

Hard Sauce (cooked)

Ingredients

1 lb. brown sugar ....
1/2 lb. butter
1/2 teaspoon nutmeg
2 egg yolks ....
1/2 cup whiskey ....

Directions (Serves 8 to 10)

Cook together in double boiler until smooth, stirring constantly. Take from fire.

Beat egg yolks well and add to above.

Add whiskey to above. You may use more or less of the whiskey as you desire. This may be stored in a covered jar in the refrigerator and used as needed. Serve over plum pudding and gingerbread.

Ethel's Famous Brandy Pudding Sauce

Water Gate Inn, Washington, D. C.

Ingredients

1 quart whipped cream ·················
1 1/2 tablespoons powdered
  sugar
3 egg yolks ·························
Brandy or rum

Directions (Makes 1 quart)

Blend sugar with the whipped cream.

Beat egg yolks until frothy and combine with whipped cream. Add brandy or rum to taste.

Fluffy Sauce

Ingredients

1 egg white–stiffly beaten ············
3/4 cup powdered sugar
Pinch of salt ······················
1 egg yolk
1/2 cup whipping ···················
  cream–whipped
2 tablespoons brandy

Directions (Makes about 1 ½ cups)

Add sugar gradually to beaten egg white, beating until mixture stands in peaks and holds its shape.

Beat salt and yolk into the above mixture.

Fold in whipped cream and brandy. Chill thoroughly.

Sauce for Mince Pie

Boston Oyster House, Chicago, Illinois

Ingredients

3 tablespoons butter ···············
2 teaspoons sugar
1 tablespoon lemon juice ···········
1/4 cup hot water
2 oz. rum
2 oz. brandy
1 pinch nutmeg

Directions (Serves 6)

Melt together butter and sugar and mix well.

Add remaining ingredients to above and when hot, pour over slices of pie.

The Duncan Hines Dessert Book

Fresh and frozen fruits and berries add color and texture to the plainest dessert.
It is easy to decorate the serving dishes with clusters of grapes or berries, fresh flowers, or leaves.

Hard Sauce (uncooked)

Ingredients

1/2 cup butter
1 1/2 cups powdered sugar

Directions (Serves 8 to 10)

Cream butter, and add sugar gradually, beating well. The longer the beating, the creamier the sauce will be. Variations may be made in this sauce by adding 2 tablespoons of brandy, Cointreau, Grand Marnier, or any other flavoring desired. If vanilla is used ½ teaspoon should be sufficient. Serve over plum puddings, gingerbread, and the like.

Remember that every picture has a frame and the frame for the dessert
is the serving dish. Crystal, colorful china or pottery should be carefully
chosen keeping in mind the enhancement of the dessert.

Remember that the right sauce can greatly enhance the appeal of a steamed or baked pudding. An "everyday" sauce can be "dressed-up" for company dinner with a dash of brandy, rum, or nutmeg.

Miscellaneous Desserts

(Fritters, Pancakes, Waffles, Cream Puffs, Doughnuts)

INCLUDED IN THIS SECTION ARE RECIPES WHICH ARE SOMETIMES OVERLOOKED AS DESSERT possibilities. They are easy to serve and easy to eat.

Pancakes and waffles are a natural for informal entertaining. Modern electrical equipment for baking waffles and pancakes is streamlined-looking, and therefore the hostess need not hesitate to bring it into the living room where places can be filled and replenished readily. Living room service also lends an air of charm to your entertaining.

Waffles make an ideal dessert base for ice cream, crushed fruit or whipped cream. The plain pancake can be "dressed up" by making thin pancakes, spreading them with jam or jelly, rolling up jelly-roll fashion, and sprinkling with confectioners' sugar. Pancakes can also be stacked in layers, spread with filling in between, and served with a sauce. For a change, the pancake or waffle batter can be enhanced by adding grated orange or lemon rind, blueberries, or chocolate chips. Cream puffs or éclairs may be filled with whipped cream, ice cream, or a custard filling, with its many possible variations. Even doughnuts can be decorated with tasty glazes, fruit sauces, or the versatile whipped cream. Fritter batter can be used for coating many fruits, such as pineapple, apple slices, apricots, bananas, strawberries and many others.

As for the origin of the pancake, waffle, doughnut, and cream puff, again we must give credit to the Europeans. Pancakes, once called "hearth cakes," have been known since the days when man first mixed flour and water to make a batter. As the original name implies, they were baked over the hearth. The dessert pancake, however, went through many stages of development before it was perfected to the light delicate dish we now know. Crêpes Suzette, the most elegant of this family, was first created to be served with afternoon tea for Louis XV and his hunters. This glorified pancake was invented for the French knight by Princess (Suzette) de Carignan who was in love with his royal highness.

The first waffle, as the story goes, came about accidentally in the 13th century. A crusader, wearing his armour, absentmindedly sat on some freshly baked oat cakes which his wife had placed on a bench to cool. The cakes were flattened and deep imprints from the crusader's steel links were made in them. Nevertheless, he spread butter on the oat cakes and ate them. His wife was delighted and fascinated with the way in which the butter stayed in the imprints made from the armour and from then on, once a week, she had her husband put on his outfit and sit on her oat cakes.

The first doughnuts were nothing more than balls of yeast dough, and back in 16th century England they were called "imported doughty cakes." Doughnuts were brought to America by the English and Dutch settlers and were eventually perfected. However, the Indians have their own version of how doughnuts began. It seems that one day, back in the 17th century, an Indian, to display his skill with his bow, playfully shot an arrow through a fried cake a squaw was making. The squaw was startled, and dropped the perforated cake into a kettle of boiling grease which was on the fire; thus she created the first doughnut.

French Pancakes or Crêpes Suzette with Southern Comfort Sauce

Mr. Francis E. Fowler, Jr., Los Angeles, California

Ingredients

Directions (Makes 5 to 6 cakes)

3 eggs–beaten ·························· Mix together opposite ingredients.

1 cup milk

1/3 cup water

1 cup flour

1/4 teaspoon baking powder ········ Sift together dry ingredients and add to mixture. The batter should be very thin.

1/2 teaspoon salt ····················· Take about ½ cup to a griddle. Bake on hot greased griddle. Turn carefully and

3 tablespoons sugar   brown the other side. When done, put on a dinner plate, sprinkle with powdered

                                  sugar and jelly and roll.

1 jigger Southern Comfort ··········· Pour over pancake and light with a match.

  to a cake

Polichinkas (Yugoslavian Crêpes Suzette)

Mrs. Frank Dieterich, Culver City, California

Ingredients

Directions (Makes about 5)

2 egg yolks ··························· Beat together opposite ingredients.

2 tablespoons sugar

Pinch of salt

1 cup sifted flour ···················· Add flour and milk and beat until smooth.

3/4 cup milk

2 egg whites ·························· Beat egg whites stiff and fold in. Batter should be thin. Pour on hot greased

Apricot jam   griddle, tipping so that batter will spread over bottom. Brown one side and turn

Powdered sugar   and brown the other. When done, spread with a thick apricot jam or any other

                         desired jam. Roll up and sprinkle roll with powdered sugar.

Banana Suzettes

Ingredients

2 bananas ································

2 egg whites

2 tablespoons flour

2 egg yolks–beaten

4 tablespoons cream

Directions (Makes 16)

Dice bananas in ¼-inch slices. Beat egg whites very stiff. Mix ingredients in order given. Fry golden brown in butter. Suzettes should be size of silver dollar. Serve with New England Sauce.

New England Sauce

1 cup sugar ····························

1 tablespoon cornstarch

1 teaspoon vinegar

2 cups water

2 tablespoons butter

(Makes 1 cup)

Mix ingredients together in saucepan. Simmer over low heat for about 50 minutes until transparent and the consistency of thin custard.

Swedish Pancakes

Ingredients

1 1/2 cups sifted flour ···············

1 teaspoon salt

1 tablespoon sugar

3 eggs–well beaten

3 cups milk ····························

3 tablespoons melted butter

Tart jelly

Directions (Serves 6 to 8)

Sift dry ingredients together into bowl.

Add milk and melted butter to beaten eggs. Pour into flour mixture and stir until blended. Pour about ½ cup batter onto hot greased griddle. Turn over when delicately brown and bake the other side. Stack the baked pancakes in layers spreading each layer with tart jelly. Sprinkle top with confectioners' sugar.

Apple Pancakes

Ingredients

Directions (Serves 4 to 6)

1 cup sifted flour ·················· Sift together opposite ingredients into a bowl.

1/4 teaspoon salt

2 teaspoons sugar

1 1/2 cup milk ··················· Stir milk into the above mixture to make a smooth paste.

4 eggs ························· Add eggs to the above, one at a time, beating well after each addition.

3 large tart apples–peeled ············· Cut apples into thin strips and cover with lemon juice. Fold apple strips into the

and cored   batter. Fry in butter in a small, hot frying pan until delicately brown; turn and

1/2 cup lemon juice   brown the other side. Serve with sugar and cinnamon.

Apple Fritters

Ox Yoke Inn, Amana, Iowa

Ingredients

Directions (Serves 8)

1 cup bread flour ················· Sift flour, salt and sugar together into a bowl.

1/4 teaspoon salt

2 tablespoons sugar

2/3 cup milk ··················· Add milk, egg yolks and butter to the above mixture. Beat until smooth. Beat egg

2 eggs-separated   whites until stiff and fold into batter.

2 tablespoons melted butter

3 tablespoons lemon juice

6 large, ripe apples–peeled ············· Cut apples into ½-inch slices. Pour over lemon juice. Dip each slice in batter. Fry

and cored   in deep hot fat 356° F. until nicely browned. Drain; sprinkle with confectioners'

sugar.

To glaze doughnuts add 1/3 cup boiling water to 1 cup sifted confectioners' sugar.
Beat until smooth and well blended. Dip the warm doughnuts into the warm glaze.

Apricot Fritters

Hotel Roanoke, Roanoke, Virginia

Ingredients

Directions (Serves 6)

1 teaspoon sugar ·························· Sift dry ingredients together.
1 1/4 cups flour
1/3 teaspoon baking powder
Pinch of salt

2 eggs ··························· Beat eggs well; add eggs, milk, and butter to the above mixture. Mix as a stiff
1/3 cup milk batter.
1/2 tablespoon butter ················ Remove stones and cut into quarters. Dust with flour and dip each apricot into
Apricots batter. Drop into deep hot fat. Fry until brown. Serve with Rum Sauce.

RUM SAUCE

1 cup mixed fruit juice ················ Mix all ingredients and cook slowly for one hour. Stir occasionally.
3/4 cup granulated sugar
1/4 teaspoon red coloring
1/4 cup rum flavoring

Banana Fritters

Ingredients

Directions (Makes about 3 dozen)

3 ripe bananas ·························· Mash bananas.
1/2 cup cake flour ··················· Sift together opposite ingredients.
2 tablespoons sugar
2 teaspoons baking powder
1/8 teaspoon salt

2 eggs–beaten ················· Combine eggs, milk and vanilla and add to flour mixture. Stir until just blended.
1/4 cup sweetened condensed
  milk
3/4 teaspoon vanilla

1/4 cup coarsely chopped, ············ Fold opposite ingredients with the banana pulp into the above mixture. (The
  salted nuts batter should be the consistency of drop cookies.) Drop fritters into deep hot fat
2/3 cup raisins 365° F. and fry for 2 to 3 minutes or until golden brown.

The Duncan Hines Dessert Book

Maple Fritters

Ingredients

Directions (Makes 16)

2 cups sifted flour ⋯⋯⋯⋯⋯⋯ Sift together dry ingredients into a bowl.
2 teaspoons baking powder
1/4 teaspoon salt

1 cup milk ⋯⋯⋯⋯⋯⋯⋯⋯⋯ Add milk to beaten egg and add to flour mixture. Stir until just blended. Drop
1 egg–well beaten   from tablespoon into deep hot fat 370° F. and fry for about 5 minutes or until
             well puffed and golden brown. Drain on absorbent paper.

Confectioners' sugar ⋯⋯⋯⋯ Sprinkle fritters with confectioners' sugar and serve with hot maple syrup.
Hot maple syrup

Pineapple Fritters

Ingredients

Directions (Serves 6)

1 cup sifted flour ⋯⋯⋯⋯⋯⋯ Sift together opposite dry ingredients.
1 teaspoon baking powder
1/4 teaspoon salt
2 tablespoons sugar
1 egg–slightly beaten ⋯⋯⋯⋯ Combine eggs, milk, and melted butter. Stir into dry ingredients.
3/4 cup milk
1 tablespoon butter–melted
1 large ripe pineapple ⋯⋯⋯⋯ Pare and core pineapple. Cut in ¾-inch slices and then cut in fourths. Dip in
             batter and fry in deep hot fat 370° F. for 3 to 4 minutes or until golden brown.
             Drain. Sprinkle with confectioners' sugar.

A heavy griddle is best for even browning of pancakes.
Modern griddles require no greasing; however, to insure success, make a salt bag
by cutting a large piece of cheese cloth, double the cloth and make a sack. Fill the bag
with salt. This salt bag cleans the griddle as well as prevents sticking.

Histulas (Little Fruit Doughnuts)

Anderson Hotel, Wabasha, Minnesota

Ingredients

Directions

1/2 cup sugar ························ Combine sugar and egg yolks.
2 egg yolks–beaten

1/2 cup sour milk ···················· Mix milk and soda and add to egg mixture.
1/2 teaspoon soda

2 cups sifted flour ·················· Sift flour, measure, then sift with salt. Add to above.
1/4 teaspoon salt

1/2 cup pecans–finely chopped ······ Add opposite ingredients to above mixture.
1/4 cup raisins–finely chopped
1/4 cup dates–finely chopped

Grated rind of 1 orange ············ Add the orange juice. Drop from teaspoon into deep hot fat 325° and fry until
2 tablespoons orange juice   light brown. Turn while cooking. Remove from fat and drain on absorbent paper.
                                    Sprinkle with sugar. (Histulas should be quite small, only slightly larger than the
                                    hole in an ordinary doughnut. It helps to drop the amount spooned out of the
                                    dough briefly into flour. Then each ball can be molded by hand. The coating of
                                    flour keeps the grease from soaking in.)

Doughnuts

Helen Gougeon, Weekend Magazine, Montreal, Canada

Ingredients

Directions (Makes 6 dozen)

1/2 lb. butter ······················· Cream butter and add sugar gradually.
3/4 lb. white sugar

6 egg yolks ························· Beat egg yolks, and add with milk to above mixture, beat well.
1 cup milk

6 cups flour ························ Sift flour and baking powder together. Add to the above, mixing well.
1 tablespoon baking powder

1 wine glass brandy ················ Add brandy and egg whites to above mixture. Pat out dough on lightly floured
6 egg whites–stiffly beaten   board. Cut doughnuts and let stand from 5 to 15 minutes before frying. Fry in
                                   370° F. fat until brown on one side, turn and brown on the other side. Remove
                                   and drain on paper towels. Frost with icing or sprinkle with fruit sugar.

The Duncan Hines Dessert Book

Cake Doughnuts

Ingredients

1 1/2 cups brown sugar
2 eggs
4 tablespoons melted butter
1 cup whole milk
4 cups sifted flour
4 teaspoons baking powder
1/2 teaspoon cinnamon
1/2 teaspoon salt

Directions (Makes 35 doughnuts)

Beat whole eggs until they are light and stir into sugar.

Stir butter and milk into above.

Add baking powder, cinnamon and salt to flour and sift again. Add to above, stirring only enough to get ingredients thoroughly blended. Place in refrigerator to chill, at least 24 hours if possible. (This prevents the doughnuts from soaking up the fat when fried.) Roll out a little of the dough at a time on floured board; cut with doughnut cutter. Fry in deep hot fat about 365° until brown on one side. Turn over and brown on the other side. Drain and roll in powdered sugar. This dough may be kept at least a week in a covered dish in the refrigerator. Break off and cook only enough of the dough at a time to fill your requirements, as freshly cooked doughnuts are better than those left standing overnight.

Orange Doughnuts

Vera Kirkpatrick, San Mateo, California

Ingredients

2 eggs
1/2 cup sugar
1/4 teaspoon salt
1/2 cup thick cream
2 1/2 cups flour
2 teaspoons baking powder
6 tablespoons butter–melted
1 teaspoon nutmeg
1/2 cup orange juice
Grated rind of 1 orange

Directions (Makes 12 doughnuts)

Beat eggs until light. Add other ingredients.

Sift flour, measure and sift again with baking powder. Add to sugar and egg mixture.

Stir butter into above mixture.

Add nutmeg, orange juice, and rind and stir until blended. Chill. Roll out and cut with doughnut cutter. Fry in deep hot fat 350° F. When cold, dust with powdered sugar.

Waffle Brownies

Ingredients

1 1/2 cups sifted flour ·················
1/2 teaspoon salt

3/4 cup shortening ··················
2/3 cup sugar
2 egg yolks

3/4 cup milk ···················

2 squares unsweetened ··················
chocolate–melted
1/2 cup chopped nuts
2 egg whites–stiffly beaten

Directions (Makes 4 waffles)

Sift together flour and salt. Set aside.

Cream shortening and add sugar gradually. Beat until light and fluffy. Add egg yolks and mix well.

Add milk to the above mixture alternately with flour.

Fold in remaining ingredients. Bake in moderately hot waffle iron about 5 minutes. Serve with a scoop of vanilla ice cream or whipped cream topped with chocolate sauce. (See Dessert Sauces Section.)

Gingerbread Waffles

Ingredients

1 1/2 cups sifted flour ···················
1 teaspoon ginger
1/2 teaspoon salt
1 teaspoon soda
1 teaspoon baking powder
3 eggs ·····················
1/4 cup sugar ··················
1/2 cup molasses
1 cup sour milk
1/3 cup melted butter

Directions (Serves 6)

Sift opposite ingredients together. Set aside.

Beat eggs until light and fluffy.
Add to eggs and beat well. Combine the liquid ingredients and flour mixture. Bake waffles in waffle iron until golden brown. Serve with whipped cream, fruit or ice cream.

Use a deep fat frying thermometer for frying doughnuts and fruit fritters.

Dessert Waffles

Ingredients

1 1/2 cups butter ··················
3 cups sifted cake flour

3 eggs ·····························
1 1/4 cups sugar
1/4 teaspoon salt

Directions (Makes 6 to 8 waffles)

Cream butter and add flour. Beat well.

Beat eggs slightly. Add sugar and salt and continue beating until light and fluffy. Add to above mixture and beat well. Bake in a moderately hot waffle iron about 3 to 4 minutes. Serve with crushed, sweetened strawberries, raspberries, or blueberries.

Cream Puffs

Ingredients

1 cup sifted flour ···············
1/4 teaspoon salt
1/2 cup butter ·················
1 cup boiling water

4 eggs ·····························

Directions (Makes 1 dozen)

Sift together flour and salt. Set aside.

Combine butter and boiling water in saucepan. Cook and stir over low heat until butter melts. Add flour mixture, all at once, and stir vigorously over low heat until mixture forms a ball and leaves the sides of the pan. Remove from heat.

Add unbeaten eggs, one at a time, beating well after each addition. Continue beating until a thick dough is formed. Drop by tablespoonfuls onto an ungreased baking sheet, about 2 inches apart. Bake in hot oven 425° about 30 minutes. When cool cut a slit in the side of each and fill with Cream Filling. (See cakes, Frostings, and Fillings Section.) May be filled with sweetened whipped cream. Serve with Chocolate Sauce. (See Dessert Sauces Section.)

Use a deep fat frying thermometer for frying doughnuts and fruit fritters.

Most waffle irons require no greasing after first seasoning.

Chocolate Cream Puffs

(Makes one dozen) Use recipe for Cream Puffs melting 1 square unsweetened chocolate with the butter and water mixture. Cool and fill with sweetened whipped cream and sprinkle with confectioners' sugar.

Eclairs

(Makes 1 ½ dozen) Use recipe for Cream Puffs. Force mixture through a decorating tube onto making sheet in strips about 1 inch wide and 4 inches long. Bake about 25 minutes. When cool, slit and fill as for Cream Puffs. Frost with Chocolate Confectioners' Frosting. (See Frostings and Fillings Section.)

Fried Cream

Ingredients	Directions (Serves 2 to 4)
3 egg yolks	Combine opposite ingredients and beat together until well blended.
1 tablespoon Jamaica rum	
1/8 teaspoon salt	
1/4 cup sugar	
3 tablespoons cornstarch	Combine cornstarch and milk and mix to make a smooth paste. Stir into the above mixture.
3 tablespoons milk	
2 cups warm cream	Add cream, to which the cinnamon has been added, gradually to the egg yolk mixture. Cook mixture in double boiler over boiling water, stirring constantly, until thickened. Pour mixture into a lightly buttered pan to a depth of about ¾ inch. Cool and cut in squares.
1/4 teaspoon cinnamon	
3/4 cup graham cracker crumbs (about)	Roll squares in cracker crumbs and dip in beaten egg. Fry squares in deep hot fat 360° F. until lightly browned.
1 egg–beaten	
1/4 cup warm Jamaica rum	Place squares on serving dish and pour rum over. Ignite rum and bring to the table.

Alsatian Pudding

Mrs. Bland Farnsworth, Bowling Green, Kentucky

Ingredients

Directions (Serves 8 to 10)

1/2 lb. butter ⋯⋯⋯⋯⋯⋯⋯⋯⋯ Cream together butter and sugar until very light and fluffy.

2 1/2 cups powdered sugar

8 egg yolks ⋯⋯⋯⋯⋯⋯⋯⋯⋯ Add yolks to the above and beat well.

1/2 cup strong cold coffee ⋯⋯⋯ Add coffee very slowly to the above.

1 dozen ladyfingers–split ⋯⋯⋯ Line an oblong pan with waxed paper and place a layer of split ladyfingers on

Rum bottom and sprinkle with rum. Next a layer of creamed mixture. Another layer of ladyfingers and sprinkle with rum and so on until mixture is used, ending with a layer of ladyfingers. Put into refrigerator overnight.

Shredded, toasted almonds ⋯⋯⋯ Just before time to serve, turn out of pan, slice and sprinkle each slice with almonds.

Date and Nut Confection

Gurney's Inn, Montauk, Long Island, New York

Ingredients

Directions (Serves 4)

1 cup pitted dates–diced ⋯⋯⋯⋯ Thoroughly mix together the opposite ingredients.

1/2 cup black walnuts–broken

1 cup granulated sugar

1 teaspoon baking powder

Pinch of salt

4 egg whites–beaten ⋯⋯⋯⋯⋯ Fold egg whites into above mixture and bake in buttered tin in 300° oven for 20 minutes. When cool, serve with whipped cream.

Fill cream puffs with whipped cream into which has been
folded sweetened strawberries, raspberries, or sliced peaches.

Ozark Bakeless Pudding

Hotel Taneycomo, Rockaway Beach, Missouri

Ingredients

1/2 cup butter
1 cup sugar
2 eggs–well beaten
1 cup chopped nuts
1 small can crushed
   pineapple–drained
1/2 lb. graham crackers

Directions (Serves 6)

Cream butter and sugar. Add well-beaten eggs, nuts and pineapple. Crush the graham crackers and in a dish place a thick layer of crackers, then the mixture and top with remainder of crackers. Let set for 12 hours in refrigerator and serve with whipped cream. (Peaches may be substituted for the pineapple.)

Peanut Brittle Delight

Hotel Roanoke, Roanoke, Virginia

Ingredients

2 cups peanut brittle
2 cups marshmallows
1 1/2 cups whipping cream
1/2 teaspoon vanilla
1/2 cup sugar
1 cup peanuts

Directions (Serves 6 to 8)

Crush peanut brittle very fine. Quarter marshmallows. Whip cream; add sugar and vanilla. Fold peanut brittle and marshmallows into whipped cream. Let stand two hours before serving. Serve in sherbet glasses. Garnish with peanuts.

Coffee Pudding Supreme

Rita Seech, Los Angeles, California

Ingredients

1/2 pint whipping cream
3 tablespoons confectioners'
   sugar
2 tablespoons instant coffee

Directions (Serves 4)

Whip until quite stiff. Stir all together and serve.

Tapioca Cream Pudding

Grace E. Smith's Restaurant, Toledo, Ohio

Ingredients

Directions (Serves 6 to 8)

1/2 cup pearl tapioca (scant) ⋯⋯⋯ Soak tapioca in water at least 12 hours.
1/2 cup water

1 quart sweet milk ⋯⋯⋯⋯⋯ Heat milk in double boiler and add soaked tapioca to hot milk. Cook 1 hour until tapioca is tender and clear. Stir occasionally.

1/2 cup granulated sugar ⋯⋯⋯ Add to milk and tapioca and cook 1 hour.

3 small egg yolks ⋯⋯⋯ Beat egg yolks and sugar in mixer until light yellow and thick. Add a little of the
1 1/2 tablespoons sugar hot mixture to the yolks. Turn off the fire. Stir yolks into milk and tapioca and mix well. Return to double boiler and cook until thickened, approximately 20 minutes.

1/4 teaspoon vanilla ⋯⋯⋯⋯ Stir in vanilla and salt and let cool, stirring occasionally until lukewarm.
1/3 teaspoon salt

Indian Tapioca Pudding

Ingredients

Directions (Serves 8)

2 cups milk ⋯⋯⋯⋯⋯⋯ Scald.

2 tablespoons tapioca ⋯⋯⋯ Mix opposite ingredients and stir into the hot milk. Cook 20 minutes, stirring
2 tablespoons Indian meal constantly until it thickens. Remove from fire.

2/3 cup molasses ⋯⋯⋯⋯ Add opposite ingredients to the above mixture; stir and pour into greased baking
1/3 cup sugar dish. Set dish in pan of hot water and bake 4 hours in 350° oven.

3 tablespoons butter

1 egg

1 teaspoon salt

1 teaspoon cinnamon

1 teaspoon ginger

2 cups cold milk

1 cup cold milk ⋯⋯⋯⋯⋯ Add milk about 1 hour before serving, but do not stir. Serve with whipped cream or Hard Sauce.

Apricot Cream Cheese Wafers

Ingredients

1 package (3 oz.) soft ·················· cream cheese
1/2 cup soft butter
1/2 cup sugar
1 cup sifted flour
1 teaspoon grated lemon rind
Dried apricot strips ····················
Milk
Sugar

Directions (Makes about 3 dozen)

Mix opposite ingredients well. Shape dough in rolls 1 inch in diameter; wrap in waxed paper. Chill and slice thin.

On one slice place a thin strip of apricot and cover with another slice. Press edges together. Brush top of cookies with milk; sprinkle with sugar. Place on lightly greased baking sheet and bake in moderate oven 350° for 5 to 8 minutes or until done.

Mrs. George P. Meier, Indianapolis, Indiana

Pecan Drop Cakes

Ingredients

1 egg white–beaten ··················
1 cup brown sugar
1 cup pecans (whole or ··············· broken)

Directions (Makes about 30)

Beat sugar into egg whites.

Add nuts and drop from a spoon onto a buttered cookie sheet. Bake in 300° oven for 40 minutes. Should be a light brown when done.

When guests are invited to my home for seven o'clock dinner, we begin the meal promptly at seven-thirty whether all have arrived or not. There is no reasonable excuse for thoughtless guests to spoil a good dinner for those who arrived at the appointed hour.

I believe there isn't any profession that requires more artistry, talent and experience than the careful preparation and cooking of good food.

Oat Cakes

Mrs. David Donald, Pittsfield, Massachusetts

Ingredients

Directions

3 cups quick-cooking oats ············· Put oats through a meat chopper.

1/2 cup corn meal ························ Add opposite ingredients to the above and mix thoroughly.

1/2 cup butter or shortening

1 cup flour

3 teaspoons sugar

1 teaspoon salt

1/2 teaspoon soda

1 teaspoon baking powder

2/3 cup hot water ························ Add water to mixture. Roll thin; cut and place on lightly greased baking sheet. Bake in 350° oven for 30 to 40 minutes.

Coffee

COFFEE, AMERICA'S FAVORITE BEVERAGE, CAN BE THE CROWNING GLORY OF A MEAL. BUT IF YOU serve poor coffee you can spoil the enjoyment of the best food.

Americans drink more than a hundred billion cups of coffee each year, and consumption is still increasing steadily. In the United States we have many different methods of preparing coffee, and some people have developed special techniques of their own to produce coffee unlike anything else wrong from a coffee bean. Someone once said that coffee is handled by experts up until the crucial moment of brewing, and then an amateur takes over. Nevertheless, we do a pretty good job of coffee making. Otherwise, it would never have become the popular drink it has since its introduction in the coffee houses and cafes of Europe more than 300 years ago.

The essentials to producing a good cup of coffee are few but the results are well worth any effort. Buy a good brand of coffee and the right grind for whatever brewing method you wish to use. Fresh coffee makes the best coffee, so do not store your supply too long. Your coffee maker should be clean and shiny. Soap has a tendency to cling to your coffee maker and will spoil the flavor, so be sure your utensil or appliance is well rinsed. Use cold water and never, never start with hot or tepid water if you want the best flavor from your coffee. For medium coffee, use 1 1/2 to 2 tablespoons of coffee per cup and vary it either way for stronger or weaker coffee. Serve your coffee as soon as possible. Cooled coffee often loses its flavor if reheated. If your coffee must stand be sure it is not in contact with the ground.

A good idea for your leftover coffee in the summertime is to pour it into an ice cube tray and freeze it. Then you will have coffee cubes for your spiced iced coffee.

The New Automatic Coffee Makers

I have found some of the new automatics to be very good. The higher cost of these units over the conventional type pots is often off-set by the pleasure you get from a better cup of coffee and from actually being able to brew a good drink with less coffee.

I especially like a coffee maker which brews out all the goodness without boiling. This is important because boiling releases the acrid oils that make coffee bitter.

Percolator Coffee

(Automatic and Non-automatic Coffee Makers)
In the percolator coffee makers the water is measured into the percolator, and then the steam and basket, holding the desired amount of coffee, are inserted. When using the automatic percolator, follow the manufacturer's directions, as different makes of electric percolators have different automatic features. If the percolator is nonelectric, place over medium heat; lower the flame when the water begins to spurt; count percolating time from the first spurt. Percolating for 5 to 10 minutes makes coffee of medium strength when 4 to 6 cups are being made.

The principle involved in the percolator coffee maker is that when the water is sufficiently heated it is forced up through the narrow stem and sprays over the coffee in the basket, which is held over the water. The spurts of water extract color and flavor from the coffee, and then return to the bottom of the coffee maker.

Vacuum-Type Coffee

The vacuum-type coffee maker consists of two separate containers. Measure the water into the lower bowl, using either cold or freshly boiled water unless the manufacturer's directions specify just cold water. The coffee is placed in the upper bowl. Heat forces the water to rise through a tube into the upper section where it mixes with the coffee. Steam pressure keeps the water there long enough to extract the desired flavor and color from the coffee. When all the water has risen to the top, the nonelectric coffee maker is removed from the heat. This causes the lower section to cool off, and the pressure is reduced; the finished coffee then filters back into the lower section.

Since vacuum-type coffee makers vary with the brand, the manufacturer's directions should be followed carefully. General directions do not apply in all cases.

Drip Coffee

Measure the coffee into the basket or middle section, which may either fit over the bottom section of the drip coffee maker or may be attached to the top section. Fit the parts together, and pour freshly boiled water into the top section. The water drips down through the coffee and into the bottom section. Remove the section holding the grounds when all the water has dripped through to the bottom. Let the coffee stand 5 to 8 minutes before serving. (This "ripens" the coffee.) To keep the coffee hot, heat the bottom section, providing the coffee maker is not made of pottery or glass which cannot be placed over direct heat. With pottery or glass coffee makers, scald the pot with hot water before using and then keep in a warm place.

Boiled Coffee

To make boiled or steeped coffee, select a rather coarsely ground coffee. Mix the ground coffee with a slightly beaten egg white and cold water just to moisten the coffee grounds. This helps to clarify the finished coffee. (Use about 1 teaspoon of egg white per cup of coffee.)

To make boiled coffee, pour fresh cold water over the coffee mixture. Place over a low flame and bring to a boil, stirring occasionally. Remove from heat at once.

To make steeped coffee, pour boiling water over the coffee mixture, and place over low heat for about 10 minutes. Do not let the water simmer.

Several tablespoons of cold water will help settle the grounds.

Café au Lait

Prepare double strength coffee. Heat some milk to the scalding point. Then pour the coffee and milk at the same time into the coffee cups, usually adding equal amounts of each. More or less coffee may be added depending upon individual preferences. Top with unsweetened whipped cream, if desired.

Spiced Iced Coffee

Ingredients

15 whole cloves
1 stick (5-inch) cinnamon
1/2 cup ground coffee
7 cups water–boiling or cold
1 cup powdered sugar
1 cup whipping cream
2 tablespoons sugar

Directions (Serves 6)

Add cloves, cinnamon, and coffee to water and brew as usual. Strain and add powdered sugar. Pour into tall glasses half-filled with crushed ice.

Whip cream with sugar. Put a scoop of whipped cream in each glass.

Café Brûlot

Ingredients

Peel of 1 orange–cut thin
4 sticks cinnamon
10 whole cloves
6 lumps sugar

1/2 cup brandy

4 cups prepared hot coffee

Directions (Serves 6 to 8)

Place the opposite ingredients in a silver brûlot bowl or chafing dish.

Pour brandy over the above mixture. Ignite brandy and keep ladling brandy over ingredients in bowl until sugar is dissolved.

Gradually add coffee, and ladle mixture until the flame dies. Serve immediately.

Café Diablo

Cameo Restaurant, Chicago, Illinois

Ingredients

6 demitasses of coffee
6 whole cloves
1/2 stick cinnamon
2 bay leaves
1 lemon peel
1 orange peel
1/4 cup whole roasted coffee
  beans
6 lumps sugar
2 oz. Jamaica rum
4 oz. brandy

Directions (Serves 6)

Use you own favorite method.

Mix remaining ingredients in a deep chafing dish and set liquor afire. Keep stirring the mixture with a ladle and very slowly add the coffee, stirring all the time to keep the flame burning. Serve in demitasse cups, using ladle and a spoon to remove coffee beans.

Coffee for a Crowd

Ingredients

1 lb. ground coffee ·····················

2 to 2 1/2 gallons water

Directions (Serves 40 to 50)

Place the coffee in one or more cheese cloth bags; never fill a bag more than one-half full. Measure the water into a large coffee pot or kettle. Let the water come to a boil. Drop the bag, containing the coffee, into the boiling water and lower the flame. Heat without boiling for 10 to 15 minutes, moving the bag through the water several times. Remove the bag; serve coffee immediately or keep hot. Another method using the same ingredients is as follows: Immerse the coffee bag in cold water. Bring the water to a boil. Remove from heat immediately and keep the bag in the water for 3 to 5 minutes. Remove the bag and serve coffee or keep hot.

Demitasse or After-Dinner Coffee

Prepare coffee using double the amount of coffee usually used, and figuring on two demitasse servings per measuring cup of water. It is served in small demitasse cups with demitasse spoons on the saucer. It is not necessary to pass cream and sugar as it is usually taken black. The hostess usually serves after-dinner coffee in the living room.

Index